COMMENTARY ON ACTS 1

COMMENTARY ON ACTS 1

STEPHEN MANLEY

COMMENTARY ON ACTS 1
© 2015 by Stephen Manley

Published by Cross Style Press
Lebanon, Tennessee
CrossStyle.org

All rights reserved. No part of this book may be reproduced in any form without prior permission from the publisher, except for brief quotations.

Scripture taken from the New King James Version®. Copyright © 1982 by Thomas Nelson, Inc. Used by permission. All rights reserved.

First Edition 2008
Second Edition 2015

Edited by Delphine Manley

ISBN-10: 0692454306
ISBN-13: 978-0692454305

Printed in the United States of America.

CrossStyle.org

CONTENTS

The Divine Activity Thing – Acts 1:1-2

Acts 1:1	A Divine Activity Thing	3
Acts 1:1	The Beginning	14
Acts 1:1	Doing and Teaching	22
Acts 1:1-2	The Ascension's Focus	34
Acts 1:2	The Eternal Flow	43
Acts 1:2	The Ordered Emphasis	51

The Promise of the Father – Acts 1:3-5

Acts 1:3	Jesus Presented	63
Acts 1:3	He Is Here	73
Acts 1:4	Let's Go Camping	82
Acts 1:4	The Announcement of the Father	92
Acts 1:4	The Promise of the Father	100
Acts 1:5	The Immersing of Jesus	109

Preceding the Ascension – Acts 1:6-11

Acts 1:6-26	Loose Ends	121
Acts 1:6-11	A Kingdom View	130
Acts 1:7-8	To Be Witnesses	139
Acts 1:8	The Unasked Question	147
Acts 1:9-11	The Ascended Lord	154

The Ascension – Acts 1:9-11

Acts 1:9-11	The Ascension's Blessing	163
Acts 1:9-11	In the Ascension	170
Acts 1:9-11	The Ascension of the Atonement	177
Acts 1:9-11	The Ascension Ministry	186
Acts 1:9-11	The Ascension Plan	194

Preparing for Pentecost – Acts 1:12-26

Acts 1:11-14	Returning to Jerusalem	205
Acts 1:14	One Accord	213
Acts 1:14	Let's Pray	222
Acts 1:14	Perseverance	230
Acts 1:15-26	Must	236

A God Ordained Board Meeting:
The Proposition – Acts 1:16-19

Acts 1:16	The Setting for Pentecost	247
Acts 1:16	The Speaking of God	255
Acts 1:16	Being a Guide	262
Acts 1:17	Aspiring to be Judas	270
Acts 1:18-19	What Do I Deserve?	278
Acts 1:19	To Know	287

A God Ordained Board Meeting:
His Preference – Acts 1:20-24

Acts 1:20	My Life in the Scriptures	297
Acts 1:21-22	A Resurrection Witness	304
Acts 1:21-22	To Be Made a Witness	312
Acts 1:23-25	What is the Right Strategy?	320
Acts 1:24	The Heart Knower	327
Acts 1:24	Surrender of Pentecost	334

A God Ordained Board Meeting:
His Place – Acts 1:24-26

Acts 1:24-25	An Aggressive Usher	345

Acts 1:25	Where Do I Belong?	352
Acts 1:25	The Ministry	359
Acts 1:25	The Apostleship	367
Acts 1:25	Traditions Beyond Jesus	375
Acts 1:25	Theology Beyond Jesus	382
Acts 1:25	Out of Shape	390
Acts 1:26	Secondary – Superior	398

About the Author   407

PART ONE
ACTS 1:1-2

THE DIVINE ACTIVITY THING

Acts 1:1

A DIVINE ACTIVITY THING

The former account I made, O Theophilus, of all that Jesus began both to do and teach, (Acts 1:1).

The former account are the first words from Luke's pen. He underscores this former account with the word **truly**, which most Bible translations do not include. It reads, **The truly former account I made.** This alerts us that only half of the story is contained in the Book of Acts. The first chapter of the Book of Acts is the former account in a summary form (1:1-11). Luke wants you to understand the framework of time in which he is writing. He begins this story in his first account. He will continue it with the same style and thrust. Luke's purpose for writing the Book of Acts is the same as his purpose for writing the Gospel of Luke, the truly former account.

With a little research, you will discover that these two books were circulated throughout the early Church as only one book, but two volumes. In its beginning form, both books were combined into what was called the Gospel of Luke, volume one and volume two. There were, however, other gospel accounts also being circulated at this time. Volume one of the Gospel of Luke became identified with the other Gospels. Thus, the stories of Jesus were linked together as the Gospels, and the volume two of the Gospel of Luke was eliminated.

The second volume is an important document from

a historical point of view. It bridges the gap between the life of Christ and the established early Church. It is also recognized as a spiritual book of instruction. Men soon came to recognize it as a writing all of its own, and it became known as the Book of Acts.

This is important information. It tells us that the theme of the Gospel of Luke and the Book of Acts are the same. Luke writes one book, not two. He has the same purpose, and he uses the same style and thrust in each volume. Thus, there is no way to grasp the Book of Acts without first understanding the flow from the Gospel of Luke. What is the theme? This is the proposition. **There is a divine God who is acting in redemptive ways. Every story, every circumstance, every scene is about a God activity thing.**

We must establish Luke's thrust in volume one, the Gospel of Luke. The first two chapters center on the birth of Jesus Christ. There are a variety of events which surround this occasion. Each event points to the truth that this is a Divine activity thing.

Mary is in the garden outside her parent's home. She is probably day dreaming about her coming marriage. She is imagining what it will be like to be married to Joseph. The plans for her new home run through her mind. Suddenly an angel appears and interrupts her dream with this announcement. *"Do not be afraid, Mary, for you have found favor with God. And behold, you will conceive in your womb and bring forth a Son, and shall call His name Jesus,"* (Luke 1:30-31). Can you imagine how troubling this announcement was to Mary? She responded, *"How can this be, since I do not know a man?"* (Luke 1:34). It is very important to Luke that we understand the birth of Christ was a Divine activity thing. *And the angel answered and said to her, "The Holy Spirit will come upon you, and the power of the Highest will overshadow you; therefore, also, that Holy One who is to be born will be called the Son of God,"* (Luke 1:35). Three times Luke relates the birth of Jesus to a Divine activity thing.

Intimately connected with this story is the account of the

birth of John the Baptist. Luke writes of this revelation coming to Mary through the angel. *"Now indeed, Elizabeth your relative has also conceived a son in her old age; and this is now the sixth month for her who was called barren,"* (Luke 1:36). Though it is not as pronounced as the birth of Christ, there is no question a Divine miracle has taken place. John the Baptist will be born through a Divine activity thing.

Luke tells us numerous times about the special presence of God involved in these two chapters. When Mary went to visit Elizabeth, the babe leaped in her womb, **and Elizabeth was filled with the Holy Spirit,** (Luke 1:41). Upon hearing the news of his wife's pregnancy, Zacharias laughed and was immediately struck dumb. He could not talk until the baby was born. At John's birth, he wrote on a tablet the name of his new Son, and immediately **Zacharias was filled with the Holy Spirit and prophesied,** (Luke 1:67).

Simeon was an old man who was waiting for the Consolation of Israel, **and the Holy Spirit was upon him,** (Luke 2:25). **And it had been revealed to him by the Holy Spirit that he would not see death before he had seen the Lord's Christ,** (Luke 2:26). When the Christ child was brought by his parents to the temple, Simeon **came by the Spirit into the temple,** (Luke 2:27). God was doing a Divine activity thing.

There can be no misunderstanding from Luke's presentation. The birth of Jesus can only be explained in terms of a Divine activity thing. God is doing a new thing! He alone has brought this to pass.

Luke gives us great insight into the childhood of Jesus. When He was twelve years old, His parents took Him into Jerusalem. When it was time to return home, they went an entire day's journey before they realized Jesus was not with them. They had left Him behind in Jerusalem. They hurried back to the city, but it took them a while to find Him. He was in the temple with the teachers. When they asked Jesus to explain what He was doing,

Part One: The Divine Activity Thing

He answered them in the form of a question. ***"Did you not know that I must be about My Father's business?"*** (Luke 2:49). Even in childhood, Jesus knew He was not here to do His own thing. He was here to do the Divine activity thing.

Now Luke moves quickly to the beginning of Jesus' ministry. He is concerned about establishing the very basis for this ministry. Jesus comes to the river where John the Baptist is ministering. Jesus insists that John baptize Him. When John takes Jesus into the river, it was as if all of heaven opened up. ***And the Holy Spirit descended in bodily form like a dove upon Him, and a voice came from heaven which said, "You are my beloved Son; in You I am well pleased,"*** (Luke 3:22). The second member of the Trinity emptied Himself of all He had as God. He became a total man. As a man, He surrendered Himself back to the Father, so the Father could fill Him with Himself. The Father acts upon the stage of Jesus' life through the Holy Spirit. The life of Jesus is a result of what the Father does through Him. He will not do what He does because He is God, although indeed He is God. He will do what He does because He is a man filled with God. His ministry will be a God activity thing.

Luke takes us immediately to the temptation of Jesus in the wilderness. The victory of this occasion is indeed a Divine activity thing. He begins to tell us about this battle with the words, ***Then Jesus being filled with the Holy Spirit, returned from the Jordan and was led by the Spirit into the wilderness,*** (Luke 4:1). This is being directed by the Father. Jesus experiences victory in every facet of the temptation because He refuses to act in Himself. He constantly rests in the Divine activity thing.

Luke reports, ***Then Jesus returned in the power of the Spirit to Galilee,*** (Luke 4:14). The first scene of Jesus' ministry takes place in Nazareth. He comes to the synagogue on the Sabbath day. They hand Him the book of the prophet Isaiah. What would be more suitable for Him to read?

> *"The Spirit of the Lord is upon Me,*
> *Because He has anointed Me*
> *To preach the gospel to the poor;*
> *He has sent Me to heal the brokenhearted,*
> *To proclaim liberty to the captives*
> *And recovery of sight to the blind,*
> *To set at liberty those who are oppressed;*
> *To proclaim the acceptable year of the Lord,"*
> (Luke 4:18-19).

All of this is about the Spirit of the Lord acting upon and through Jesus. He surrenders Himself totally to the Father. He does this in order to demonstrate who the Father is! His life is a product of a Divine activity thing.

Jesus called His disciples. Now it was a time in their training, when He should give them something of Himself. He wanted to share with them what was happening in Him, (Luke 9:1). It was time for them to experience the reality of the action of God through them. He sent them out to minister. When they returned, they were extremely excited. The demons came under their control. But Jesus was fearful, lest they did not understand the focus of the Divine activity thing. He began to instruct them, **saying, "The Son of Man must suffer many things, and be rejected by the elders and chief priests and scribes, and be killed, and raised the third day,"** (Luke 9:22). The heart of the Divine activity thing is the cross style. The flow of the Divine life can never be used for self promotion. If they are to continue to experience this life, they must have the mind of Christ, the style of the cross.

It soon became evident that the disciples did not grasp His message. On their way to Jerusalem, they passed through Samaria. James and John were sent to a village to secure a place to spend the night. The leaders of the village would not allow Jesus and His disciples to stay there. James and John were extremely

Part One: The Divine Activity Thing

upset. Their suggestion to Jesus was, ***"Lord, do You want us to command fire to come down from heaven and consume them, just as Elijah did?"*** (Luke 9:54). The disciples wanted to use the Divine activity thing to satisfy their own desires.

Jesus immediately rebukes them. He says ***"You do not know what manner of spirit you are of. For the Son of Man did not come to destroy men's lives but to save them,"*** (Luke 9:55-56). The disciples do not express the attitude, or the Spirit, of the Divine activity thing. Jesus always pours His life out to others. The heart of the Father, expressed through Jesus, is always redemptive.

Jesus stands at a crisis point in His ministry. He attempts to win three major cities in order to form an evangelistic basis to win the whole world. It failed! He wants to win the leadership of Israel. That, too, ends in failure! His ministry plans are not being fulfilled. He is at a crossroads in His life and ministry. What will be His response to this apparent set back? ***In that hour Jesus rejoiced in the Spirit and said, "I thank You, Father, Lord of heaven and earth, that You have hidden these things from the wise and prudent and revealed them to babes. Even so, Father, for so it seemed good in Your sight!"*** (Luke 10:21). Jesus believes this is all under the control of the Divine activity thing.

Jesus was aware that the disciples were worried about many things. If they could only have His eye sight, then they could see the great provision of the Divine activity thing (Luke 12:22-40). The Divine activity thing made provision for the ravens (Luke 12:24). It had also made provision for the grass (Luke 12:28). Surely the Divine activity thing would provide for the disciples!

Jesus finds the disciples arguing intensely over position. ***Now there was also a dispute among them, as to which of them should be considered the greatest,*** (Luke 22:24). Jesus continues His explanation of the style of the cross. His desire is for them to grasp the fundamental of the Kingdom of God! He ends the discussion by informing them that it is a Divine activity thing which establishes positions and Kingdoms (Luke 22:29).

Jesus prays three prayers in the Garden of Gethsemane. The central issue of each prayer is a focus on the Divine activity thing. He prayed, ***"Father, if it is Your will, take this cup away from Me, nevertheless not My will, but Yours, be done,"*** (Luke 22:42). Even the death of Christ is a Divine activity thing. Hanging upon the cross, Jesus cries out, ***"Father, into your hands I commit My spirit,"*** (Luke 23:46).

Surely the theme of volume one, the Gospel according to Luke, is plain to us. The second member of the Trinity emptied Himself of all He knows as God and becomes a total man. As a man, He surrenders Himself to the Father. He becomes a stage upon which the Father can demonstrate Himself. What is done through Jesus is not because He is God, although He is, but it is because He is a man totally surrendered to God. God is doing a Divine activity thing through the life of Jesus.

If you are thinking at all, I'm sure you are beginning to understand where this is leading. I am going to be asked to be like Jesus. That may be a proper goal, but it is idealistic in this life. Jesus is always right, and I am always wrong. Jesus is always wise, and I am always foolish. There is absolutely no way I can reach to the high state of being the demonstration of the Father as Jesus did.

BUT WAIT! Now we come to volume two, the Book of Acts. Here is a group of people just like us. They are mean, nasty, legalistic, over come with tradition and ceremonies, and they destroy the lives of other people. They fight for control and position. They use each other for their own benefits. All of a sudden something dramatic takes place in their lives, and they experience the Divine activity thing, just like Jesus.

From the very outset of volume two, we are reminded of the words of Jesus, ***"But you shall receive power when the Holy Spirit has come upon you; and you shall be witnesses to Me in Jerusalem, and in all Judea and Samaria, and to the end of the earth,"*** (Acts 1:8). Immediately after this introduction, we are

Part One: The Divine Activity Thing

exposed to the great Day of Pentecost, (Acts 2:1). ***And they were all filled with the Holy Spirit and began to speak with other tongues, as the Spirit gave them utterance,*** (Acts 2:4). Luke makes a great effort to inform us correctly. The entire ministry of this volume can only be explained by the Divine activity thing. Just as Jesus' ministry was a product of God's activity within Him, volume one, so the disciples will experience the same thing.

A large crowd has gathered. They are wondering what is going to take place. Peter stands in front of them all. Some of the crowd begin to mock. Surely when Peter is confronted he will do as he has always done. He will deny, cower, and run away. But Peter doesn't seem to be the same. He presents a powerful sermon of bold truth. It is a result of the Divine activity thing taking place in his life.

In the heart of Peter's message he exposes the Divine activity thing which took place in Jesus. ***"Men of Israel, hear these words: Jesus of Nazareth, a Man attested by God to you by miracles, wonders, and signs which God did through Him in your midst,"*** (Acts 2:22). He explains that the cross was the Divine activity thing (Acts 2:23). Even the resurrection was a Divine activity thing as it took place in the life of Jesus (Acts 2:24; 32). It was a Divine activity thing that made Jesus both Lord and Christ (Acts 2:36).

Peter and John go to the Temple (Acts 3:1). A lame man sits at the gate of the Temple called Beautiful, begging and asking for alms. Peter had no money to give, but he did have a Divine activity thing to share. The man was healed and created quite a scene of rejoicing. The people began to respond to Peter and John as if they had done this great feat. ***So when Peter saw it, he responded to the people, "Men of Israel, why do you marvel at this? Or why look so intently at us, as though by our own power or godliness we had made this man walk?"*** (Acts 3:12). Peter rushed into a discourse of explanation about the greatness of the Divine activity thing.

This greatly upset the leaders of Israel, and they rushed in to take the disciples into custody (Acts 4:3). The leaders of Israel, who were in charge, confronted them, saying, *"By what power or by what name have you done this?"* (Acts 4:7). Luke takes great care to be sure we understand the source of this miracle. *Then Peter, filled with the Holy Spirit, said to them. ...* (Acts 4:8). It is intriguing to notice the reaction of the leaders of Israel to Peter's answer. *Now when they saw the boldness of Peter and John, and perceived that they were uneducated and untrained men, they marveled. And they realized that they had been with Jesus,* (Acts 4:13). Is there any question? All of this is a product of the Divine activity thing.

Upon their release from custody, Peter and John return to the early Church fellowship and share all that has taken place. *And when they had prayed, the place where they were assembled together was shaken; and they were all filled with the Holy Spirit, and they spoke the word of God with boldness,* (Acts 4:31). It continues to be a demonstration of the Divine activity thing.

The leaders of Israel continue to respond to this demonstration by taking the apostles captive again. The council said to them, *"Did we not strictly command you not to teach in this name? And look, you have filled Jerusalem with your doctrine, and intend to bring this Man's blood on us!"* (Acts 5:28). And what was the response of Peter and the apostles? They simply said they could not help themselves. There was within them a passion and fire. *"We ought to obey God rather than men,"* (Acts 5:29). It was a Divine activity thing taking place in them.

Stephen was full of faith and power. This resulted in many great signs and wonders being done through him among the people. A certain religious group came to dispute him. Luke's emphasis is not upon the educational talent of Stephen, but upon the Divine activity thing. *And they were not able to resist the wisdom and the Spirit by which he spoke,* (Acts 6:10).

Here we go again! *Now the angel of the Lord spoke to Philip,*

Part One: The Divine Activity Thing

(Acts 8:26). ***Then the Spirit said to Philip, "Go near and overtake this chariot,"*** (Acts 8:29). A eunuch of great authority, under Candace the queen of the Ethiopians, was riding in his chariot. He was reading the Scriptures in an attempt to understand the truth. Philip joins him and leads him to a knowledge of Jesus as his Savior. An entire nation will be influenced. This was not the result of clever Church planting or careful marketing; it is a Divine activity thing.

Then Saul, still breathing threats and murder against the disciples of the Lord, went to the chief priest and asked letters for him to the synagogues of Damascus, (Acts 9:1-2). The early Church had a real problem with Saul of Tarsus. At a high rate of speed, and with extreme zeal, he was striving to eliminate the entire Christian church. Who in the early Church would plan a strategy to win Saul? Will the chief evangelist confront him? Certainly the one who knows the evangelism plan the best should be selected for the job. But you know the story well. God came in a blinding light and struck him from his horse (Acts 9:3-4)! No one would be able to say, "I was the one who led Saul of Tarsus to Christ." It was a Divine activity thing.

All of this is summarized for us in one tremendous statement. ***Then the churches throughout all of Judea, Galilee, and Samaria had peace and were edified. And walking in the fear of the Lord and in the comfort of the Holy Spirit, they were multiplied,*** (Acts 9:31). In a period of 70 years, the early Church won over a million people to Christ. Christianity became the world religion. This great growth of the Church can only be explained as coming from one source. It was a Divine activity thing.

Luke clearly states his theme. In volume one, we discover the second member of the Trinity empties Himself of all He knows as God. He becomes a total man, and He surrenders Himself back to God. God now acts upon the stage of His life to demonstrate Himself in this world. The entire ministry of Jesus can only be explained by the Divine activity thing.

But it would be impossible for us to live in a similar manner. Christ's likeness is the ideal. We can only try, but we can never attain. Yet, we see in volume two, a tremendous happening in the lives of people just like us. They have the background of sinful defeat, just as we do. But the Divine activity thing, which demonstrated Himself through the life of the man, Jesus, is now doing it again through the lives of the disciples. It is the only explanation for what took place in the early Church. It is a Divine activity thing.

Do you suppose He wants to write a volume three with you and me? Could the same Divine activity thing, who acted through Jesus, and then through the disciples of old, now demonstrate Himself through you and me? It is the most desperate need of our lives. We have produced an anemic Christianity, which is a product of the best that we can do. We long for our lives to be the product of the best that He can do!

There is only one hindrance to this. Will we surrender to Jesus in the same way He surrendered to His Father? Will we push aside everything we depend upon outside of Him? The talent and skills, so carefully developed, can no longer be the source of our ministry. The knowledge and wisdom, which we have accumulated through education and experience, can no longer be our basis of operation. If we can surrender to Jesus in the same way Jesus surrendered to His Father, we will know the Divine activity thing.

What other answer is there to the great need of our lives? This is our only chance. Jesus would never have been victorious in redeeming a world through the cross, nor would the disciples have ever experienced the conquering of their world, without the Divine activity thing. This is our only chance as well. Our family, our personal victory, and our evangelism are all dependent upon one factor - the Divine activity thing!

Acts 1:1

THE BEGINNING

> *The former account I made, O Theophilus, of all that Jesus began both to do and teach, until the day in which He was taken up, after He through the Holy Spirit had given commandments to the apostles whom He had chosen, to whom He also presented Himself alive after His suffering by many infallible proofs, being seen by them during forty days and speaking of the things pertaining to the kingdom of God,*
> *(Acts 1:1-3).*

In chapter one of Acts, the first three verses constitute one long sentence. This significant statement sets the boundaries of the first volume. If you diagram the sentence, you will establish the main verb, the subject, and other details of the verses. However, when you get the correct grammar, you do not really discover the key to the whole thought Luke is trying to give us. The thrust of the statement is contained in the idea of one translated word. It is contained in the word which is translated **began**. Everything else in the sentence gives content to this one word.

The Gospel of Luke is the first volume. When we discover and understand the content of the first volume, we have a proper perspective of the second volume, the Book of Acts. Volume one tells us what God the Father did through Jesus the Son. In volume two, we read what He did through the apostles. Volume three is being written now. God desperately wants to continue, in you and me, what He did in Jesus and the disciples. The content of volume one is our key to understanding all that is taking place. The idea which seems to unlock this is contained in the sentence which begins with the word **began**.

A simple definition of the word is this, "to be the first to do anything, the beginning." It is amazing how many times this word is used in the New Testament. There are several different emphases of this word which we need to note.

In relationship to CIRCUMSTANCES, the word "began" has to do with "to begin, to make a beginning." The word seems to revolve around the idea that something began, meaning it had never been done. Therefore, something which had not been in existence, was actually being done. In the context of our passage, this means Jesus was the first to do something which no one else had ever done. Perhaps it would be better to say what Jesus was, or what He became, no one else had ever been. If it had been in existence before, it had been so long ago that no one remembered. He started something brand-new for His hour.

In relationship to a PERSON, this word refers to being a chief, to be a leader, or to be a ruler. It is often translated pioneer, captain, or author. It originated from the idea of hero or founder. In days of old this word was used to describe the hero, or the founder, of the city. It was used to describe the person whose insight and resources brought the city into existence. In the context of our passage, it is Jesus who is the beginner. He is the chief, the leader of this new something. He is the beginner, the author, the captain, the pioneer of this new something. He founded a new city and new people by His own resource.

When you apply the word "began" to TIME, it actually refers to the point in time when something, which had not been in existence, came into being. It speaks of this point in time as the new beginning. In the context of this passage, the time span of the life of Jesus on earth is the beginning point of this brand

Part One: The Divine Activity Thing

new something. From His birth through to His death, from the resurrection to the ascension, is the time span when this new set of circumstances was brought into existence. During this time, our hero, by His own resource, began something new. The new something, of which Jesus is the pioneer or starter, happened about two thousand years ago.

There is also the PHILOSOPHICAL application of this term. It is used to refer to the original material from which the new something evolves. The new circumstances come from a new substance. This makes perfect sense, since it has not been in existence. If the circumstance, or being, is not of this new substance, then it is not the new beginning. In the context of our passage, Jesus is the material, the substance from which this new something began. Every time you find this new something, or any place you find it, you will find His substance. He is the material from which the new something is made. There have been many attempts to duplicate this material, but they are all fakes. There is only one authentic material, and it is Him. If in passing, you view what looks like this new something, it would be well to stop and examine it closely. It may look like the new something Jesus has brought into existence, but if it does not have Jesus' substance it is not authentic. It must smell, taste, and feel like Him, or is not the real thing.

The word **began** tells us that Jesus Christ brought into existence a whole new something which has not been in existence. He began it during the time He was on earth, from His birth to His death and resurrection. He is the hero, and founder, of this brand new something. He is the substance of this new something. If He is not the substance, then it is not authentic.

If you are like me, you are now crying out, "What is this new something of which Jesus is the author, the beginner? What is this new something which has not existed before Him, but is now made from the material of His being?"

Volume one and volume two seem to have the answer to this

question! The second member of the Trinity emptied Himself of all He knew as God and became a total man. As a man He surrendered Himself back to the Father, who began to act upon the stage of His life to demonstrate all He, the Father, was. It was a Divine activity thing (volume one). Then a group of people, just like us, appear on the scene. They have all of our shortcomings and flaws. Yet, this same Divine activity thing happened in them, and they began to manifest the same demonstration (volume two). From the demonstrations, there is a strong teaching that God wants to write a volume three with us.

When you look at what Jesus was as a man, and what the early disciples became through the Divine activity thing, what would you call them? It appears they should be called "Sons of God." They are born of God and experience the very nature of God. They have become partakers of the Divine nature (2 Peter 1:4). Jesus was the very first Son of God. What He was, we are to be. God dreamed of many sons who would look like Him and demonstrate who He is.

It is exciting to go through the Book of Acts (volume two), and see the various places and usages of this word "began." For instance, Peter and John go to the Temple. There is a man who lies daily at the gate of the temple which is called Beautiful. He is begging for alms. Peter tells him they do not have any money, but they have a Divine activity thing, which they will be glad to share with him. Immediately his feet and ankle bones receive strength.

Rejoicing and praising are the result. It is quite a scene. The people who are watching begin to think Peter and John are the ones responsible for this miracle. Immediately Peter breaks into a sermon. He preaches a tremendous message in which he tells them a Divine activity thing brought about this miracle. He describes how Jesus was delivered up to be crucified. Then he gives a confrontational statement. ***"But you denied the Holy One and the Just, and asked for a murderer to be granted to you, and killed the Prince of life, whom God raised from the***

dead, of which we are witnesses," (Acts 3:14-15). Notice the phrase, ***the Prince of life.*** The word ***Prince,*** and the word ***began*** (Acts 1:1), are the same word. Peter tells this great crowd that Jesus is the beginner, the author, the source, and the material of a whole new existence of life. A new breed of humanity has been started with Christ. These are called Sons of God. There has never been anyone quite like them. They are the demonstration of the Divine activity thing.

The leaders and Israel have already threatened the apostles about teaching in Jesus' name. I guess they thought their threat would end the whole matter. But the power, acting within and through the disciples, was much bigger than their threats. The disciples were brought in before the council again. The enemies of the Divine activity thing tell us how extensive their witness really is, when they say, ***"Did we not strictly command you not to teach in this name? And look, you have filled Jerusalem with your doctrine, and intend to bring this Man's blood on us!"*** (Acts 5:28). What is the disciples' response? They say they just could not help themselves. God is doing something within them, and through them, and they could not stop it. Peter goes on to preach another message to the leadership of Israel. He tells them God raised Jesus from the dead. It is the very Jesus they murdered. ***"Him God has exalted to His right hand to be Prince and Savior, to give repentance to Israel and forgiveness of sins,"*** (Acts 5:31).

As we said before, the word ***Prince*** is the same word translated ***began*** (Acts 1:1). He is the founder, the Prince, the author, the beginner, the captain, and the trailblazer of a whole new thing. It has never been in existence before. It has to do with forgiveness of sins and a brand-new substance from which a new breed of people will come into existence. They will be the result of a Divine activity thing.

You cannot read through the epistles of the New Testament without running into this special word and its concept. The

Book of Hebrews clearly states it as it gives a clear picture of the superior Jesus. The author declares Jesus as superior to angels, (Hebrews 1). Now he quotes from David's Psalm (Psalms 8:4-6). David is questioning his significance. In light of the greatness of the creation around him, why would God care about him? Man was made a little lower than the angels (Hebrews 2:7), and yet he finds himself crowned with glory and honor. So the order of things is God, angels, and then mankind. Yet man has received the dominion over all the creation of His hands.

But the tragic part of the message is in the "Fall." *But now we do not yet see all things put under him,* (Hebrews 2:8). Man has become dominated instead of dominating. His circumstances and his surroundings have overcome him. All is in dismay. *But we see Jesus, who was made a little lower than the angels, for the suffering of death crowned with glory and honor, that He by the grace of God, might taste death for everyone,* (Hebrews 2:9). Jesus leaped from His throne, but He did not become an angel. Instead He stooped to the lowest, and He became a man. He did this for a purpose. It was to *taste death for everyone.*

In his commentary, Adam Clark, tells us the custom of that day from this verse. If a man was to be punished by death for his crimes, he was given a cup of poison. Fully aware of what was taking place, the criminal would hold the cup of poison in his hand. By the movement of his own muscle, he would bring the cup of poison to his lips. He would drink it all and die. Behold the scene! Every man, every woman, every boy, and every girl is standing shoulder to shoulder from every generation. A cup of poison has been placed in every hand. Everyone is guilty and worthy of death. The first one begins to bring the cup of poison to his lips. He will drink it and die. *But we see Jesus!* He comes to the first man, and snatches the cup of poison from his hand. Jesus drinks it all! Christ rushes to the next person in line and drinks his poison as well. Onto the next, and to the next he goes, until every cup of poison is consumed for every person.

Part One: The Divine Activity Thing

Why would Jesus do this? What does He hope to accomplish? In the very next verse the author says, ***For it was fitting for Him, for whom are all things and by whom are all things, in bringing many sons to glory, to make the captain of their salvation perfect through sufferings,*** (Hebrews 2:10). In the beginning part of the verse he is obviously referring to God, the Father. He is the One ***for whom are all things and by whom all things.*** It seems He has a dream! He wants ***many sons*** in glory. He does not want one, or several, but ***many.*** How can this be accomplished? He will make the ***captain of their salvation perfect through sufferings.***

The word ***captain*** is the same word Luke uses for ***began*** (Acts 1:1). Jesus is the trailblazer, the pioneer, the scout, the beginner, and the author of a brand-new happening. He broke a hole through the wall. He made a door where there was no door. He invaded territory where no one else had ever gone. He established a new category called Sons of God. When Jesus accomplished it, He turned around and grabbed a hold of you and me, and He pulled us through also. We, too, have become Sons of God. He was the first one (volume one); the early disciples were the second and third, etc. (volume two). Jesus now wants to continue with you and me (volume three). It is the substance of the Divine activity thing, making us Sons of God.

The blood of Christ is one of the great themes of the Bible. The epistles are filled with this emphasis. It is the blood of Christ which brought about this new breed of humanity called the Sons of God. We find a proper understanding of this theme in the Old Testament. ***For the life of the flesh is in the blood,*** (Leviticus 17:11). The word, ***life,*** and the word, ***blood,*** are synonymous. When you take a man's life, you take his blood. When we speak of the blood of Jesus, we highlight the eternal life of God.

There are deep ramifications to the usage of the word for blood. There is a distinct reference to the idea of conception. It is as if contained within the blood is the seed of life itself. On the cross, more than just physical blood was spilled. On the cross, in a moment of time, the eternal life of God was injected into a world. A whole new breed of humanity was born. They were unlike anyone has ever been.

What does this new breed of humanity look like? What kind of people are they? They are like Jesus (volume one). The second member of the Trinity emptied Himself of all He knew as God. He became a total man, offering Himself back to God, the Father, in total surrender. God began to act upon the stage of His life. Jesus was a demonstration of the Divine activity thing. The only explanation for the life of Jesus on this earth was God acting through Him. He was the first Son of God.

Then came a group of people who had a background of sin, just like you and me. Something happened in a moment of time, and they were filled with the Divine activity thing (volume two). They were born from above. They experienced the life of God and became demonstrations of the person of God. They were Sons of God who were born from a cross.

But where are these Sons of God today? Do we just read about them in ancient history? We are to be volume three! Luke wrote the former account to tell us all that the pioneer, captain, trailblazer, author, beginner, founder, and hero did and taught. He is the substance of a brand-new thing. He was the first of this brand new breed of people. But was it only for one man? No! Volume two is about the spread of the Divine activity thing through the lives of hundreds of people just like us. The very life of God, living through Jesus, comes now to live through them. They shake their world in an immeasurable way.

He wants to do it again through us. We are to be volume three. What Jesus began, He wants to continue through us. Who is available?

Acts 1:1

DOING AND TEACHING

The former account I made, O Theophilus, of all that Jesus began both to do and teach, (Acts 1:1).

Even before greeting his reader, Luke reminds him of this former account. This seems to be very important to Luke. The former account is essential to understanding what is happening in volume two (The Book of Acts). Luke wrote volume one (The Gospel According to Luke) with the same theme and thrust as volume two (The Book of Acts).

The theme of volume one is the Divine activity thing. The second member of the Trinity leaped off His throne. He emptied Himself of all He knew as God, and He became a total man. As a man, He surrendered Himself back to the Father, allowing the Father to act upon the stage of His life. Everything happening in the life of Jesus can only be explained by the Father's action through Him.

The same theme, the Divine activity thing, is true in volume two. The Divine activity thing is acting through the lives of people just like us. They are mean and nasty. They are legalistic and filled with a self-will. But suddenly, in a moment of time, they become a product of the Divine activity thing. The same life style which Jesus had is now being lived through them. The same source of life has come to indwell them. Now we come into the picture. The same Divine activity thing wants to write a volume three, and He wants to do it in us.

As you look at the former account to understand its happenings, it is clear that it is about what Jesus began. Jesus started something which had not been in existence. He is the pioneer, scout, author, and the beginner of the new deal. He broke a hole through the wall and made a door where there was no door. He created a new breed of people. They are called sons of God. Jesus was volume one. The early church was volume two. We are volume three. What Jesus was, the early disciples became, and we are to be. We can experience the same thing in our lives. ***Jesus began!***

There are some important details in the content of **Jesus began.** He began **both to do and teach.** If Luke had simply written about "all that Jesus began to do," he could have filled two volumes. The dynamic miracles of Jesus reached every area of life. He raised the dead and cast out demons. The doings of Jesus could occupy us for eternity. If Luke had written about "all that Jesus began to teach," he could have filled two more volumes. The teachings of Jesus are a wonder to study and ponder. We could study for all eternity and not grasp the depth of meaning in the Sermon on the Mount. Alone with His doings, or alone with His teachings, there is more content than we can assimilate.

However, there is a definite attempt by Luke to link the doing and the teaching together. He writes, ***of all Jesus began both to do and teach.*** He links doing and teaching with the conjunction **and.** This would be sufficient to link the two, yet, he goes on to emphasize this linkage with the word **both.** He does not want to miss the intimate tie between doing and teaching. He presents them as a unit, a whole. They cannot be divided in the ministry of Jesus.

This linkage has a huge scope. Therefore, we need to examine it a part at a time.

Part One: The Divine Activity Thing

Doing Is Teaching

This is not a new idea. We have heard this truth all of our lives. It appears in statements like, "What you do speaks so loud, I can't hear what you say." Doing is a forceful teacher. It overrides the lectures you give. I learn from you, not by what you tell me, but by what you do before me.

This was certainly true for Jesus. His actions were the out spill of His teachings. Jesus was the expressed image of the invisible God. He taught us the heart of God. We now know how God feels, thinks and acts. We do not know this because Jesus told us, although we did hear Him speak and were moved by what He said. We do not know this from diagrams of Jesus' theological persuasion of God. We know this because Jesus demonstrated it to us through His life style.

We can understand what Jesus said because we saw it in the very style of His life. What He said was profound, but it was far removed from where we live and act. It was completely out of our reach, and there was no way we could grasp it in a practical manner. He communicated to us by what He lived and taught. In a combination of His doing and teaching, He captivated us with the possibility that we could have this too.

Luke records the Sermon on the Mount in chapter six (Luke 6:20-49). In it, Jesus gives the Beatitudes. He expounds the principles of love and compassion. He said things like, **"Love your enemies,"** (Luke 6:27). But what exactly does He mean? How, exactly, am I to express love? Is this the same love I have for God, or my dog, or my wife, or my car? Perhaps I am to simply tolerate him when he comes near me. And who is my enemy anyway? I know my enemy is the one who has done unmentionable things to me. But there are other people I just do not like to be around. Which ones of these is Jesus instructing me to love?

Then suddenly Jesus answers the question about my enemy. He concludes His message and goes to the streets with His sleeves rolled up. He is approached by a centurion. This man has a servant who is dying, and he believes Jesus can help him. A Jew would never help a Roman centurion. He is the head of the Roman garrison which polices their town. He is the hated symbol of the enemy who has harmed and conquered them. Why is Jesus embracing this man? He speaks the word and the servant is healed. He demonstrates what He said in the Sermon on the Mount. This must be what He meant when He said, *"Love your enemies."*

In the life of Jesus, we can see Him move from one teaching and doing to another teaching and doing. He always demonstrated what He taught by His actions. He never taught without linking with it a doing. There is no mistaking what Jesus meant because of the Divine activity thing through Him. He never proposed a spiritual concept but what He acted it out in His life. We heard Him, then we saw Him.

If we trace the linkage of teaching and doing we will end up at the cross. What Jesus taught us about the Father was acted out on the cross. The way to save your life is to lose it. That great truth is seen in reality in the cross resurrection event. If He had escaped this moment, could we ever have believed what He said? Doing is teaching!

This is Luke's proposition in volume one. **What God, the Father, taught us through Jesus Christ, the Son, is exactly what God did through Jesus.** We heard it, and we saw it! Jesus, by His very life, was the pattern of exactly what the Father wants to do, in and through us. What Jesus is, we are to be. What He did, we are to do. What He became, we are to become.

It is important to teach everyone that "God is love." We put it on our church's billboard for all to see. But the neighbors are aware that a new church building is under construction at the edge of town. Who is starting a new church? It is the group who

Part One: The Divine Activity Thing

heatedly left the church with the billboard that reads, "God is love." What happened to the love of God in their midst? This church split contradicts their billboard, and it cannot be repaired, because doing is teaching.

I place my child on my knee and proceed to teach him this children's chorus.

> "Jesus loves the little children,
> All the children of the world.
> Red and yellow, black and white,
> They are precious in His sight.
> Jesus loves the little children of the world."

But I interrupt my teaching with a conversation with my wife. She wants to know about the decision made at the recent board meeting of the local church. I tell her we voted to relocate the church. The neighborhood around our present building has become dangerous. After all, those ethnic groups have taken over our community, and we just do not feel safe anymore. Which message is my child learning? After all, doing is teaching!

I can tell people about the cross, but what I say is meaningless, unless they see it in the style of my life. To yell it from the pulpit or the class room, and not live it on the streets, contradicts the truth of the message; because doing is teaching. The message of forgiveness is wonderful. Jesus forgives every sin. He forgives seventy times seven. But who can believe the truth of such a message when we do not forgive each other? Doing is teaching.

We continually encourage people to seek the heart of God. When you tell me to respond to God, but I never see you do it, I do not know how. When I see you seeking, then I learn how. If I never see you at the altar, kneeling in openness before God, I do not know how to respond in openness. Doing is teaching. I am going to be just like you. If you do not show me, I will not learn.

There is a second linkage between doing and teaching.

Teaching Is Doing

When you do, you teach. The reversal is also true. What you teach is what you do. If your life style does not match your teaching, you will adjust your teaching. You cannot stand a contradiction between your life style and your teaching, therefore, you make the adjustment in your teaching. If we did not do this, we could not live with the guilt it produces in us.

We can see this clearly in volume one (The Gospel According to Luke). Jesus has come to a time in His ministry when He needs to test His disciples. He has given them "on the job training" for over two years. Are they grasping the truth as He is doing and teaching? He asks them, *"But who do you say that I am?"* (Luke 9:20). Of course, Peter has the answer. He jumps to his feet and cries, *"The Christ of God!"* That is the right answer, but do the disciples really understand what that means? Do they grasp the concept of what it means to be *The Christ of God?* Jesus explains to them the essence of the Divine activity thing through Him. He says, *"The Son of Man must suffer many things, and be rejected by the elders and chief priests and scribes, and be killed, and be raised the third day,"* (Luke 9:22). He spends a good bit of time developing this theme for them. He explains the Mount of Transfiguration to them (Luke 9:28-36). He focuses on the valley experience when they returned (Luke 9:37-45). He explains again the content of the Divine activity thing. *He said to His disciples, "Let these words sink down into your ears, for the Son of Man is about to be betrayed into the hands of men,"* (Luke 9:44). Did the disciples understand it?

The next scene that Luke records tells of an argument. The disciples are fighting about position. *Then a dispute arose among them as to which of them would be greatest,* (Luke 9:46). This is a representation of division in the local church. The next recorded event is John's report to Jesus. He says, *"Master, we saw*

Part One: The Divine Activity Thing

someone casting out demons in Your name, and we forbade him because he does not follow with us," (Luke 9:49). This represents division between the denominations, or groups of believers. In the next scene, James and John return from a Samaritan village. The people of this village rejected their request for lodging for Jesus and the disciples for that night. How do the sons of thunder respond? **They said, "Lord do You want us to command fire to come down from heaven and consume them, just as Elijah did?"** (Luke 9:54). This represents division among the races.

It is obvious the disciples have not grasped the style of the cross which Jesus has tried to communicate to them. Why do they reject what He says? If being the Christ of God means death on a cross, then they will have to embrace a cross as well. After all, can the disciples be greater than their Master? This was the major problem. The disciples do not want to live the cross style. They want big positions. They desire to be superior to others, and certainly to other races. If they were going to live for themselves, then they had to believe that the Messiah lived for Himself. A cross style Messiah would not do for them. He did not match their life style. How could they embrace Jesus, who pours His life out for everyone, but continue to live in their self style? They had to adjust their belief to match their life style, because teaching is doing.

There are people who have hurt me deeply. I am waiting for the day when God Himself will bring judgment upon them. After all, they need to be punished for the way they have treated me. They deserve it, after all I have suffered. So I cannot fully embrace a Jesus who dies on the cross for everyone, then turns to His enemies and says, "Father forgive them, for they know not what they do." I need a God who sets in the sky and condemns all the bad people to hell. I need a God who makes all the bad people suffer. That way, I do not have to love the people who have hurt me, because after all, God is that way too. You understand teaching is doing, do you not?

I really like, and need, a God who lives in the church. He accepts my tithe, and my proper sacrifices at the altar. That way, I do not have to get involved in the hurting people of my world, because God doesn't do that either. If my Jesus lives on the streets, involved in the lives of hurting people, I might have to leave the four walls of my church and think about the people with whom I work. There is more comfort in worshiping the God of the sky than the Christ of the cross. My belief must match my life style, because teaching is doing.

Is the Jesus you serve the real Jesus, or is the Jesus you serve one who is shaped by your lifestyle? Have you developed the way you want to live into a tradition which has shaped and determined the Jesus you serve? It is very possible to shape your perception of Jesus by your lifestyle, because teaching is doing.

Doing and Teaching Are Him

There is a third aspect to this linkage. "Doing" is not doing as you may think of it. For most people, the concept of doing means action. When doing is an action of the hand, you can separate what you do from what you feel inside. Suppose you hit another person in the face with your fist. You can rebuke your hand for its doing, and you can punish your hand by putting it in your pocket. But what about the anger within your spirit? What about the rage on your face and the elevation of your blood pressure? Did you lose your temper? Or was it simply an action of your hand? Your hand was doing the action, but your emotions are more important.

The Hellenists (Acts 6:1), were a group of people in Jesus' day who thought the action of the hand and the inside feelings had nothing to do with each other. The New Testament was written in Greek, due to the strong influence of the Greeks. This group had adopted the Greek culture and philosophy of living.

Part One: The Divine Activity Thing

All Jews had been strongly influenced by Greek thinking, but the Hellenists adopted the Greek patterns into their Jewish beliefs in a more radical way.

The intellectual emphasis of the Greek philosophy dominated the Hellenists' thinking. I hesitate to use the word "intellectual," because I am not negative against using the mind and thinking. I believe the more open we are to thinking, the more likely we are to find the truth. But there is a difference between grasping the truth and being academic. Academic fact is not truth, because the academic fact leaves out the interplay between the teaching and the doing.

This was very evident in Jesus' day. The teachers of that day were steeped in academic pursuit. They studied the law of God. They spent hours debating questions concerning the law. The longer the debates continued, the more righteous they felt. In many circles, the study of the law was held in higher esteem than the doing of the law.

Jesus' life was remarkably absent of this academic emphasis. When the Pharisees approached him with the debate about the greatest commandment, He quickly cut through the academic pursuit and said, "Oh, love God with your whole being and your neighbor as yourself, and get on with it." They wanted to consider the academic facts of doing without dealing with the inward motive and condition of the heart.

The issue of music has become a war in the evangelical movement of our day. Congregations are divided and often split concerning the music played in their churches. I have visited many of these churches. The first few rows are filled with young married couples and teens who are worshiping God. They sing the new choruses with their hands raised in praise and worship. Sitting behind them, are several rows of older adults with their arms folded. Their complaining spirits are written on their faces.

If you were to talk to those senior adults, they would express their concern in the terms of the academic fact. They would tell you the value of the hymns which they have enjoyed all of their lives. They will tell you they cannot stand for very long. They feel there is importance in sitting in the presence of God. These are all academic facts. There is value and truth in what they say, but go beyond the academic fact and look at their inward hearts. What is the motive of their heart, and what feelings are coming from within them? Why do they not feel joyful that these young people are praising God? Why are their spirits filled with negative complaints? We can argue loud and long about the academic facts, but the heart is what really matters.

The neighborhood in which I live is going down. I have no choice but to sell my house and move to a better section of town, even if I lose most of my equity. It is an academic fact that people of the lower class have moved into my neighborhood, causing the economy of the neighborhood to depreciate. My closest neighbors have fifteen kids, and they are all hoodlums. They break my windows and steal everything I leave out. They have six junk cars in their yard, and they never mow their lawn. I just cannot live like this. Did you notice that all of my complaints are about academic facts? Why do I feel this way? What is at the heart of my feelings? I prayed this very morning, asking the Lord to give me the opportunity to minister to someone. Yet I have never gone over to my neighbor's house and offered to take their children to Sunday School. I have never offered my hand to the parents in friendship. I simply hide behind the academic facts and justify my actions.

Luke wrote about this in his gospel account of Jesus. The Greek language paints word pictures for us to see. The Greek word for "doing" has a strong undercurrent to it. It is the picture of an artist painting a picture. He is in his studio. The morning sun is shining through the window. He is dressed casually. There is soft music playing in the background. The creative juices are flowing within him. He expresses this creativity in the strokes he makes upon the canvas. Is he doing? Yes, in a sense, but it

Part One: The Divine Activity Thing

comes from within.

There is another Greek word which also means "doing." But this word has an entirely different meaning. It is the doing of an assembly line worker. His responsibility is to put a nut on a bolt. All day long he stands in one place. He puts one nut on a bolt, and then another nut on another bolt. He is bored and waiting for his break. He can hardly wait for the week end to come. Is he doing? Yes, but it is not the same kind of doing the artist does.

The word "doing," which Luke uses to describe Jesus, is the doing of the creative juices. It is the Divine activity thing. God is flowing through Jesus. He is doing so to demonstrate and teach the truths far beyond mere academic facts.

It is easy to go to the evangelism seminars and learn the academic facts about evangelizing your world. We can memorize the right Scriptures and learn the correct questions to ask. But seventy-five percent of the people who learn these facts never win anyone to Jesus. Evangelism is a flow of the Divine activity thing through the human heart.

It is easy to produce programs and slogans. We find ourselves putting a nut on a bolt, a nut on a bolt, and another nut on another bolt. We do all the right things, and we keep all the right rules. We maintain the necessary activities to be called the church. But the passion of the soul is missing. Does the Divine activity thing flow through us?

In volume one, Jesus is seen as a product of the Divine activity thing. He was filled with the heart of God. God flowed out in what He taught and what He did. He could not help Himself! He had become the stage upon which the Father acted. Volume two is the story of the early disciples, who were filled with the same heart of God, and they could not control it. Spontaneously, they spilled God out into their world in doing and teaching.

Volume three must be written in you and me! It will not happen by our learning of the academic facts, putting nuts on bolts. It can only happen as we experience the Divine activity thing from within, allowing Jesus to act upon the stage of our lives. Our world is dying to see it!

Acts 1:1-2

THE ASCENSION'S FOCUS

> *The former account I made, O Theophilus, of all that Jesus began both to do and teach, until the day in which He was taken up, after He through the Holy Spirit had given commandments to the apostles whom He had chosen,*
> *(Acts 1:1-2).*

Verse one of volume two is the statement of the proposition. Luke relates it to volume one, the former account. He focuses it on **all that Jesus began to do and teach.** Jesus' life was the product of a Divine activity thing. Verse two is the exposition of the proposition. He restates, expands and gives the details of what **Jesus began both to do and teach.**

There are three aspects to this exposition.

The Ascension

Verse two is not as it appears in the English translation. I have no criticism of the English translation, because there is no way to translate from the Greek to the English to give the impact of what Luke says in this verse. When verse two is read in the English, the main focus of the verse seems to be upon the ascension. It is forcibly stated at the beginning of the verse, and it overshadows all other ideas.

At the outset of the verse is a double statement of the ascension. Luke writes **until the day.** This refers to the Day of the Ascension. Often in the New Testament, the word *day* is used in reference to an event. Luke is not writing about a twenty-four-hour period. He is highlighting the event of the ascension. He continues with the phrase, **He was taken up.** This phrase is one word in the original language of the Bible. It is a word used to describe the ascension. This verse begins with such a heavy emphasis on the ascension, you cannot see anything else.

This is not true in the Greek language, however. The order of the words is not the same as given in the English translation. It you take the English translation and move the phrase, **He was taken up,** to the end of the verse, you will have the original order. It will read like this, "Until the day, He through the Holy Spirit had given commandments to the apostles whom He had chosen, He was taken up."

That gives a completely different emphasis. Luke sets the perimeters in the verse. He begins with *"until the day,"* and he ends with, *"He was taken up."* These two phrases surround everything else. The phrases act as parenthesis around the material Luke presents to his readers. Both phrases refer to the same thing, which is the ascension. This is significant, because the thrust of the verse is not on the ascension. Luke wants us to view the ascension as the framework in which something else takes place. The ascension is the lens through which we are to view the rest of the verse. We are to interpret the rest of the verse through the emphasis on the ascension.

What is this emphasis? **He was taken up,** is the actual translation from the Greek. It is different from the word Luke uses on other occasions. Luke establishes a contrast between two different emphases, one at the end of volume one and one at the beginning of volume two. In their original form, these volumes were in a scroll. As the reader unrolled the scroll, finishing the

Part One: The Divine Activity Thing

Gospel of Luke (volume one), he would immediately see the beginning of the Book of Acts (volume two). The Gospel of Luke ends with the story of the ascension. Luke writes, **Now it came to pass, while He blessed them, that He was parted from them and carried up into heaven,** (Luke 24:51). The Greek word translated **carried up** (Luke 24:51), is different from the Greek word translated, **He was taken up** (Luke 1:2).

At the end of volume one, Luke emphasizes the fact that Jesus offered Himself to the Father. The Greek word which Luke uses is often related to the cross and the sacrifice Jesus made. He offered Himself as a sacrifice upon the cross. It is in the imperfect tense, which indicates repeated and continual action. It is in the passive voice, which means Jesus was doing the offering. It is the indicative mood, which means it is a simple statement of fact. So Luke says Jesus offered Himself to the Father at the ascension moment, and it was a continual offering, or lifting of Himself to the Father. The focus there is upon Jesus offering Himself to the Father.

But in Acts 1:2, the word is altogether different. The word used here for the ascension has the idea of something being received. The focus is not on Jesus offering Himself, but it is upon the Father receiving Jesus. It is in the aorist tense, which means we translate it in the past tense, and it is in the passive voice, which means Jesus is the recipient of the action. It is also in the indicative mood, which makes it a simple statement. The focus in the Gospel of Luke is on what Jesus is as an offering, but in Acts it is upon the Father, who is receiving the offering.

If the focus of this verse is contained within the framework of the ascension, then it must be seen through the lens of the Father's Divine action. It is a Divine activity thing. What Luke really wants to say to us in this verse, he presents upon the stage of the ascension. The focus is about the Father's Divine action. The Father is receiving Jesus. He wants us to interpret the truth of verse two in light of the Divine activity thing, which has been his theme from the beginning.

We need to think carefully about this contrast. There is something great about the surrender of Jesus to the Father. His yielding was absolutely necessary. The Divine activity thing could not have happened in the life of Christ without Jesus' total surrender. But the other emphasis is equally important. The Father pulls Jesus to Himself. This Divine activity makes the surrender of Jesus possible. In His intimacy with the Father, Jesus found the ability to surrender to the Father. During the ascension, Jesus did not offer Himself to the Father to be lifted up; rather the Father pulled Jesus to Himself, and Jesus responded to what the Father was doing.

This gives us insight into our personal need. For my entire life, I have focused my attention on my surrender to God. I have never felt like I was truly adequate in offering myself to God. If I could just surrender the way I should. But I do not know how. Perhaps my focus has been wrong. The concentration should be upon the Father, who receives me.

Even my surrender is a Divine activity thing. I am so bad, I cannot surrender like I should, but the Father constantly pulls me to Himself. If I will stop my struggling and relax in Him, He will draw me to Himself in surrender. I am so bad I cannot even die right. If I stop trying, and rest in Him, He will bring me to death. Even my surrender is a Divine activity thing. Will I allow Jesus to bring me into full surrender to Himself?

We hear a lot about "my part" and "God's part" in Christian talk. When I hear this discussion, I know we do not understand holiness. We think if we do our part, God will respond with His part. The difficulty with that comes in the fact we have never adequately done our part. When have I been righteous enough? When have I prayed enough? When have I surrendered to God enough? The truth is, I never have done my part. The answer is obvious. If I have never adequately done my part, then God has never done His part, and I am miserably lost.

Part One: The Divine Activity Thing

Prevenient grace says God is not waiting for me to do my part. I have no part. He will do the surrendering for me, if I will let Him. He draws me to Himself, if I will not resist. I do not have to struggle to surrender. I only have to respond to the movement of God within me. Even my surrender is a Divine activity thing.

The second aspect of the exposition is the appointment.

The Appointment

Now we come to the heart of what Luke is saying in verse two. He begins with the ascension, and he closes with a focus on the same event. He sandwiches his main emphasis in between this concept of the ascension. He wants us to see it through the eyes of the Divine action of the Father, who is receiving Jesus unto Himself.

Here is the main truth of the verse. **He through the Holy Spirit had given commandments to the apostles whom He had chosen,** (Acts 1:2). It seems that Luke makes a double emphases upon the idea of Jesus choosing the disciples. It would have been quite adequate for Luke to have written, **He through the Holy Spirit had given commandments to the apostles**. Everyone understands the word **apostles.** The definition means "being chosen or sent." When Luke adds the phrase, **whom He had chosen,** we know there is a double emphases.

There is a parallel between this statement from Acts and the actual account Luke gives in his Gospel concerning Jesus choosing of the apostles (Luke 6:13). This verse must be viewed in the context of the entire story. Luke gives a different picture of the choosing of the disciples than Matthew gives in his Gospel account. Matthew tells of Jesus' baptism by John the Baptist (chapter 3). Jesus is then led by the Spirit into the wilderness temptation (Matthew 4:1-11). Then Jesus began the process of choosing His disciples before there is any mention of the multitudes following Him (Matthew 4:18).

Luke relates Jesus' launching of His ministry with the baptismal experience (Luke 3:22). Jesus is filled with the Holy Spirit. He is led by this same Spirit into the wilderness to do battle with Satan (Luke 4:1-12). The same Divine activity thing takes Him from Galilee to Nazareth. He begins His preaching ministry there. Before He goes very far in ministry, people are already so upset with Him, they try to kill Him (Luke 4:29). The crowds are building because of Jesus' miracles. *And the report about Him went out into every place in the surrounding region,* (Luke 4:37). The *multitude pressed about Him to hear the word of God,* (Luke 5:1). More miracles are done and His fame builds. *However, the report went around concerning Him all the more; and great multitudes came together to hear, and to be healed by Him of their infirmities,* (Luke 5:15). Jesus and the leaders of Israel are in conflict. The leaders of Israel are upset with Jesus over the Sabbath activities (Luke 6:1-11). *They were filled with rage, and discussed with one another what they might do to Jesus,* (Luke 6:11).

Up to this point, Luke does not mention the choosing of the disciples. He writes, *And when it was day, He called His disciples to Himself;* (Luke 6:13). The indication is that there were a vast number of disciples. They formed the bulk of the multitude, which had been following Jesus. Luke says, *"and from them He chose twelve whom He also named apostles,"* (Luke 6:13). Jesus chose the twelve apostles from among the multitude. These men formed the group Luke calls Jesus' disciples.

The word, *"chose"* (Luke 6:13), is the same identical word used in Acts when he writes, *apostles whom He had chosen* (Acts 1:2). In Acts, this word is in the middle voice, which suggests the action of the subject is for Himself, or for His own benefit. Think of the significance of this truth! Jesus chooses us in order to satisfy the desires of His heart. There is something deep within Jesus, which causes Him to want to choose us. It

Part One: The Divine Activity Thing

is a passion which Jesus must fulfill. He loves us and seeks us for Himself.

The word ***chosen*** comes from the combination of two basic words. One is the little word which means "out of." The other word is translated "to speak" or "to call by name." The idea is He called them out of the group, by their names, which is exactly the scene Luke has painted for us in chapter six. This was a group of disciples, and from that large group, Jesus called these twelve to be apostles. They were to act as His representatives. What Jesus was to the Father, they are to be to Jesus. This is the reason He calls them.

How did He get their names? What determined which twelve He would call? Did He hold interviews in order to find those who were best qualified to fill the positions? Did He look for leadership qualities or talents? Perhaps He was looking for certain personality traits, which would blend together to make a harmonious group of apostles. ***Now it came to pass in those days that He went out to the mountain to pray, and continued all night in prayer to God,*** (Luke 6:12). The decision on whom to call was made by the Father. The Father called the twelve apostles through Jesus. Jesus would reveal Himself to the world through the disciples, just as the Father revealed Himself to the world through Jesus. It is all about the Divine activity thing.

You should, by now, begin to see the sense of this verse (Acts 1:2). We are to see the main idea of the verse through the lens of the ascension. The focus is in the Father's action upon the life of Jesus, and Jesus' response to that action. It is a Divine activity thing. After praying all night to the Father, Jesus chooses the twelve disciples from a larger group of disciples. The emphasis of the choosing is a Divine activity thing.

This concept comes into greater focus when we go to the third aspect of this verse.

The Avenue

Luke begins with the ascension, and he ends with the ascension. The main truth of the verse is contained within this framework. The truth is this, **He through the Holy Spirit had given commandments to the apostles whom He had chosen,** (Acts 1:2). The significance of this statement seems to be in the word, ***through.*** This word is a primary preposition, denoting the channel of action. Luke clearly tells us the actions of Jesus were done through the Holy Spirit. Jesus was a channel through which the Divine activity thing took place. Jesus did not do anything except through the Divine activity thing, and, therefore, the Divine activity thing did everything through Jesus. We are back to the major theme of both volumes one and two.

Another way to state the theme is this. Jesus was an avenue for the flow of the Divine activity thing. Certainly you understand what it means to be a channel. A channel does not produce anything. A channel is not the source. A channel is an avenue through which something else flows or is expressed. It is not good or bad. An avenue has no merit and receives no praise. The entire focus is upon what flows through it.

The idea of being an avenue for the flow of the Divine activity thing is a real shift from the Old Testament doing and law structure. It is a shift from trying, striving, doing better than others, to relaxing, leaning, depending and surrendering. It is a shift from doing for Jesus to allowing Jesus to do through you. It is the complete opposite thought process from the Old Testament legalism. We are not being called to work harder, do more, and get our act together. The message of the Gospel is a call to death, to the cross style life, and to respond to Jesus.

It is time to give the responsibility and control to the one who is in charge. You can no longer be in charge. That is Jesus' responsibility. In the Old Testament the focus was upon us. We

Part One: The Divine Activity Thing

were constantly being measured to see if we had achieved the standard. But in the New Testament, Jesus is being measured. The focus is on Him, not upon us. It is not about what we do, but about whom we allow Him to be, in and through us.

In the Old Testament, the focus was upon talent, discipline, ability and performance. If we had the ability, and the will power, we could keep the law, and thus be what we were required to be. But in the New Testament, the focus is upon His flow through us. What are the obstacles which keep this from happening? We must die to our self-centeredness and everything connected to it. We must respond to the cleansing flow of the Divine activity thing as He moves through us.

In the Old Testament, with its emphasis upon the law and our doing, there was no evangelism. The Jews did not win their world. They isolated themselves from all who might defile them. It was one of the major conflicts the leaders of Israel had with Jesus. But Jesus was an expression of the avenue of the Father's flow. When the flow of the Divine activity thing came to the world (Acts), there was an evangelistic thrust. In seventy years, the early disciples won their entire world to God. Christianity became the world religion.

Here is the secret of evangelism. It is not in our programs or techniques. It is in the flow of the Divine activity thing. God wants to demonstrate Himself to our world through us. Will we be the avenue for Divine action?

Acts 1:2

THE ETERNAL FLOW

Luke's first words in the second volume (Book of Acts), are a reminder of ***the former account,*** (Acts 1:1). The theme of the Gospel According to Luke (the former account) is also going to be the theme of the Book of Acts (volume two). He is determined to remind you of this, and he gives a tremendous summary of the former account. The first eleven verses of the first chapter of Acts are Luke's attempt to bring us up to date. Then he can begin volume two.

Luke divides the summary of the former account (Acts 1:1-11), into two sections. Verses one through five form the first section, and verses six through eleven form the second. We have been concentrating on the first section.

Luke begins the first section with these words. ***The former account I made, O Theophilus, of all that Jesus began both to do and teach,*** (Acts 1:1). He is writing expositionally. He presents his main proposition in verse one. In the next few verses, he exposes and expands this proposition. His proposition is found in the phrase, ***all that Jesus began both to do and teach.*** This is a simple statement of summary for the former account.

As he proceeds, Luke takes this statement and gives additional content to it. There are three basic breakdowns to this statement. Verse two is about the commandments Jesus gave to His apostles. Coupled with the commandments, Luke emphasizes that the apostles were chosen from the heart of

Part One: The Divine Activity Thing

God, through the Divine activity thing. The second thrust is found in verse three. It is about the resurrection appearance of Jesus, which took place over a forty-day period. These were the infallible proofs concerning His resurrection. Luke gives the third presentation in verses four and five. He emphasizes that what took place in Jesus, would also take place in the disciples, through the Holy Spirit. These disciples were going to be volume two of the Divine activity thing.

In this chapter we look specifically at the first point of his exposition in the first verse. Something great was happening during this time when Jesus was doing and teaching. ***He was giving commandments to the apostles whom He had chosen.***

It is important to understand the structure of this verse. When you read it in the English translation, it is a bit misleading. You walk away with the idea that the important thing, which Luke highlights, is the ascension. But this is not true. When you go to the Greek language of the Bible, there is an altogether different awareness. This is not a criticism of the English translation. There is no way to adequately translate what is being said in the Greek.

In the original language of the Bible, the opening phrase of verse two is ***until the day in which.*** The closing phrase of the verse is, ***He was taken up.*** The middle of the verse, which is sandwiched in by these two phrases is, ***He through the Holy Spirit had given commandments to the apostles whom He had chosen.*** If you take the phrase, ***He was taken up,*** in the English translation, and put it at the end of the verse, you will have the way it is in the Greek language.

The main thrust of the verse is surrounded by the two phrases about the ascension. ***Until the day in which*** is about the ascension. ***He was taken up,*** is definitely about the ascension. These become the parentheses around the main idea which Luke presents to us. He wants us to see this truth in light of the ascension. The ascension is the lens through which we must view, *He had given commandments to the apostles whom He had chosen.*

Luke is writing here to emphasize the ascension as the direct action of the Father on the life of Jesus. *He was taken up,* is one word in the Greek language. The emphasis is upon the Father's receiving of Jesus. The focus is upon the Divine activity, which the Father is performing for, and upon, Jesus. This is in direct contrast to the way Luke writes about the ascension at the end of the Gospel of Luke, volume one. The emphasis there is upon Jesus offering Himself to the Father. But here, Luke is staying with his major theme. It is about the Divine activity thing.

The Divine activity thing is the theme of the Gospel of Luke, volume one. The second member of the Trinity leaped off His throne and emptied Himself of all He had as God. He became a total man, who surrendered Himself totally back to God, the Father. The Father began to act upon the stage of the life of Jesus, the Man. Everything which happened through Jesus was a direct result of the Divine activity thing. His birth, His childhood, the beginning of His ministry, His victory over the Devil, and the miracles He did, were all a result of the Divine activity thing.

The resurrection was also a result of the Divine activity thing. In the picture Luke presents, the Father reaches out and brings Jesus unto Himself. In the moment of the resurrection, Jesus did exactly what He had been doing for every moment of His life. He responded to the Father. He was allowing the Father to act upon the stage of His life. He was not acting out of His Godness, although He was God. He had set that aside, and as a man, Jesus was totally surrendering to the Father. The ascension was a result of the God activity thing.

We cannot get away from the truth Luke wants to present to us. Every phrase is full of it! The ascension was a Divine activity thing, and Luke uses it as a lens through which to view the primary phrase of verse two. *He through the Holy Spirit had given commandments to the apostles whom He had chosen.*

Part One: The Divine Activity Thing

In the choosing of the disciples, I must remind you of the phrase, **whom He had chosen.** Jesus prayed all night before He came to the place of choosing the apostles (Luke 6:12). He did not do this on His own. He did not choose these men because He had become special friends with them. It was not based upon interviews with them, or on their qualifications or talents. It was a Divine activity thing. God, the Father, gave Jesus the names of the ones Jesus was to choose.

The other phrase in the verse is this. ***He through the Holy Spirit had given commandments to the apostles.*** What is the emphasis of this phrase? It is a Divine activity thing. The Holy Spirit was the channel through which Jesus received the commandments, which Jesus then gave to the disciples. It was a Divine activity thing. Jesus did not do this on His own. He was totally surrendered to the Father, and the Father, through the Holy Spirit, ministered through Jesus.

Therefore, in verse two, we have three different references to the fact that Jesus' life was a product of the Divine activity thing. The event which we call the ascension was a Divine activity thing. Jesus' act of knowing whom to choose as disciples was a Divine activity thing. And the commandments which Jesus gave to the disciples came through knowledge received through the Divine activity thing. There was nothing in Jesus' life which was not the result of the Divine activity thing.

So, we return to the amazing truth! Volume one tells us the second member of the Trinity emptied Himself of all He knew as God, and Jesus became a total man. As a total man, He offered Himself back to God in complete surrender. God, the Father, filled Him and began to act upon the stage of His life. His birth, His childhood, the beginning of His ministry, the miracles He performed, and His ascension were all a result of the Divine activity thing.

But I cannot be like that. Jesus was always good; I have always been bad. He was always right; I have always been wrong.

But wait! There is volume two, the Book of Acts. Here is a group of people just like me. They are deniers, betrayers, murderers, liars, legalists, and now they are filled with the same Spirit which Jesus had. They, too, are a product of the Divine activity thing. They are moving their world. Could He write a volume three with me?

But this is old truth. It is great truth, but we have said all of this before. Isn't there something new in this verse? Yes! It is startling! Luke takes this concept of the Divine activity thing and expands its duration. Up to this time our focus has been on the here and now. We have concentrated on the earthly ministry of Jesus and all the things which happened in the thirty-three years of His time on earth. Was Jesus only dependent upon the Father for the brief thirty-three years He was on this earth? It may seem that way. The miracle of Jesus' virgin birth could only have come through the power of the Father. He depended on the Father for the power to do the miracles. He did not return from the dead in His own power, but it was the Father who raised Him. Jesus' resurrection was a Divine activity thing. But now He has been raised from the dead. He is in His ascension form, and He will soon float off to glory and take His prepared place on the throne. He looks back at the God activity thing and thinks how wonderful it was. It was a great experience, but it is over.

But wait! This is not what Luke tells us. Yes, Jesus' birth was a Divine activity thing. His earthly ministry was a Divine activity thing. Yes, the resurrection was a Divine activity thing. But this did not mark the end of it. The Divine activity thing was not just a span of thirty-three years. Luke is very specific about this. Do you see the focus of verse two? **He through the Holy Spirit had given commandments to the apostles?** When did this take place? It happened after the resurrection, at the time of the ascension. The Divine activity thing did not cease with the resurrection. The Father lived through Jesus in the struggles of the world, and the Father lives through Jesus in the bliss of the eternal Kingdom. The Divine activity thing is an eternal activity.

Part One: The Divine Activity Thing

Jesus gave many commandments to His disciples in the three years they walked with Him. Luke is not referring to all of these commandments (Acts 1:2). Many of these were very specific commandments, such as those Jesus gave in the Sermon on the Mount. When He sent them forth to minister, He gave them special commands for their ministry (Matthew 10). But none of these are included in reference to the commandments in our present passage. These are the specific commandments Jesus gave just prior to His ascension. You can read this entire account at the close of Luke's Gospel account (Luke 24:44-53). These commandments are also referred to in verse four. ***And being assembled together with them, He commanded them not to depart from Jerusalem, but to wait for the Promise of the Father,*** (Acts 1:4). Luke tells us the commandments Jesus gave during this time were a result of the Divine activity thing. Jesus was still experiencing the Divine activity thing in His glorified state.

Jesus was a fully resurrected man. He is called, ***the firstborn from the dead,*** (Colossians 1:18). This does not mean He was the first individual to be raised from the dead. Jesus raised Lazarus from the dead (John 12:1). Jesus also raised the Ruler's daughter from the dead (Matthew 9:25). At the crucifixion, when Jesus yielded up His right to live, ***and the graves were opened; and many bodies of the saints who had fallen asleep were raised;*** (Matthew 27:52). Jesus is ***the firstborn from the dead,*** because He is the first one to go into the grave and be raised on the other side. All others came forth from the grave, reentered the time zone, only to die again.

Jesus was raised from the dead, just as you and I will be raised from the dead. We are to be like Him in life, and we will be like Him in death. We are to be like Him in the resurrection, and we are to be like Him in His eternal state. His living state, the method by which He lives in the eternal realm, is the same as He lived in the bracket of time. It is a Divine activity thing.

This has startling ramifications for us. Jesus was the first of a new breed of people in volume one. The out spill of that continues through the disciples in volume two. God wants to write a volume three through us, making all that was true about Jesus, and all that was true about the disciples, true about us. As the Father lived through Jesus for thirty-three years, so Jesus wants to live through me now. As the Father lives through Jesus in the eternity, so He wants to live through me forever. Heaven is going to be an experience of the Divine activity thing. This is His eternal plan. I am forever, and forever, going to be one with Him. Leaning, depending, surrendering, and trusting, I will allow Jesus to act forever upon the stage of my life.

There is no question about the fact I need Jesus in the struggles of my life. How can I make it through my job without His activity through me? Depression would overwhelm me without His Divine flow. There would never be victory over sin, in the midst of temptation, without His Divine strength. How could I minister adequately without His Divine power flowing through me? But do I understand that the fullness of the Spirit, the Divine activity thing, is not a safe guard in times of trouble. It is who we are! It is the very essence of what we have become as Kingdom people. It is the very structure of the Kingdom itself. It is forever. It is for the time when there will be no more struggle. You and I will need Him not one bit less in heaven than we need Him right now. He is not a fire escape; He is life itself. Without Him, Christianity ceases to exist!

Adam was made perfect by God. He was without sin, and God gave him a beautiful Garden in which to live, The Garden of Eden. He was built to be dependent upon God. He was designed by God to be the flesh of God. God made Adam in His image, expressing the very essence of Himself. God enthralled Adam's life with His presence. Adam was filled with the very Spirit of God. It was how God moved and had being. What was the tragedy of sin? Man decided to become independent instead of dependent. Man decided to be filled with himself instead of

Part One: The Divine Activity Thing

being filled with God. Man became his own God, when God alone was meant to be God in his life. Adam was built as a man to live in the Divine activity thing. This is normal humanity.

Man became abnormal and lived in the flow of his own selfishness. His sons and grandsons continued the pattern. Man became so used to living out of himself, he thought it was normal. It is terrible when we have been abnormal for so long, we forget and think it is normal. God recognized the need to do something about the situation. He needed to show man once again what a normal man was to be. Only this time, instead of making a man, God Himself became the man. We call Jesus the second Adam (1 Corinthians 15:45). Jesus was a normal man, living in the Divine activity thing.

Do you see that God is not some aid to get you through this life? He is not a plus factor to help you have a better life in the struggles of this day. The Divine activity thing is the very nature of all we are as mankind. When man is all God wants him to be, He lives as Jesus, the man, lived (volume one). This will be forever in eternity!

The great parable of the vine and the branch (John 15:1-6), reminds us of this same truth. He is the vine, and we are the branches. We live by the very flow of the life of the vine. We bear fruit because of the life sap of the vine. In our appearance, we look like the vine, because we are a product of the life of the vine. It is who we are as the branches. If we are separated from the vine, we are dead (John 15:6). In eternity, we will be all who we were meant to be. We will be attached to the vine, flowing with the life of the vine. It is who we are! This has strong application to our lives now. The life of God, living through us now, is not an option. You cannot go to heaven without it. It is the nature of who we are as Kingdom people. Do you live in the Divine activity thing? Is He the life by which you live? Is He the source by which you exist? Do you live moment by moment in His Divine flow? It is the only way to live!

Acts 1:2

THE ORDERED EMPHASIS

The former account I made, O Theophilus, of all that Jesus began both to do and teach, until the day in which He was taken up, after He through the Holy Spirit had given commandments to the apostles whom He had chosen, (Acts 1:1-2).

  The disciples have lived with Jesus for three years. This time has not been without the struggles of development. They now see the Kingdom of God clearer than they have ever seen it. The cross emphasis, and its style, has been hard for them to grasp, but it is coming into focus in their hearts and minds. The days of His crucifixion and death were tough. Their lives were crushed. It seemed they had no reason to continue. The disciples had left all to follow Jesus, believing He was the Messiah. Following His death, they spent hours analyzing the events, trying to make sense of it all. Judas, one of them, had betrayed the Christ, and none of them had been faithful to Him.

  The resurrection had stretched their understanding. They had actually walked with Him in His resurrected presence. What an experience that was for them! They ate with Him and talked with Him. It was beyond their belief. According to verse three, this continued for forty days. This was not a hazy appearance of a form in the distance. They could identify Him. They spent hours with Him. Think of the teaching which Jesus gave them during this time. What tremendous insight they gained. They were now ready to listen and comprehend. Surely Jesus reviewed all He had taught them before, only now they were receptive to the truth. There could be no question in their minds concerning the resurrection, not after the forty days of His resurrected presence among them. It was an experience of ***infallible proofs*** (Acts 1:3).

But this time with the resurrected presence of Jesus was coming to an end. As the Father had led Him into the wilderness to be tempted (Luke 4:1), so the Father was leading Him now to the moment of the ascension. Luke uses the very same word for the ascension of Christ that is used in the Septuagint (the Greek translation of the Old Testament) for Elijah's translation. The Father is acting. When God translated Elijah, it was not a result of anything Elijah did. God did it! So it will be with Jesus. He was going to leave them in the physical sense, but, oh, the promises He made to them. His presence with them would be more real than even the physical experience they were now having. He was going to indwell them. The same experience He had with His Father, He would now have with each of them. As Jesus was the physical presence of the Father in the world, so they would be the physical presence of Christ in the world.

What could Jesus say in these parting moments? They had been through so much together. The future was full of promise. What words would be adequate? Just before His ascension, Jesus turns to the disciples and says, *"These are the words which I spoke to you while I was still with you, that all things must be fulfilled which were written in the Law of Moses and the Prophets and the Psalms concerning Me." And He opened their understanding, that they might comprehend the Scriptures. Then He said to them, "Thus it is written, and thus it was necessary for the Christ to suffer and to rise from the dead the third day, and that repentance and remission of sins should be preached in His name to all nations, beginning at Jerusalem. And you are witnesses of these things. Behold, I send the Promise of My Father upon you, but tarry in the city of Jerusalem until you are endued with power from on high,"* (Luke 24:24-29). These are powerful words!

Luke begins his second volume (The Book of Acts) with a reference to, *The former account I made, O Theophilus, of all that Jesus began both to do and teach,* (Acts 1:1). He then proceeds with a summary of the former account (Acts 1:1-11). His purpose is to bring us up to date with the flow of his account, launching us into the truth of the second volume. Volume one (The Gospel According to Luke) ends exactly where volume two (The Book of Acts) begins.

It is important for us to notice the content Luke includes in his summary. He does not give any of the content of the Sermon on the Mount. He tells nothing of the miracles Jesus did, or the parables He told. He does not mention the Mount of Transfiguration at all. One would think these would be the kinds of events Luke would have highlighted in his summary of volume one.

Luke focuses the bulk of his summary of the former account on the last days which Jesus spent with His disciples. He speaks strongly of the resurrection appearances of Christ, which took place during the forty days following the resurrection (Acts 1:3). He highlights the command Jesus gave them not to leave Jerusalem. They were to wait for the Promise of the Father, which is the fullness of the Holy Spirit (Acts 1:4-5). Luke writes of the question the disciples asked Jesus, *"Lord, will You at this time restore the kingdom of Israel?"* (Acts 1:6). Their question was off the subject at hand. Jesus brings them back to the power of the Holy Spirit. They are to win their world, and that is to be their only concern. The Father will take care of everything else, and they can trust Him with it all (Acts 1:7-8). Luke then briefly describes the ascension (Acts 1:9-11). The summary of volume one focuses on the post resurrection time.

We find a summary of the summary in verse two. The

closing statement is the heart of the verse. It reads, **He through the Holy Spirit had given commandments to the apostles whom He had chosen.** In the Greek, it is not the closing statement, but it is the middle of the verse. The statement is sandwiched in between two phrases. Both phrases focus on the ascension. Luke begins the verse with the words, **until that day,** and he ends the verse with the phrase, **He was taken up.**

The Father was receiving Jesus unto Himself. It is a focus of the Divine activity thing working in the life of Jesus again, even in the ascension following the resurrection.

The middle statement is, **He through the Holy Spirit had given commandments to the apostles whom He had chosen.** It must be understood in the framework of the ascension. You must approach it in the framework of the Divine activity thing. The commandments, which Luke makes reference to, are not the commandments which Jesus gave throughout His ministry. The focus of his summary is upon what Jesus said to the disciples during the day of His ascension. The main thrust of the verse concentrates on these **commandments.**

Let us begin with an investigation of the word, **commandments.** Jesus is giving a command. The Greek Lexicon gives the definition of the original word in terms of "enjoin." The dictionary's definition of "enjoin" is "to direct or impose with authority or emphasis." Luke is not describing the rules, commandments, or orders which Jesus gave at His ascension. He is describing the emphasis, or the focus, of what Jesus is saying. Jesus was not relating specific activities, or ceremonies, which the disciples should accomplish. He was not giving the standards of holiness practice. He was talking about the concentration, or focus, which the disciples should have in their lives in the days ahead.

We must investigate the grammar of the word. The English translation says, **had given commandments.** This is in the past tense. I propose to you that this is not quite correct. The translators translated it in the past tense in the English because it is in the aorist tense in the Greek. There is no English equivalent to the aorist tense, so it is normally translated into the English past tense. That is usually sufficient to grasp the meaning, but not in this case.

The actual aorist tense disregards the past, present and future idea and focuses on a moment in time, when the action takes place. This is difficult for us to understand, because we cannot think in terms of anything that is not past, present or future. But the aorist takes you immediately into the moment of the event's occurrence. It emphasizes a point in time beyond the present, most often, the reference to the time when the action took place is in the past.

In this case, we believe it to be a "gnomic" aorist. It is used in the ancient Greek literature with maxims and proverbs. "A fool learns by experience." "Beauty is either wasted by time or withered by disease." These verbs are all in the gnomic aorist. It expresses a general truth. It states a past occurrence, leaving the reader to draw the inference from a concrete case that what has occurred is typical of what often occurs. This is true in the past, but it is true in the present and the future as well. It is always true.

That is the point Jesus wants to make with the disciples (Acts 1:2). Through the Holy Spirit, Jesus gave commandments to His disciples. He did not give rules or orders. He gave them a focus which would be true in the past, present and future. Jesus presents the disciples with a fundamental of Christianity, which will always be true. In every generation, for all people, it will be the focus for life.

Jesus always focuses on the Divine activity thing. The ascension was a Divine activity thing. It was a reality for Jesus in the past. It is the explanation of His birth, His miracles, and His resurrection. His total ministry can only be explained in terms of the Divine activity thing. God acted upon the stage of His life. Jesus depended on the Father in the past, but it is true of the present also. In Luke's description of the ascension,

Part One: The Divine Activity Thing

Jesus depends on the Holy Spirit to give the proper instructions and emphasis to the disciples. He is ready to ascend and be received by the Father. This will be a Divine activity thing. But it would not end here. Whether in His earthly life, or in the eternal Kingdom of God, the Father was living through Jesus. The Divine activity thing is always the pattern of truth for Jesus.

If this was the pattern of truth for Jesus, it is even more true for the disciples. Jesus does not come to the ascension and give the disciples a new focus. He does not tell them to wait in Jerusalem for a new truth. The focus He taught them during His three years with them remains the focus for this time in their lives. He does not set it aside. The Holy Spirit will not come with something new. No! No! The focus is the same as He gave them in the past. It is to be their concentration for the present, and it will remain true into and throughout eternity.

And what is this emphasis? It is Jesus! He is to be their only focus. They are to center their passion on Him. He is to be all they talk about. He is going to be the Divine activity thing through them. As Jesus concentrated and focused on the Father, so the disciples are to concentrate and focus on Jesus. As the Father demonstrated Himself through Jesus, now Jesus will demonstrate Himself through the disciples. They will know nothing but Him. He will be the talk of their lips, the message of their preaching, the beat of their hearts, the joy of their souls, and the shine on their faces. He will be their entire emphasis, focus and concentration.

Let us return to the enjoining Jesus did as recorded in Luke. Jesus said to the disciples, ***"And, you are witnesses of these things,"*** (Luke 24:46-48). What are these things? Jesus had told them,

"Thus it is written, and thus it was necessary for the Christ to suffer and to rise from the dead the third day, and that repentance and remission of sins should be preached in His name to all nations, beginning at Jerusalem," (Luke 24:46-47).

It is all about Him! It is His death and His resurrection. It is the style of the cross! Luke summarizes this for us in Acts 1:1-11. Jesus said, *"And you shall be witnesses to Me in Jerusalem, and in all Judea and Samaria, and to the end of the earth,"* (Acts 1:8).

This takes place throughout the Book of Acts. Every sermon preached was about Jesus, His death and resurrection. They consistently talked about Jesus. Peter is preaching on Pentecost Day, and he says, *"Men of Israel, hear these words: Jesus of Nazareth, a Man attested by God to you by miracles, wonders, and signs which God did through Him in your midst, as you yourselves also know - Him, being delivered by the determined purpose and foreknowledge of God, you have taken by lawless hands, have crucified, and put to death; whom God raised up, having loosed the pains of death, because it was not possible that He should be held by it,"* (Acts 2:22-24).

Peter and John went to the temple. They were confronted by a man with a desperate need. They did not give him alms. They had but one thing to give him. *Then Peter said, "Silver and gold I do not have, but what I do have I give you: In the name of Jesus Christ of Nazareth, rise up and walk,"* (Acts 3:6).

The people who witnessed this miracle responded aggressively. They thought Peter and John had done this thing in their own power. Peter was horrified they would even have such a thought. He immediately set them straight in a powerful sermon. He said, *"The God of Abraham, Isaac, and Jacob, the God of our fathers, glorified His Servant Jesus, whom you delivered up and denied in the presence of Pilate, when he was determined to let Him go,"* (Acts 3:13).

The apostles were brought in before the Sanhedrin because of the miracle. Even then the disciples could not keep silent. Their lives were at stake, but they continued their one focus. In this concentration on Jesus they said, *"Let it be known to you all, and to all the people of Israel, that by the name of Jesus Christ of Nazareth, whom you crucified, whom God raised*

Part One: The Divine Activity Thing

from the dead, by Him this man stands here before you whole," (Acts 4:10).

The leaders of Israel were irate. They threatened the disciples, and told them not to preach in the name of Jesus again. They wanted everything about Jesus to simply fade away. Undoubtedly they thought their threats would end the matter. But that was not the case! They had the disciples again brought in before the council. The leaders of Israel said, **"Did we not strictly command you not to teach in this name? And look, you have filled Jerusalem with your doctrine, and intend to bring this Man's blood on us!"** (Acts 5:28).

Can there be any doubt about what Luke is saying? At the ascension of Christ into heaven, Jesus gave to His disciples the focus and emphasis they were to have in their lives. It was all about Him. They were to be talking about Him, living Him, and depending upon Him. Their entire lives were to be about Jesus. This was to be in the past, the present and in the future. It would continue into their lives in heaven. There will never be a time when there will be anything but Him.

This is the heart of the Divine activity thing. We see it in volume one. Jesus always demonstrates the Father. Everything He does is through the Father. The Father is His life. Even after the resurrection, it is still the Father acting through Him. His ascension is the Father receiving the Son unto Himself. All eternity will be about the Father.

What is the focus of volume two? It is about the disciple's focus on the Divine activity thing. They concentrate on Jesus. As Jesus concentrated on the Father, so the disciples are focused on Jesus. They talk Jesus. They preach Jesus. They fill Jerusalem with Jesus. It is true in the past, it is true now, and it will be true in heaven. There is nothing but Jesus!

If the Divine activity thing is the issue of all Christianity for my life, how can I know if I am living in that flow? Here is the test:

- *Are you demonstrating Him consistently in your life?*
- *Do you relate everything that happens to you to Him?*
- *Is He the focus and concentration of your entire being?*
- *Do you always end up talking about Him?*
- *Is He the moment by moment experience of your life?*

The main issue of our lives is not about being evil. We are not wrong, but we are greatly distracted. That leads to possible destruction. The circumstances of our lives easily distract us from Jesus. Happenings allure us from Him. Just being religious will not help us. We must concentrate completely on Him. He wants to be the center of every event of our lives. He must be the moment by moment presence in every step we take. You are never to do anything in life without intimately involving Jesus. Practice His presence! Are you focused on Him?

PART TWO
ACTS 1:3-5

THE PROMISE OF THE FATHER

Acts 1:3

JESUS PRESENTED

The person of Jesus is central to the resurrection. The authors of the Gospel accounts were not interested in giving us a new philosophy of eternal life. They did not care about a theology of the life after death. Their supreme desire was to show us Jesus. He is not a Jesus of history or concept. He is alive, functioning, and the active person we see in the Gospel accounts. It is my delight to focus on Him.

Christianity is not the acknowledgment of a creed or religious practice. Christianity is the personal embrace of this person called Jesus Christ, and is the experience of an intimate relationship with Him. Do you know Him? Has the Spirit of Christ indwelt you? **Christ in you** is the hope of glory (Colossians 1:27). The dividing line between a Christian and a non-Christian is the person of Jesus Christ. If you have Him, you are in the Kingdom. If you do not have Him, you are not in the Kingdom. He is the sum total of all things. Jesus is the answer to all of life's questions.

In Luke's summary of the *former account* (Acts 1:1), he focuses on the person of Christ. It is an account **of all that Jesus began**, (Acts 1:1). Jesus started a new and radical breed of humanity. These men were born from the cross. Jesus was the very first of this breed, and He established the means for **bringing many sons to glory** (Hebrews 1:10). He is the substance and material from which sonship is formed and has its being.

Part Two: The Promise Of The Father

God focused on Jesus for the fulfillment of His plan and dream.

The new beginning is highlighted in **both to do and teach** (Acts 1:1). The Sons of God are going to do, but it is a different kind of doing than has been up to this time. There is such a radical change from the old doing. It is not even proper to refer to their actions as doing. Their doing is not self-initiated, but it is always Spirit-initiated. Spirit-initiated doing flows from the creative juices of the Divine Activity within the person. Jesus never claimed credit for anything which flowed from Him. He always acknowledged the Father's action through Him. He was the perfect example of the kind of doing of a Son of Glory.

Luke reminds us of this in the next verse. **Until the day in which He was taken up, after He through the Holy Spirit had given commandments to the apostles whom He had chosen,** (Acts 1:2). The focus of the ascension is on the action of the Father. He reached out and brought Jesus to Himself. When Jesus chose the disciples, He spent an entire night in prayer, receiving the instructions of the Father. Every command Jesus gave, before the resurrection and at the ascension, was given to Him through the Holy Spirit. He found His total source in the Holy Spirit, and this new kind of doing focuses on the activity of God through Jesus and through us.

Luke's focus does not change as he writes the conclusion of this sentence. **To whom He also presented Himself alive after His suffering by many infallible proofs, being seen by them during forty days and speaking of the things pertaining to the kingdom of God,** (Acts 1:3). Luke focuses this section on the person of Jesus Christ. He does not present a mere concept, but he presents a real person. We can see this in the **infallible proofs** of Jesus' resurrected person. The disciples saw the person of Christ for forty days. He was not a vision in the distance. They did not imagine Him. He spoke to them **of the things pertaining to the kingdom of God**. Christ, Himself, continued **both to do and teach**.

We can see this clearly in the subject and verb of this prepositional phrase, *to whom He also presented Himself alive after His suffering by many infallible proofs, being seen by them during forty days and speaking of the things pertaining to the kingdom of God,* (Acts 1:3). *He* is the main subject of this phrase. This pronoun is referring to *Jesus*, (Acts 1:1). When you view this statement in the original language of the Bible, you discover this pronoun is a part of the verb itself. *He presented* is one word, and the pronoun is given in the ending of the verb. This is the usual method of writing in the New Testament.

However, in this prepositional phrase, Luke gives the pronoun again. We translate it, *Himself.* With both pronouns present we translate it, he, himself. It is a double emphasis, or focus, on the person of Jesus. Luke is very careful in declaring the evidence of the resurrection. What was presented to the disciples during the forty days of *infallible proofs* was not a likeness of Jesus. What they saw was not Jesus' clone. They did not see a vapor image, which passed away when the sun shone brightly. They saw Jesus. The same physical Jesus they knew for three years of ministry is now spending an additional forty days with them, *speaking of the things pertaining to the kingdom of God.*

It seems as though the authors of the New Testament want to convince us that Jesus is the same. The resurrection brought about a significant change in the position of Jesus Christ, and we understand that. In one sense, things would never be the same again. But the apostles wanted to make sure we understood Jesus did not change in attitude or motive. He did not change in relationship to the cross style. As He poured out His life for others before the resurrection, so He will pour out His life for others after the resurrection. What He taught His disciples before, He is still teaching them now. He is the same Christ with the same goals and purpose.

We can gain amazing insight from the verb *presented*. The Greek language is a picturesque language. It paints a vivid picture, enabling us to see what is being said. It is so with the word *presented*. Luke is conveying a concept far beyond simply "to show." Jesus did more than present His body, which had been physically raised from the dead. He wanted to accomplish more than just persuading His disciples that He was physically alive. Luke could have used another Greek word to accomplish that. Ten lepers came to Jesus for healing. After He healed them, He gave them these instructions. *"Go show yourselves to the priests,"* (Luke 17:14). The word show is not used in relationship to the resurrection appearances of Jesus. What Jesus is doing here is far beyond show, and it has to do with presented.

Servanthood
Acts 1:3

The word, *presented*, in the context of verse three, shows us servanthood. This word paints the picture as it is in the royal courts. At the heart of the word is the idea of service. But the service is not menial or insignificant. It implies dignity, but also dependence. We read of angels presenting themselves in such a manner. *Now there was a day when the sons of God came to present themselves before the Lord, and Satan also came among them,* (Job 1:6). This was the position of the priests and Levites. *At that time the Lord separated the tribe of Levi to bear the ark of the covenant of the Lord, to stand before the Lord to minister to Him and to bless in His name, to the day,* (Deuteronomy 10:8). The same word is used to describe the prophets being used of God. *And Elijah the Tishbite, of the inhabitants of Gilead, said to Ahab, "As the Lord God of Israel lives, before whom I stand, there shall not be dew nor rain these years except at my word,"* (1 Kings 17:1).

Jesus *presented Himself alive after His suffering* for the purpose of service. Does that surprise you? There is never a tone of "I told you so," contained in any of the resurrection appearances. Jesus never gives a hint of judgment or condemnation in any of His conversations. His purpose has not changed. He was a servant before, and He is a servant after the resurrection. He came to serve.

Often in our speech and in our songs, we indicate that when Jesus returns the second time, He will not be like He was on His first coming. He came the first time as a lowly babe in a manger, but He will return as a King in glory. He came to die on a cross the first time, but when He returns the second time, He will come as the Conqueror. Though these statements of His second coming are true, we must look closely at the attitude. He has not changed inwardly. The circumstances have changed, and He does not need to die again for the sins of a world, but the burn of His heart is still the cross style. He came the first time to pour out His life, and He will come again to pour out His life the second time. Redemption was the purpose of His first coming, and He will come for redemption the second time also. He has not changed on us.

Perhaps you will remember this story. Two brothers, disciples of Jesus, came to Him desirous of the right and left-hand positions in the coming Kingdom. Their mother, who was the sister of Jesus' mother, came with them. They hoped to use her influence to swing things in their favor. When the other disciples realized what they were asking, they were indignant. A great dispute arose among the group. Jesus proceeded to give them some spiritual insight. *"And whoever desires to be first among you, let him be your slave - just as the Son of Man did not come to be served, but to serve, and to give His life a ransom for many,"* (Matthew 20:27-28). Jesus had a driving passion to serve. He demonstrated that in three years of earthly ministry, and it ended with His death and resurrection. That driving passion has not yet subsided! Jesus presents Himself to the disciples after the resurrection as a servant, just as He has always done.

Jesus' inner heart is that of the cross and its style. How can He pour out His life for His disciples? How can He help mold them into what God has dreamed they can be? How can He be redemptive in these days following His resurrection? He is totally available to the Father. Jesus will make as many resurrection appearances as the Father desires. Jesus spent forty days with His disciples, giving them instructions *of the things pertaining to the kingdom of God.* He was born to serve, and now He is raised to serve.

This remains true for your life in this hour. The Hebrew author states it this way. *"Therefore He is also able to save to the uttermost those who come to God through Him, since He always lives to make intercession for them,"* (Hebrews 7:25). As surely as *He also presented Himself alive after His suffering by many infallible proofs* to His disciples then, so He comes to you. He will do whatever is necessary to get this truth to you. Jesus is prepared to give whatever time it takes to bring you to the full awareness of spiritual truth. He has one focus and one desire. He has come to serve you.

Spotless
Acts 1:3

Another part of the word, *presented*, is spotless. This should not surprise you. Spotless is ingrained into the fibers of the Kingdom of God. Jesus came to proclaim it to the disciples and to us. If you could fully comprehend what Jesus left to come to us, you would better appreciate spotlessness. In His first coming, Jesus embraced the sin of an entire world. He did not touch it, and then run away from it. He went to the very heart of sin and became what it is. *For He made Him who knew no sin to be sin for us, that we might become the righteousness of God in Him,* (2 Corinthians 5:21). Jesus embraced the guilt of our sin, as if it were His own, as if He had committed the deeds Himself. Think of how this must have crushed Him, when He was without sin before. In a moment of time, He experienced it all in its mature state with its full consequences.

But this is not His condition now! With His death on the cross, Jesus conquered sin and hell. Jesus paid the penalty of sin, and God robbed hell of the presence of His Son. No touch of sin remains on Jesus now. You cannot find one twist in one fiber of His character. The righteousness He lived among the disciples before His death is the same righteousness He experiences as He presents Himself to them again.

The truth is revealed when the word, *presented*, is linked with the righteousness of Christ. The righteousness of Christ is linked with the service He wants to render. *For we do not have a High Priest who cannot sympathize with our weaknesses, but was in all points tempted as we are, yet without sin. Let us therefore come boldly to the throne of grace, that we may obtain mercy and find grace to help in time of need,* (Hebrews 4:15-16). He serves us in holiness.

It is important for us to understand Christ's righteousness in the resurrection appearances. Jesus never did any sinful deeds, but that is not why He is holy. Holiness does not come through abstaining from evil deeds or keeping the rules. Jesus' holiness is derived from the Father. His holiness was not accomplished by His own actions. It flowed from the Divine Activity of the Father within Him. Jesus had totally abandoned self-initiated action. He lived the crucified life, and that enabled the Father to flow through Him. Service to others naturally flowed from this attitude.

As it was between Jesus and His Father, so it is to be between us and Jesus. Christ derived His righteousness from the Father. God constantly acted within Him through the Spirit. Pay close attention to this statement from the Book of Hebrews. *How much more shall the blood of Christ, who through the eternal Spirit*

Part Two: The Promise Of The Father

offered Himself without spot to God, cleanse your conscience from dead works to serve the living God? (Hebrews 9:14). Christ offered Himself without spot to God. Because of His offering, we have the continual, redemptive process of Christ operating in our lives. But how did He offer Himself? He offered Himself through the eternal Spirit! This continues to happen as Jesus presents Himself to the disciples in the infallible proofs of the resurrection.

Let's return to the verse we quoted earlier. *For He made Him who knew no sin to be sin for us, that we might become the righteousness of God in Him,* (2 Corinthians 5:21). Now we are confronted by the truth of His service in righteousness. Jesus wants to do in and through us what the Father was doing in and through Him. God presented Jesus in righteousness for cross style service, and the resource for this service came to Jesus through the Father. In like manner, Jesus presents us in His righteousness for cross style service, and our resource comes through Jesus.

Now look at this statement. *Yet now He has reconciled in the body of His flesh through death, to present you holy, and blameless, and above reproach in His sight,* (Colossians 1:21-22). There is no more estrangement between God and us. We are no longer alienated, nor are we His enemies. We have become one with God as sons. Christ has presented us. As God presented Jesus to the disciples, so Jesus now presents us to our world. Jesus was not righteous on His own, but He derived His righteousness from the Father. So we are not righteous on our own, but we derive our righteousness from Jesus. We no longer live a self-initiated life, but the Spirit of Christ flows through us, and our purpose for life is to live the cross style.

The heart of cross style is focused on evangelism. *Him we preach, warning every man and teaching every man in all wisdom, that we may present every man perfect in Christ Jesus,* (Colossians 1:28). We are to participate in the redemption of our world. The word, *present*, is always linked with righteousness and service. Paul writes, *that He might present her to Himself a* glorious *church, not having spot or wrinkle or any such thing, but that she should be holy and without blemish,* (Ephesians 5:27). He is speaking about the church. This presentation follows the statement: *that He might sanctify and cleanse her with the washing of water by the word,* (Ephesians 5:26). Jesus is involved in redemptive service in order to make this presentation. Included in the context of these verses is the picture of how a husband is to treat his wife. It is the pattern of redemptive service. What Jesus is, we are to be. What He is doing, we are to do.

Surrender
Acts 1:3

The third part of the word, *presented*, is surrender. There is such an undercurrent from the ideas of servanthood and spotlessness that it might not be necessary to mention surrender. Jesus would not have been able to do either of the two without surrendering to the Father. He did not surrender out of force or discipline. Often, when we think of surrender, it comes with the sense of straining. However, this surrender was not out of Jesus' effort, but it came from the action of the Father, bringing it to pass in Him. He relaxed His life into the Father's hands. In this relaxation, the Father became a reality, and the flow was spontaneous.

Paul calls us to this same process. In the sixth chapter of Romans, Paul states what we call positional theology. In Romans 6:2, he says we have died to sin. It is seen is the symbolism of our baptism (Romans 6:3). Therefore, we have joined Jesus in His death and resurrection. *Now if we died with Christ, we believe that we shall also live with Him,* (Romans 6:8). While this is our position in Christ, how does this practically demonstrate itself in the real world? ***And do not present your members as instruments of unrighteousness to sin, but present yourselves to God as being alive from the dead, and your members as instruments of righteousness to God,*** (Romans 6:13).

When we present ourselves to Jesus, He can flow His resurrection life through us. Righteousness then manifests itself in our redemptive service to others. This is the pattern of Christ. He has ***presented Himself alive after His suffering by many infallible proofs,*** (Acts 1:3). He came to His disciples in cross style service. His focus during the forty days was on them, not on Himself. He was washing their feet in another way. As Jesus served the disciples, He rendered righteousness and holiness to them. He became sin for us. He, by the Spirit, conquered sin completely, and we see righteousness in His Spirit-initiated service. This was all based on Jesus surrender to the Father. When Jesus relaxed in surrender, the Father flowed the righteous service through Him.

Jesus calls us to such a surrender.

Acts 1:3

HE IS HERE

Jesus is the focus of verse three in the first chapter of the Book of Acts. The prepositional phrase of this verse gives us the basis for this focus. It says, ***to whom He also presented Himself alive after His suffering by many infallible proofs, being seen by them during forty days and speaking to the things pertaining to the Kingdom of God,*** (Acts 1:3). These words end a three-verse sentence which introduces the second volume written by Luke. It all focuses on Jesus.

We can see this focus in the subject of the prepositional phrase. *He* is the subject, which refers to Christ. In the original language of the Bible, this pronoun is a part of the ending of the verb *presented*. The subject and the verb appear as one word in the Greek language. Immediately following the verb is the pronoun, ***Himself***, which makes a double emphasis upon the Person of Christ. It is translated, ***He presented Himself***. A physical figure appears to the disciples. He is not a clone of Jesus. He is not an image in vapor form. It is really Jesus, and He is the same Christ the disciples knew during three years of ministry.

This prepositional phrase holds more important information. It is found in three participles contained within the verse. They are ***alive, being seen***, and ***speaking***. A participle gives content to the main verb. These three participles act as adverbs describing the action of the verb. Luke uses them to give us the details concerning the appearance of Jesus after His resurrection.

Each one of these participles is present tense. They indicate that these actions were taking place as Jesus presented Himself. As we view the details of the presentation, we discover it was forty days in duration. During this forty-day presentation, Jesus is *alive*, *being seen*, and *speaking*. Each one of these participles is translated as if in the active voice. *Alive* and *speaking* are definitely in the active voice, while *being seen* is in the middle voice. When translating the middle voice into English, we consider it active in nature. The active voice means the verb is the action of the subject. This indicates again, a clear focus on the Person of Jesus. Luke boldly presents us with the living, visible, speaking Christ. He is the same Christ we knew before His resurrection. He has not changed. He is embracing us.

We have nowhere else to turn, but to Jesus. He is the complete focus of Christianity. Outside of Jesus, there is no life. He is the sum total of all things. Christ is the answer to our every question. From His person, we derive all the needs of life. But do not think you must search to find Him. **He** has **presented Himself alive** to you. There is no way to avoid Him. He is in your pathway.

He Is Alive
Acts 1:3

In the first participle, Luke attempts to establish the infallible proof that Jesus was, and is, physically *alive*. The most basic meaning of the word, alive, has to do with physical life as compared to physical death. There was a physical resurrection from the dead. Jesus physically stood before the disciples in His resurrected form. His actions during the forty days of His appearance were physical actions. He cooked fish, ate, traveled, spoke, instructed, and related to individuals, as well as groups. He expressed His love, had a recognizable physical appearance, and the list goes on and on. All of these actions have to do with

His physical resurrection from the dead.

However, in the New Testament sense, when Luke uses this word, *alive*, he gives us a much deeper sense than simply physical appearance. Something has happened which is completely beyond the mere physical. It is not completely new, but it is completely fulfilled. Luke does not give us the sense that this life was not present before the resurrection. The throbbing heart of God was manifested in Christ for three years of ministry. Christ was alive in His teachings. The crowds saw this aliveness when it was contrasted with the deadness in the teachings of the scribes. Matthew records the astonishment of the crowds to the Sermon on the Mount (Matthew 7:29), *for He taught them as one having authority, and not as the scribes,* (Matthew 7:29). The word, authority, has to do with the inner flow of the person.

Life is highlighted at the resurrection of Lazarus (John 11:1). Jesus responded to Martha's distress and disappointment that He did not come when Lazarus was sick. He said, *"I am the resurrection and the life. He who believes in Me, though he may die, he shall live. And whoever lives and believes in Me shall never die. Do you believe this?* (John 11:25-26).

This aliveness is not completely new. Jesus **presented Himself alive**. We see this aliveness most vividly when it is contrasted with death. Did you notice Luke attached the phrase, *after His suffering?* (Acts 1:3). Luke shows the aliveness of Christ against the backdrop of His death. But it is not just a moment of death, or the fact He stopped breathing. We actually translate **suffering** as "passion." The week which includes Good Friday is called "Passion Week." This week included all of the suffering which took place before the death of Christ. The soldiers mutilated the body of Christ beyond recognition. They pulled His beard out by its roots. They punctured His brow with a crown of thorns. They laid His back wide open with their scourging, until His flesh hung in ribbons, exposing His inner organs. This all took place before the actual crucifixion on the cross. Who can adequately describe the suffering after His physical death? Who can tell of the experience of hell? That was a spiritual death in its completeness. But He is **ALIVE**.

Jesus aliveness has always been vital and of great importance to us. It is our only hope. ***And if Christ is not risen, then our preaching is empty and your faith is also empty,*** (1 Corinthians 15:14). What Jesus is in His resurrection is what we will become. He is the ***firstborn from the dead,*** (Colossians 1:18). ***He also presented Himself alive.*** He is our only chance.

He Is Available
Acts 1:3

Jesus is alive. He appeared to the disciples following His resurrection, and He gave them many infallible proofs, ***being seen by them during forty days.*** The second participle, translated ***being seen***, is only used one time in the New Testament, and it is in this passage. This fact causes a Bible scholar to look closely at what is being said. This one time usage is usually for the purpose of giving a special definition to the word. But that is not so in this instance. Here the participle gives special form to the verb. Luke wants to state, definitely, that the disciples really did see Jesus. Jesus did not only appear to the disciples, but they saw Him, and they comprehended what they saw. This participle is in the middle voice, but in most cases, it is translated into the English as active voice. In many translations it is stated, ***appeared to them***. It can also be translated in the passive as ***being seen by them.*** This strongly emphasizes that Jesus was clearly seen by the disciples in His resurrected form.

The statement, ***during forty days***, is linked with the phrase, ***infallible proofs.*** This gives strong support to the idea of Jesus being seen. ***Infallible proofs*** means "beyond doubts." This word is only used one time in the New Testament. It becomes very significant when you remember the profession of the author. Luke was a medical doctor, a scientist. He was very interested in research and the validation of facts. Luke uses this word to demonstrate the evidence of the resurrection. We can contrast this with the evidence which was provided by witnesses. Those who witnessed the resurrection shared important evidence, but the proof to the disciples was not the testimony of others. The resurrection was proven for them by touch and sight. Luke recorded this in volume one when he wrote, **He said to them, "Behold my hands and My feet, that it is I Myself. Handle Me and see, for a spirit does not have flesh and bones as you see I have,"** (Luke 24:39). In his first epistle, John wrote, **That which was from the beginning, which we have heard, which we have seen with our eyes, which we have looked upon, and our hands have handled, concerning the Word of life** (1 John 1:1).

Can you imagine this incredible experience? The disciples' interaction with the resurrected Lord erased all of their doubts. How could they not believe in Jesus? He did not come to them in a withdrawn state. He did not appear in dreams or visions. He came and made Himself totally available to them for forty days. They ate with Him. In the closing scene of John's Gospel account (John 21:12), Jesus cooked fish on the open fire and invited the disciples to eat breakfast with Him.

Many Bible scholars believe **being seen by them during forty days** refers to the various appearances of Jesus during that time. You can understand why one could come to this conclusion. The appearances of the resurrected Christ, as recorded by the Gospel accounts, indicate He would come to them, and then He would leave. The disciples never knew when Jesus would appear again. But I am convinced there is another indication in the Scriptures. There is no doubt Jesus spent a consistent amount of time with the disciples. Day after day, Jesus was with them. He gave them many hours of training and teaching on the principles of the Kingdom of God. They touched Him with their hands. They ate with Him. He was totally available to them.

Does that surprise you? Has He not always been available to them? From the lowly task of washing their feet to the lofty position of being their Redeemer, Jesus had always been available to them. Every question they wanted to ask, regardless of the significance of the subject, Jesus was there to listen. Was it any different after the resurrection? He was still there for them, giving them what they needed.

What Jesus was to the disciples, He is to us! We have seen His *infallible proofs*. He has brought us from death to life. Oh, we have seen Him in rare appearances at an altar of prayer, but that has not been our proof. It is in the day in and day out presence of His indwelt Spirit that we are convinced of His aliveness. He is totally available to us. We do not lack for His attention. There is no limit to the supply of His resource. We feel Him. We see Him. We eat with Him. The experiences we have had with Jesus have been translated into our cultural setting. Jesus is not out of date for our fast paced generation. He is totally available to us.

He Is Addressing
Acts 1:3

Jesus is *speaking*. That is third participle of this verse. Luke says Jesus was *speaking of the things pertaining to the kingdom of God*. It will help us to understand the progression of the word, *speaking*. The basic meaning of the word is "to gather" or "to assemble" or "to put together." The idea of "to count" is attached to the word, because it has to do with the mental activity of gathering similar things. This leads to the idea of "enumerating" or "drawing up" or "to entering on a list." From this conclusion, we get the idea of narration, which gives us the sense "to speak."

Jesus was living and available to the disciples for forty days. He gathered all He had told them about the Kingdom of God during the three years of ministry, and now He put it into the new context of His resurrection. Because they had experienced the crucifixion and the resurrection, they now had a new understanding and openness to the Kingdom style. Jesus was now the firstborn from the dead. Just think of the astounding perspective He could give them as He spoke from the realm of eternal life. Jesus and the disciples must have had incredible conversations as they quizzed Him about the operation of the Kingdom of God.

It is essential we understand the Kingdom of God as Luke refers to it here. He wants us to understand the sovereign authority and rule of God in the lives of His people. It is more than an area of territory, or even the people, over which God rules. An appropriate equivalent to the Kingdom of God is "the rule of God" or "God's ruling." Understanding this distinction is very important in understanding all of the New Testament.

Jesus did not talk with the disciples about the size of the territory over which He was Lord. The square miles of land, or the number of continents, was not the issue. The number of people living within these spaces is not significant either. The focus is on God's rulership. Jesus explained the completeness of the flow and resource of God was to empower an individual for the full expression of his created purpose. He painted a picture of a kingdom which would operate on an altogether different principle than we have known in this world.

Jesus never forces dictatorship. He has not conquered us by might and ability, against which we cannot defend ourselves. He is not even King, as a member of the royal family, who has inherited the position. He has won our hearts, and we leap at the chance to be under His Lordship. His death and resurrection

Part Two: The Promise Of The Father

have expanded His Lordship to a level of pure love.

But we have not yet described it adequately. This Kingdom is for the individual, but it is also corporate. From the view of our world, we understand a corporate Kingdom. It engulfs groups of people, who are all under the reign of the King. But the Kingdom of God has a different flavor. While it is definitely community, it is likely to function as a body, and it is distinctly individual. The King is not "over there," ruling over hundreds of people, not knowing their names.

This King "is here," indwelt within the individual, bringing intimate linkage with the individual. This individual seems to have the entire Kingdom of God within his person. He has relationship with the King. While Jesus, the King, is certainly Lord, He is also a brother to the individual. In the corporate sense of the Kingdom, He is a brother to each individual in the Kingdom. This brings new perspective to the corporate linkage of this Kingdom. It brings the individual members together in a body process unlike any other Kingdom.

Think of what it must have been like for the disciples to hear Jesus explaining this brand new way. He was leading them into the promise of verses four and five. He was going to indwell them through the Spirit. As the Father exploded the Kingdom of God through Jesus, so Jesus would explode the Kingdom of God through them. As the Father ruled through Jesus, bringing life, so Jesus would rule through the disciples, and they would experience His resurrected life.

Jesus, and the very presence of His person, confronts everything else which rules. How can you tell what is ruling you? That which rules you is visible, and can be seen in what controls you. Think of the wonder of Jesus being in absolute control of life itself. He will determine the way you respond to every circumstance or problem under His presence. It is not that Jesus is King, and you should imitate Him, but Jesus is enthroned within you, and He will act through you. He is not in control of making laws or rules for you to follow, but you are submissive to His attitude, and you respond to His person. He does not give you a list of activities which He wants you to do for Him, but He indwells and empowers the fulfillment of His dreams through your being. Do you know such a Kingdom? ***He* has *also presented Himself alive, being seen, and speaking.***

Acts 1:4

LET'S GO CAMPING

In the last chapter we completed our study of the first sentence in the Book of Acts (volume two), and now we must stop and get our perspective. This one sentence was not an easy journey. It required diligent and significant climbing. Three verses were contained within this one sentence. Luke began this volume like a well-versed expositional preacher. He presented us with **THE PROPOSITION** (Acts 1:1). He made us fully aware of the Divine Activity Thing. The Person of Jesus Christ, the Man, demonstrated the Divine Activity Thing. He began a new breed of persons called Sons of God. These Sons of God will know God's production of His life in their living.

Luke reminds us of **THE PERSPECTIVE** (Acts 1:2). As we look through the lens of the ascension, we realize the viewpoint is the Divine Activity Thing. The ascension was the action of the Father upon Christ. The Father gave commandments through Christ, even after His resurrection. The Divine Activity Thing is the perspective of eternity. It is not a crutch to help us through the hard times of life. It is the nature of who we are as Kingdom people.

Luke reminds us of the content of the Divine Activity Thing in this sentence (Acts 1:3). It is found in **THE PRESENTATION**. After His resurrection, Jesus *also presented Himself alive* to His disciples. During these forty-days, He gave them *infallible proofs*. Jesus presents Himself as a servant, Who has come to stand before the disciples to aid them, as if they were the King. That sounds like Jesus. He demonstrated the reversal of roles. Jesus is the King, and yet, He is again serving His disciples in their moment of need. Jesus is revealing the cross style in the eternal realm. This is the motive of the Divine Activity Thing. God is playing out His heartbeat on the stage of a Man's life. It is the cross. God is serving us!

Now we come to the second sentence of the first chapter (Acts 1:4,5). It is **THE PROMISE** of the Divine Activity Thing. Everything within this sentence seems to focus on the Promise. Without even knowing the details of the Promise, we know it is significant that God has made us a promise at all. When you think of Who He is and who we are, there is no reason for Him to make us a promise. He is not obligated. There is no way we can be worthy. God simply made us the Promise. The sentence gives us something of the details of the setting of the Promise.

The Communion
Acts 1:4

Luke gives the circumstances in which Jesus reminds the disciples of the Promise. *And being assembled together with them*, is its context. *Being assembled together with them* is actually one word in the original language of the Bible. There seems to be some controversy concerning this word. This makes it difficult to boldly declare the complete definition of the statement. The Greek language is very picturesque and gives us the tone and atmosphere of what is taking place during this time.

The verb may have two different meanings. It may derive from a stem meaning "eat salt together." If this is true, it possibly refers to a meal, and we can translate it, "while He was eating a meal with them." But it may come from a root word meaning, "camping out with" or "stay with," and could be translated "while He was staying with them." The fact that Luke began this sentence with, *And,* lets you know this verb has a direct connection with the previous verse. He just told us of Jesus being with His disciples for forty-days, giving them infallible proofs, and teaching them anew about the Kingdom of God. This was not a casual gathering for a brief moment, which leads you to the idea of "camping out with."

Luke closes the Gospel according to Luke (volume one) with the fact that Jesus ate with the disciples. "Salt" was the symbol of hospitality. Thus, we have the idea of "eat salt together with" or a meal. ***But while they still did not believe for joy, and marveled, He said to them, "Have you any food here?"*** (Luke 24:41). Since the disciples and the resurrected Lord were together for forty-days, it is not hard to believe they ate meals together.

However, the actual Greek word translated, ***being assembled together with them,*** indicates another strong emphasis by Luke. Even the translation hints at this emphasis. Luke makes a double statement about the fact of their being together. The Greek word is two words put together. The main root word means, "to gather together," while the prefix also means, "together." This intensifies the meaning of gathering together. It might actually be translated, "And when they were gathered together, together." In other words, they were really together.

This speaks of the kind of intimacy Jesus desired to have with His disciples. He was not interested in a casual meeting, on a surface level. He came to present Himself in resurrection power. His mission was to give them necessary insight into the Kingdom of God. But He wanted to do much more than teach them. In the midst of this intimate kind of gathering, Jesus would reveal the Promise of the Father. The disciples would see and understand things they could never know without this kind of being together.

Have you not found this to be true? You do not discover the heart of God in a casual meeting with Him. You do not obtain great insight from lectures about the Biblical truth. You do not find the mind of God in the latest Christian book. Oh, God may choose to use any, or all, of these things to bring revelation, but those avenues without "being gathered together, together," will not benefit the soul. You have certainly found this true in the corporate body's worship of Christ. You can have the best music and the greatest preaching, but those things are lifeless without His coming. Unless the Spirit of God visits the corporate body, the music and the preaching are only performance. When God's presence moves in the midst of our gathering together, something takes place in the minds and hearts of those gathered, which cannot be experienced without Him.

I admonish you to obtain the best Bible study material you can find. Stretch yourself by gaining all of the education for ministry available to you. Attend every seminar you can which is designed to aid you in church growth. But above all, seek the heart of God. You cannot survive without the Divine Activity Thing operating in our heart. Only in His presence will you find what you need. You cannot keep appointments with Him, coming into His presence once in a while, thinking you know Him. It is "being gathered together, together," which is day after day, moment by moment abiding with Him that makes your life livable. Saturate in His presence. Never let a second pass by without allowing Him to permeate your very being. This is where you will know the heart of the Father. This is where the wonder of His promises will come to you!

The Command
Acts 1:4

To really understand a part of something, you must first of all understand the whole of it. This is true of the next phrase Luke writes. It is found in verse four. He says, **He commanded**

them not to depart from Jerusalem but to wait.... The word ***command*** is the heart of the verse. It is the main verb, and speaks of the action of Jesus. It is a different word than we find in, ***He through the Holy Spirit had given commandments to the apostles*** (Acts 1:2). The word, ***commandments***, has to do with emphasis or focus. Jesus was not giving them rules to keep, or orders to carry out, but He was giving them a concentration for their lives. But now He is going to ***command*** them. Jesus is making an announcement, coupled with the idea of coming alongside. It has the flavor of the military, and it is a word used for a watch word passed from man to man.

Again you see the idea of Jesus and His disciples being together. Jesus is not the top sergeant, yelling an order to the troops. This is the picture of soldiers in the fox holes, passing the word down the line from man to man. The commander is in the trenches with them. He has just come from the cross. He has just been resurrected. It is now time for the next step in the great plan of God. Jesus gives the order in this "gather together, together," experience.

The command which Jesus gives has two elements which are closely linked together. Contained within the order is ***not to depart*** and ***but to wait***. The focus is on the city of ***Jerusalem***. Jesus asks His disciples ***not to depart from Jerusalem***. The idea is not to be separated, severed, or divided. He does not want them to leave the city, but He wants their physical presence in Jerusalem.

The last verses of volume one (Luke 24:50), indicate these words from Jesus were actually spoken to the disciples at the Mount of Olives. We know the disciples did not spend the fifty days between the crucifixion and Pentecost in Jerusalem. According to Matthew, Mark and John, they returned to Galilee some time after the resurrection. Galilee was their home. Jesus told them He wanted to meet them in Galilee (Matthew 28:10). He gave them the great commission at the mountain in Galilee. They were surrounded by familiar territory. They made their living from the Sea of Galilee. In fact, the disciples had decided to return to fishing (John 21:3).

The disciples had been in Jerusalem during the Feast of the Passover. They returned to Galilee following the resurrection of Christ, as He had requested them to do. Now they were back in Jerusalem for this time of the Ascension. Jesus let them know His desire for them. "Don't go back to the comfort of your home, your old patterns, and your former business. Stay here in the middle of Jerusalem."

Can you imagine how hard it was for them to remain in Jerusalem? They had been doing quite well for themselves before they came to Jerusalem. They had a successful ministry among the multitudes of Galilee. Jerusalem was the beginning of their troubles. Everything had gone well until they entered this city. If they had stayed away from Jerusalem, Jesus would not be dead. They would still be performing miracles, and the crowds would still be following them. Hope would have remained with them. Now, in light of all they have experienced, and knowing the wrathful strength of the leadership of Jerusalem, it is only natural they do not want to return there, leaving the safety of Galilee.

But Jesus commands them ***not to depart from Jerusalem, but to wait.*** But there is another thought which is more difficult for them to handle. They are not only to stay in the scene of their trouble, but they are also ***to wait.*** They are not to simply remain in Jerusalem, but there is the idea of expecting, focusing on, and wanting. This is the only time in the New Testament this word is used, which always means we must pay close attention to the emphasis. The word is in the present tense, the active voice, and the infinitive mood. This word could be translated "to keep on waiting for."

Jesus commands the disciples to remain in the midst of their trouble. He does not want them to run back to their home environment, which would be less threatening and safe. But they are to do more than remain in the problems. They are to hope,

Part Two: The Promise Of The Father

trust, focus, expect, and watch for the Promise of the Father. They will experience all God has for them in the pressure of their trouble, while they anxiously look through the eyes of faith.

They would not have to wait long. From the Feast of the Passover (the cross event) to the Day of Pentecost, was fifty days. Three of those days were spent waiting for the resurrection. From the resurrection until the ascension was a period of forty days. During this time period, Jesus appeared to them and instructed them on *the things pertaining to the kingdom of God,* (Acts 1:3). This means the time from the ascension to the Day of Pentecost was only seven days. They only waited seven days after the command.

What did they do during their seven days of waiting in Jerusalem? Certainly they did not lock themselves in the Upper Room, hiding from Jerusalem. If they had hidden, it would have been a form of departing from Jerusalem and their troubles. Luke gives us clear insight into their activities. *And they worshiped Him, and returned to Jerusalem with great joy, and were continually in the temple praising and blessing God,* (Luke 24:52-53). They were right in the middle of the leadership of Israel and the people of Jerusalem. They were hoping, trusting, expecting and proclaiming while they remained in Jerusalem. They fulfilled the command of Jesus.

Were they not in an upper room? According to Luke, after the ascension, *they returned to Jerusalem from the mount called Olivet, which is near Jerusalem, a Sabbath's day's journey. And when they had entered, they went up into the upper room where they were staying,* (Acts 1:12-13). But that does not mean they remained in the upper room for seven days. Luke indicates they spent their days in the temple praising God, witnessing, and worshiping. He does not specify where they actually were on the Day of Pentecost when the fullness of the Spirit came. Luke says *they were all with one accord in one place,* (Acts 2:1). He says the manifestations of the Spirit *filled the whole house where they were sitting,* (Acts 2:2). The word, house, could mean the upper room, or it could also mean the temple. As you read on in chapter two (Acts 2:5), the large crowd which saw and heard in their own languages, could indicate the disciples were actually in the temple among the people when Pentecost came. They were keeping the commandment of Jesus. They did not depart from the scene of their trouble, but they stayed in the presence of the leadership of Israel and the very people who were responsible for the cross of Christ. They were praising and worshiping Christ. They were, no doubt, proclaiming Him as Lord even then. The Promise of the Father came as they were expecting, anticipating, focusing, and hoping, in the midst of the scene of their trouble.

This is a truth which we must grasp. We have had this scene repeated in each of our lives again and again. Jesus calls us to remain in the midst of our trouble. He does not call us to run away to the safety of our traditions. He does not want us to retreat to the safety of how we have always done it. He calls us to stand in the middle of the pressure and to hope, trust, look, and concentrate on the Promise He has made to us. Here is where we will find all He has for us! It is not just what He has for us, but for our world as well. In the Promise of the Father, there is an evangelistic thrust which will shake the world.

The Commitment
Acts 1:4

You might think we have covered the concept of commitment in the material just discussed? After all, if you stay in the midst of Jerusalem, the scene of your trouble, and expect the fullness of God to come, are you not committed? That is absolutely correct! But the commitment discussed at the end of verse four is not about us. It is about the Father. Jesus told the disciples, *to wait for the Promise of the Father, "which,"* He

Part Two: The Promise Of The Father

said, "you have heard from Me;" (Acts 1:4).

This is a message of the Father's commitment to you. The Greek word translated, **the Promise**, is very significant. The promise is free, without solicitation. The Father has given us a promise without any pressure from us. We did not ask Him to do it. We certainly had nothing He wanted or needed so as to bargain with Him. There was no way to get Him obligated to us. It is a free promise.

If you really grasp this concept, you will break into joyous praise. The sovereign God has decided to commit Himself to us. He is not under any pressure. Where is the one who could make God do anything? The Promise comes from the depth of His love for us. There is no other explanation. It is an expression of the total dream He has for you as an individual.

How strong is His commitment to you? We can only answer this in the light of the character of His person. All the resource of His being is highlighted in the Promise. It is as sure as the Person of God is sure. But we are not without ample evidence of the security of His Promise. In the unfolding of the pages of an Old Testament is the revelation of a Promise made by God to Abraham. Abram was not looking for a Promise. God simply came alongside of him and gave him a Promise. It spilled forth from the dream of God for His world. God had a heart for the redemption of mankind. The Promise to this man had significance for the entire human race. Best of all, we have seen the unfolding of this Promise. We witnessed the tremendous resource God poured into keeping the Promise to Abraham and his seed. He kept it to the great sacrifice of His own being. The cross was a result of the Promise.

The Promise He gives to us is not unlike this. The same commitment He made to Abraham, he gives to us. All of God's resources bend to fulfill the Promise in our lives. God commits Himself to us. His dream will be fulfilled. What an opportunity we have!

Jesus wants to camp out with us. Saturating in His presence, we will hear His direction and command. It is in the moment by moment involvement in His being, the continual flow of His person, that we begin to understand His desire for us. He does not want us to run away from the pressure of our trouble, and He certainly does not want us to run away from our world. But as we stay, looking with anticipation, hope and faith, we will find the Promise clearly revealed. It contains the best God has for us. It is the destiny of our living.

Acts 1:4

THE ANNOUNCEMENT OF THE FATHER

What a privilege it would have been to be able to hear the voice of Jesus as He gave this commandment to His disciples. All Jesus was about, and everything He had done, was pointing to the coming moments when the disciples would receive the Promise of the Father. As a member of the Trinity, Jesus had dreamed about this from the first moment of man's sin. What man had lost in the Fall would now be restored in the Promise of the Father. This Promise contained the purpose for which God created man. The lost purpose was finally going to be restored. Suppose you have worked and saved all year to purchase a Christmas gift for someone you love. The gift has been bought, it is wrapped and secured in your home, and you are waiting for the moment to reveal it on Christmas morning. That is what it was like for Jesus. Everything He accomplished since He leapt from His throne to His death and resurrection, was a part of the provision of this one gift. It is the Promise of the Father.

Do you think the voice of Jesus trembled with excitement when He told the disciples about the Promise? Did He gesture with His hands? Did His face show the thrill of excitement? He desperately wanted this for His disciples. They needed it. Think of the intensity and the air of anticipation as you view this scene again.

And being assembled together with them, He commanded them not to depart from Jerusalem, but to wait for the Promise of the Father, "which," He said, "you have heard from Me;" (Acts 1:4). In the middle of "being gathered together, together," Jesus slips alongside His disciples and orders them not to leave Jerusalem. He wants them to remain there, even though they are uncomfortable. They are not to return to the safety of their homes, back to the familiar, but they are to remain in the middle of the symbol of their trouble, Jerusalem. Here, in the pressure and the threat to their lives, they will experience *the Promise of the Father*. They are *to wait* for the Promise with hope, trust, and anticipation.

Jesus reminds them *the Promise of the Father* is not a new or recent revelation. *He said, "you have heard it from Me;"* (Acts 1:4). As we investigate the context of what Jesus is saying about the Promise, we see a concept begin to develop. This preliminary concept is necessary if we are to understand the fullness of *the Promise of the Father*.

There is no doubt this Promise is from old. Jesus distinctly reminds His disciples this has been the plan all along, and they should have understood it. You can clearly see this in the word *Promise*. The original word meant "announcement." Though the content of the Promise may have been a "mystery" it was certainly not a secret. God has boldly declared it. Paul refers to it as *the mystery which has been hidden from ages and from generations, but now has been revealed to His saints,* (Colossians 1:26). Man has never understood the Promise in its fullness. Its full details have not been declared, but it has been announced again and again. We have not been caught off guard.

The actual Greek word for *Promise* is primarily a law term. It points to "a summons." The basic word means "to proclaim or announce," while the prefix is the word, "upon." All of this points to the atmosphere of a declaration from old. The Promise has been told by Jesus and announced by the Father.

Part Two: The Promise Of The Father

Ezekiel, the prophet, heard the voice of the Father. He was speaking to him about the great restoration of Israel. He said, ***"Then I will sprinkle clean water on you, and you shall be clean; I will cleanse you from all your filthiness and from all your idols. I will give you a new heart and put a new spirit within you; I will take the heart of stone out of your flesh and give you a heart of flesh. I will put My Spirit within you and cause you to walk in My statutes, and you will keep My judgments and do them,"*** (Ezekiel 36:25-27). God was establishing a New Covenant with Israel. It was the ***Promise of the Father***. There would be a new purity involved. The emphasis would shift from the external to the internal. The heart of man would be changed so the very desires of God could be accomplished from the source of the Spirit of God, now within man. No one hearing this Promise in Ezekiel's day would have understood what it would be like to experience this. But it had been boldly declared by the Father.

Isaiah gave insight into the coming redemption of mankind. He gave amazing descriptions about the suffering Messiah, Who would change things for everyone. You would expect to find the ***Promise of the Father*** contained in his pronouncements. The Lord said to Isaiah,

*"For I will pour water on him who is thirsty,
And floods on the dry ground; I will pour My Spirit on your descendants, And My blessing on your offspring"*
(Isaiah 44:3).

Peter, on the Day of Pentecost, as the ***Promise of the Father*** was being fulfilled, reminded everyone present this was a declaration from days gone by. When the Promise was fresh upon him, he addressed them saying,

"Men of Judea and all who dwelt in Jerusalem, let this be known to you, and heed my words. For these are not drunk, as

you suppose, since it is only the third hour of the day. But this is what was spoken by the prophet Joel: 'And it shall come to pass in the last days, says God, that I will pour out My Spirit on all flesh; Your sons and your daughters shall prophesy, Your young men shall see visions, Your old men shall dream dreams, And on My menservants and on my maidservants I will pour out My Spirit in those days; And they shall prophesy. I will show wonders in heaven above and signs in the earth beneath: Blood and fire and vapor of smoke. The sun shall be turned into darkness, and the moon into blood, before the coming of the great and awesome day of the Lord. And it shall come to pass that whoever calls on the name of the Lord shall be saved'" (Acts 2:14-21).

Peter was quoting from the *Promise of the Father* as stated in Joel 2:28-32.

However, even more significant than this was Jesus' declaration and demonstration of the *Promise of the Father*. The theme of *the former account* (Acts 1:1), as well as the Book of Acts, is the Divine Activity Thing. God was acting upon the stage of the life of Jesus. When it was time for Jesus to launch His earthly ministry, He came to John the Baptist to be baptized. Little did John know what would happen as he placed his leathered hands upon the flesh of Christ. *The Holy Spirit descended in bodily form like a dove upon Him, and a voice came from heaven which said, "You are My beloved Son; in You I am well pleased,"* (Luke 3:22).

Jesus was beginning something new. He was establishing a new category called "Sons of God." He was the very first one. These "Sons of God" would be characterized by the fullness of the *Promise of the Father*. Every son of God would be possessed by the same Spirit. Every son of God would partake of this Divine life. God would re-create the life of Christ through him. God would take him from the death of trespasses and sins into the resurrected Life of Christ. Jesus promised this experience to His disciples and boldly demonstrated it in His own life.

Christ boldly declares the Promise. According to ***the former account*** (Acts 1:1), Jesus announced the ingredients of the Divine Activity Thing to the disciples. This activity always demonstrated itself in the cross style (Luke 9:22). By nature, the Divine action will always be redemptive, not destructive (Luke 9:56). The fulfilled Promise lives in constant rest, not worry (Luke 12:22ff). It was the good pleasure of the Father to give the resource Jesus demonstrated to the disciples. Jesus told the disciples of a son who was hungry and asked for bread. Would any father among them be so wicked as to give him a stone? Or if a son would ask for a fish, would any father among them be so wicked as to give him a scorpion? Jesus clearly said, ***"If you then, being evil, know how to give good gifts to your children, how much more will your heavenly Father give the Holy Spirit to those who ask Him!"*** (Luke 11:13). The disciples had ample revelation of the ***Promise of the Father, "which,"*** He said, ***"you have heard from Me;"*** (Acts 1:4).

But there is a problem. Though the disciples have seen the demonstration and heard the message about **the Promise of the Father**, they have not grasped the reality of this truth. The words, **you have heard** (Acts 1:4), are translated from the usual word which denotes, "to hear." When this verb is used transitively, as the direct object is expressed, it is sometimes in the accusative case, and sometimes in the genitive case. When the verb is expressed in the accusative case, the focus is on the hearing of the meaning or message of the voice. In other words, they heard or grasped the meaning of what was said. However, sometimes the verb is expressed in the genitive case, which indicates a "sensational perception," simply meaning the Lord's voice was sounding. In this instance (Acts 1:4), the verb is in the genitive case. The emphasis is then upon the fact Jesus spoke to them about the ***Promise of the Father***, but they did not really hear Him. Even though Jesus demonstrated the quality of the

Promise, the disciples did not see it. They did not understand what He was telling them.

But this was a different day! What an experience it must have been! In the new light of the resurrection experience, the minds of the disciples have an openness as never before. They were shaken from their normal patterns of understanding. Jesus will spend forty days **speaking of the things pertaining to the kingdom of God,** (Acts 1:3). If you remember from our previous study, the word, *speaking*, comes from the idea of gathering together, numerating, or forming a list. In other words, Jesus was making an organized presentation concerning the Kingdom of God. He gathered all He had taught the disciples before His death and now presents it to them in light of His resurrection. He spent forty days covering the material and bringing them to this focus on the **Promise of the Father**.

Do you think you would have clapped your hands at the end of this seminar? Would you have stood to your feet and cheered? Yes, you would have responded like that! You would have packed your bags and returned to your local church, ready to put all of these great suggestions into practice. The pages and pages of notes which you carefully took will keep you enthused and on course. You will arrange meetings with the key leaders in your church to share this information and make plans. You are ready to do it! You are ready for action!

But Jesus stops you at the door and says, ***"Wait for the Promise of the Father!"*** Will you argue with Him? You do not want to wait. After all, you have all of the information. You have been through forty days of intense training under the greatest teacher of all times. He has clarified the three years of training you experienced before the cross. You already know how to cast out demons and handle great multitudes of hungry people. There is no reason to wait! You have all of the knowledge and truth to do the job.

But Jesus tells us the resource is not found in just knowledge or truth. The resource is in His Person, the One who is Truth. You need to experience the ***Promise of the Father***. This will be vividly portrayed in the unfolding of the Book of Acts. Time and time again the highly educated people of Israel will confront the disciples. The scholars will drill them about their doctrine and practices. But it will not be the philosophical or theological knowledge of the disciples which will impress these educated leaders. It was **when they saw the boldness of Peter and John, and perceived that they were uneducated and untrained men, they marveled. And they realized that they had been with Jesus,** (Acts 4:13). They saw the disciples were resourced with the Person of Christ Himself. The power of Christianity has never been doctrine, ceremonies, or legalistic practices. It has always been the indwelling presence of Christ.

The Apostle Paul was highly educated for his day. Yet, he was deeply aware of this tremendous truth. In writing to the people of Corinth, he reminded them of the ministry he had with them. He wanted them to remember he *did not come with excellence of speech or of wisdom declaring to* them *the testimony of God. For,* he stated, *I determined not to know anything among you except Jesus Christ and Him crucified. I was with you in weakness, in fear, and much trembling. And my speech and my preaching were not with persuasive words of human wisdom, but in demonstration of the Spirit and of power, that your faith should not be in the wisdom of men but in the power of God,* (1 Corinthians 2:1-5). What had the Apostle Paul gained from the wisdom of man. He had followed the best religious minds this world could produce, and he had become a killer of men, women, and children. He had persecuted all of them for naming the name of Christ. What was the great argument which convinced him to convert to Christianity? What man had the wisdom to show him the true pathway to life? It was not done by the knowledge of man, but Christ knocked him off his horse with a blinding light. The resource was in the person of Christ Himself!

Seek education; learn all you can learn; read all you can read. But far beyond any effort or focus spent there, seek the heart of God! Do the academic work necessary to gain the platform from which you can demonstrate the power of God, but note this, it is His person Who is the resource of the demonstration. Name any area of conflict, then understand the answer will only be found in the resource of the Person of Christ. We will never evangelize our world with better programs or with studies of cultural qualities. We need the resource of the Person of Christ. We must demonstrate the Person of Christ, as we are resourced by Him. We need the ***Promise of the Father.***

Acts 1:4

THE PROMISE OF THE FATHER

The Promise of the Father has a definite ring about it for those who are aware of who the Father is! When you have seen Jesus' demonstration of the Father, you know this ***Promise*** is significant. This Promise has been talked about since the days of old. Jesus said to the disciples, **"which you have heard of Me,"** (Acts 1:4). The Father revealed the Promise to prophets generations ago. Ezekiel spoke of it (Ezekiel 36:25-27). Jeremiah gave the same message (Jeremiah 31:31ff). Isaiah was thrilled at its announcement (Isaiah 44:3). Peter quoted Joel on the Day of Pentecost, telling about the ***Promise*** (Acts 2:14-21). The Father has planned for the Promise for a long time.

The Promise is the climax of all God has dreamed for mankind. He has poured out all of His resources into fulfilling this Promise, and He has dreamed of giving it to His children. Everything God did in the Old Testament was for the purpose of bringing the Promise into reality. Jesus Christ is the redemptive resource to make the Promise possible for His sons. It has been the total focus of God's purpose for mankind from the very beginning. The ***Promise*** is the heartbeat of God for us.

Jesus made the clarification that whatever is contained within the Promise will resource the Kingdom of God. He made it easy to understand that the ***Promise*** and the Kingdom are the same. Israel, and even the disciples, had a twisted view of the Kingdom. They viewed the Kingdom as a military endeavor.

It would have been easy for God to have resourced that kind of kingdom. It would not have taken any sacrifice on behalf of the Trinity. But the Kingdom of God, as Jesus described it, would demand a new kind of resource. He spent forty days giving His disciples a new perspective of the Kingdom in the context of the resurrection (Acts 1:3). This Kingdom would never be resourced by information or knowledge. It would not be a new program which a man could practice and accomplish. The Kingdom would not be brought about by discipline. It would only be resourced by the *Promise of the Father*.

It is such a marvel! The *Promise of the Father* is freely given to us. The concept of this free gift is found in the meaning of the word *Promise*. The giving does not come from an exchange or a bargain. It is a lavish gift of the Father. No one can obligate God. The motivation of the gift is strictly love, and it flows from His heart.

All of the ideas, as stated above are valid and good, but they are only aspects of the main idea of the Promise. It is very important for us to grasp and understand what the complete thrust of the *Promise* really is. We must never reduce the Promise of the Father to an experience one has at an altar of prayer. To the average evangelical Christian, the *Promise of the Father* is equated with the baptism of the Holy Spirit. Many view the Promise in the context of the Day of Pentecost, and they see their surrender to Christ as their personal Pentecost. As great a moment as that might be, it is cheap and small in comparison to what is really contained in the *Promise of the Father*.

The *Promise of the Father* is greater than an experience. God wants a relationship with you which will last throughout time and eternity. He wants true intimacy between you and Christ, as Jesus lives His life through you. The realm of the Kingdom of God, as Jesus discussed it with His disciples (Acts 1:3), is the *Promise of the Father*. God is looking for a group of individuals through whom He can do exactly what

He did through Jesus, the Man. All the resources God placed within Christ, which demonstrated the Father, is a part of the Promise of the Father. The Promise of the Father has to do with who we are as Kingdom people, as a branch abiding in the vine, as the flesh which He wears, as a platform upon which He can act, and as a glove into which He can place His hand.

Absolute Resting

Let us examine this concept in light of the context of our passage. Let us view the absolute resting. This highlights the trust factor. Trust must be present if we are to experience the fulfillment of the Promise. Jesus experienced the ***Promise of the Father***. In ***the former account***, we see Jesus living a life of total faith. He never wavered in His confidence in the Father. His great faith is what activated the reality of the ***Promise*** in His life. Jesus never lived one self-initiated moment. He was always living out of the resource the Father provided through the ***Promise***.

Jesus had a definite experience as recorded in Luke 3:22. The fullness of the Holy Spirit descended on Him when He was baptized by John the Baptist. But this was not the complete ***Promise of the Father***. This was a part of the Promise. It was important for the ministry to flow through the life of Jesus, but it cannot be labeled as the ***Promise of the Father***. Luke had the same theme for the Gospel of Luke (volume one) and for the Book of Acts (volume two). The baptism of Jesus by the Holy Spirit cannot be considered the ***Promise of the Father***. Neither can the Day of Pentecost be labeled as the ***Promise of the Father*** for the disciples. Both are a part of the Promise, but they are certainly not the whole. The Promise is much broader than an experience. The Promise means absolute trust in the Father's total provision for life. In maintaining that trust, Jesus experienced the moment by moment life of the Father.

The Promise of the Father | Acts 1:4

The essence of trust, or faith, is highlighted in the idea of the Promise of the **Father**. The Promise does not come from a Cosmic Begetter or a National Protector. Begetters and protectors fulfill their roles with fear and manipulation. You can see that in the pagans of the Old Testament. They were fearful of their gods. They attempted to manipulate them with their sacrifices and prayers, trying to get their needs met. Religion for them became a constant hassling of their gods. They tried to bargain with them, merit their favor, and appease them. They did all of this in order to get what was necessary to fulfill their own plans and dreams.

But this is not the Promise of the **Father!** We can clearly see it in *the former account.* Jesus trusted the plan of the Father. He did not have an agenda of His own. He did not attempt to get the Father's resource to fulfill His plan. NO! The Promise is always the Father's business (Luke 2:49). How can I fulfill the Father's will (Luke 22:42)? Do not worry, for Jesus always lives in the Father's provision (Luke 12:22-30). Even when it came to the issue of life or death, Jesus gave His total trust to the Father (Luke 23:46).

The disciples witnessed this in the three-year ministry of Jesus. They should have had no difficulty doing the same. This was also the content of Jewish thought and heritage. In the middle of a sea of paganism, which viewed God as the Cosmic Begetter, or National Protector, Judaism was an island of different content. For the Jews, God was their Father. He was the Father of the covenant people, and they had relationship with Him. He was not their Father in the sense of begetting them, but He was their Father in attitude and action. He fulfilled the role of Father in the highest sense. He actually cared about His people. Again and again, they used the personal pronouns, our, your and my. When Judaism expressed their feelings about God, they said, **"Father."**

Jesus clarified this idea in more vivid terms. He taught

us the heart of the Father. It was through Jesus the Father's attitude was demonstrated in practical action in our world. God is the **Father** Who knows what we do not know. He has long range dreams, and we have been born out of His dreams. He is absolutely trustworthy. We can trust Him with our lives more than we can trust ourselves. Therefore, we can live a life of total rest in the ***Promise of the Father.***

Abiding Relationship

Once the absolute rest is understood, we begin to see other important aspects of the ***Promise of the Father***. As the Book of Acts (volume two) is viewed, we immediately see there is ***the former account***, (Acts 1:1). The Gospel of Luke (volume one) informs us of the manifestation of the life of the Father through Jesus Christ. The opening statement, ***Jesus began***, gives us a summary of the former account. The action of the Father, through Jesus, is the beginning of a new set of circumstances which have never been in existence before. Jesus was like no one ever born before. He was the Hero, the Founder, the Captain (Hebrews 2:10), the Prince (Acts 3:15), and the Beginner of a new circumstance or category. This time period for this new category was from His birth through His ascension. He was the first example of what God dreamed others would become.

This new category is called "Sons of God." Jesus became the substance of this new category. We are called His brothers (Hebrews 2:11). We have the same life source. The very substance, which resourced Jesus, is now resourcing us. Peter wrote, ***as His divine power has given us all things that pertain to life and godliness, through the knowledge of Him who called us by glory and virtue, by which have been given to us exceedingly great and precious promises, that through these you may be***

partakers of the divine nature, having escaped the corruption that is in the world through lust, (2 Peter 1:3-4).

It is in the context of this sonship, when we share the life of Jesus as His brother, we understand the ***Promise of the Father***. The ***Promise of the Father*** is sonship. We must view it, not as an experience, but as a relationship. This category is not a moment to remember, but it is a moment by moment living of Jesus' life through us. It is not a special anointing by the Spirit for a one time feat, but it is the flow of Divine life resourcing our lives in a demonstration of Him. This is a continual relationship, destined to live forever. It is not a temporary, for the moment happening. The Promise of the Father moves us from the temporal life, across the line into the eternal life, which we now possess in Him.

We experience the ***Promise of the Father***, in the cry, **"Abba, Father,"** (Romans 8:15). The fullness of the Spirit makes us children. ***For as many as are led by the Spirit of God, these are sons of God,*** (Romans 8:14). We become sons of God in a relationship with God. This relationship is one of complete resting in God, being resourced by Him, and knowing His life rather than ours. It is in this context of being sons of God that we now know the full scope of the ***Promise of the Father***.

We must carefully remove the limitations we have placed upon the ***Promise of the Father***. We must see it through the eyes of Christ, Who experienced the Promise by being the complete demonstration of its fullness. You and I are invited to the same kind of trust Jesus had. Then we can experience the same kind of sonship which He knew. What a Promise God has given to us! It is His dream for us through the ages, and He has fulfilled it in our time.

However, there is a greater purpose in view through the Promise. God does not want sons for the mere sake of having sons. There is greater destiny involved in the fulfillment of the plan. We see it in the third aspect of the ***Promise of the Father***.

Part Two: The Promise Of The Father

Accented Revelation

The Father gave the Promise. Jesus was the complete revelation of the Father. In fact, it was the *Promise of the Father* which made Jesus this demonstration. The revelation of the Father is the *Promise of the Father*, and the *Promise of the Father* is the revelation of the Father. If the *Promise of the Father* is contained in sonship, it is natural to assume the Son looks like His Father. If the *Promise of the Father* is found in the fullness of the Holy Spirit, we understand it is this Holy Spirit who is the life of the Father. The Father gives birth and life to the son. We see this in Jesus (volume one), and in the disciples (volume two). Other men must see it in us (Volume Three). The natural evidence of this reality is displayed in the revelation of the Father as seen in the Son.

Jesus, the Beginner and Captain of this new sonship, taught this vividly. We see it everywhere in *the former account,* the Gospel of Luke. John, in his Gospel account, forcibly states this concept. *And the Word became flesh and dwelt among us, and we beheld His glory, the glory as of the only begotten of the Father, full of grace and truth,* (John 1:14). One of my favorite verses paints the picture so clearly. *No one has seen God at any time. The only begotten Son, who is in the bosom of the Father, He has declared Him,* (John 1:18). The message of Divine fatherhood relates to revelation. In a sense, the focus of Divine fatherhood narrows. God is not primarily the Father of all, but the Father of the Son who reveals Him. The Father is the Giver of revelation, and the Son is the Revelator of the same.

Jesus explained this to the disciples. *"All things have been delivered to Me by My Father, and no one knows who the Son is except the Father, and who the Father is except the Son, and one to whom the Son wills to reveal Him,"* (Luke 10:22). The revelation of the Father is contained within the responsibility of being the Son. The **ABSOLUTE TRUST** is clearly stated in this verse from *the former account*. *"All things have been delivered to Me by My Father…"* The Son knows no resource except the Father. He is totally dependent upon the Father. The only *things* the Son has, have been given to Him by the Father. The **ABIDING RELATIONSHIP** is also stated in this verse. Jesus says the Father is *"My Father."* In fact, He says, *"no one knows who the Son is except the Father, and who the Father is except the Son."* This is a very tight relationship. This verse also clarifies **THE ACCENTED REVELATION**. It is the Son's responsibility *to reveal Him*.

The truth of this verse is enough to astound us into a long meditation. We could spend our lifetime reflecting on the relationship between Jesus and His Father. But when you come to volume two (The Book of Acts), suddenly a new meaning appears.

What the Father was doing through Jesus, the first Son, He now wants to do through us in Christ. All the resource Jesus had as a Son, He now gives to us. The birthing and revealing thrust of the Holy Spirit now becomes ours. We, too, are the revelation of God to our world. As Jesus revealed the Father, so we are to reveal Jesus. We are birthed and resourced by the same life. It is the *Promise of the Father*.

The Son acts, and is about *"My Father's business,"* (Luke 2:49). He acts only as He sees the Father act. As the Father has given the Kingdom *(Promise of the Father)* to Jesus, so Jesus is now giving the same Kingdom to us (Luke 22:29). The Son set aside His own will in favor of the Father's will, He knows the Father's will is far superior to His views and desires (Luke 22:49). The Son realized, even in the midst of death, the Father is worthy of trust (Luke 23:46). The Father is revealing Himself through the Son. Jesus continually speaks about the Father. To **know** and to see the Son is to know and to see the Father. To be the Son is to be the Revelator of the Father.

But everything written about Jesus in the above paragraph

Part Two: The Promise Of The Father

can be written about us. Everything Jesus was, in and through the Father, is exactly what we are in and through Jesus. Jesus has given the Kingdom (Promise of the Father) to us (Acts 2:33). We are setting aside our will in favor of Jesus' will. In the midst of life, or death, we know Jesus' will is far superior to our views and desires. Jesus reveals Himself through us, the sons. We continually speak about Jesus. To know, and to see us, the sons, is to know and see Jesus. To be a son is to be the revelator of Jesus.

This is the content of the ***Promise of the Father***. Are you experiencing it?

Acts 1:5

THE IMMERSING OF JESUS

And being assembled together with them, He commanded them not to depart from Jerusalem, but to wait for the Promise of the Father, "which," He said, "you have heard from Me; for John truly baptized with water, but you shall be baptized with the Holy Spirit not many days from now," (Acts 1:4-5).

As we come to this verse, it is essential for us to see it as the climax to all Luke has written. The Book of Acts is not a separate writing from the Gospel account. It is the second volume of one presentation written by Luke. ***The former account*** (Acts 1:1), are Luke's words which relate us back to the Gospel according to Luke. The early church read it as one book. Therefore, this verse is based upon all of the previous verses in the Gospel account.

This verse is the spring board from which we launch into the reality of the ***promise of the Father*** (Acts 1:4). The actions we will see in the rest of the Book of Acts are the fulfillment of this promise. Luke lays a foundation to help us understand this demonstration. He begins in Acts with the **PROPOSITION** (Acts 1:1). Jesus has shown us the Divine Activity Thing. All Jesus did was a result of the action of the promise of the Father. From there Luke moves us to the **PERSPECTIVE** (Acts 1:2). Here we discover the eternal promise. We see the action of the Father, the Divine Activity Thing, in the framework of the ascension. The Divine Activity Thing is the promise of the Father forever.

Part Two: The Promise Of The Father

He secures the means by which we will live eternally. The Father demonstrates the **PRESENTATION** (Acts 1:3), in Jesus. This is a reversal of roles. Jesus, the King, presents Himself as the servant to meet the needs of the disciples. He demonstrates the heartbeat of the Divine Activity Thing. After Luke solidly lays this foundation, he brings us to the **PROMISE** (Acts 1:4-5). This is the climax of what we have learned.

This *promise of the Father* is so important to Luke that he naturally flows into a discourse. He does not introduce the verse with the words, "He said." He gives no other indication he is moving into a direct quotation. The translators have injected the words, "He said," into the verse to help us understand, but in the original language these words are not present. One moment we read what Luke is writing, and the next moment we hear the voice of Christ. Luke focuses on Christ when he emphasizes the phrase, *which you have heard from Me* (Acts 1:4). Then Luke continues in the next verse with the words of Christ, which gives us the content of the promise of the Father. Jesus said this before the resurrection, but the disciples now understand the content more than they did then.

Luke presents the *promise of the Father* as a contrast. We could make many distinctions between the type of baptism by John and the type of baptism by Jesus. John's baptism was outward and Jesus' baptism was inward. John's baptism was physical, but Jesus' baptism was of the Spirit. John's baptism was done in the River Jordan, but Jesus' baptism is in the river of God's grace. We could go on describing the types of baptism, but Luke's purpose was not to contrast the differences between John's and Jesus' baptisms.

As we get into the heart of what Luke is saying, it becomes evident the contrast is not between water baptism and the spiritual baptism of the Holy Spirit. The contrast is between the two persons, John the Baptist and Jesus. This is where we find the full content of the *promise of the Father*.

The Immersing of Jesus | Acts 1:5

We need to review, taking a closer look at the person of John the Baptist. John was a prophet who was calling Judah back to God. During his brief ministry, there was a beginning to a great revival. This revival was a part of his responsibility as the forerunner to the Messiah. John the Baptist was paving the way for the great journey of the Christ (Matthew 17:11-13).

The platform from which John preached extended over one hundred feet. It was the River Jordan. He undoubtedly used every bit of it. He was a strange man in every way. He lived as a hermit in the desert (Luke 1:80). The open sky was the only roof over his head. When he appeared on Sunday morning to deliver his message, he did not have the common garb of the day. He wore a strange garment made of camels' hair, (Matthew 3:4). Just to look at him created an itching sensation. If you got close to him you could smell the locust on his breath, and he had some honey in his beard from his last meal.

His hair was bushy and uncombed. His beard was always untrimmed. This hair bounced around and his beard swung back and forth as he ran up and down the banks of the Jordan River. He gave the appearance of a wild man. He only had one message. *He went into all the region around the Jordan, preaching a baptism of repentance for the forgiveness of sins* (Luke 3:4). He was ruthless in his approach. He did not spare any man, nor consider any too great to make him aware of his sin. When the Pharisees and the Sadducees appeared in his services, John was quick to make the message plain (Matthew 3:7). John even called the King to repentance (Luke 3:18-20). It is not surprising this ministry was short lived. John only lived six months after this confrontation, before the King took his life (Matthew 14:9-10).

Think of the greatness of John the Baptist. He was the best the law could produce. As predicted before his birth, John took a lifelong Nazirite vow. An angel told Zacharias, the father of John the Baptist, that John **will be great in the sight of the Lord**

Part Two: The Promise Of The Father

and he will drink neither wine nor strong drink, (Luke 1:15). Along with not drinking wine or liquor, the vow also included never cutting the hair or touching anything that was ceremonially unclean, such as a dead body. Many Jews, both men and women, took a Nazirite vow for a few months or a year. But Samson (Judges 13:7 and 16:17), Samuel (1 Samuel 1:11), and John the Baptist are the only three persons mentioned in Scripture who took the vow for life. Theirs was a lifelong, voluntary commitment to self-denial as an act of devotion to God.

John's role as a prophet was superior. There were no prophets during the time period between the Old Testament and the New Testament. Four hundred years of silence was finally broken by John the Baptist. He was the prophet called of God to break the pattern. He was unlike any prophet had ever been. He did not predict the coming of the Messiah, but was the actual voice who cried out that the Messiah was present. Other prophets pointed a great finger at His coming, but John the Baptist actually pointed out this Great One. John the Baptist stood on the shoulders of all of the other prophets as the last in the long line.

Think of the statements Jesus made to His disciples! He said, *"Assuredly, I say to you, among those born of women there has not risen one greater than John the Baptist;"* (Matthew 11:11). John the Baptist was the best the Old Testament law could produce. But this was not all Jesus said in this statement to His disciples. He continued, *"but he who is least in the kingdom of heaven is greater than he,"* (Matthew 11:11). The greatest the Old Testament could produce is less than the least of those who experienced the *promise of the Father*.

John was quick to admit this himself. He said, *"I indeed baptize you with water; but One mightier than I is coming, whose sandal strap I am not worthy to loose. He will baptize you with the Holy Spirit and fire,"* (Luke 3:16). In the great revival, with all who were baptized, with all of the disciples and the vows, John boldly says he does not even begin to compare with Jesus. My first reaction was agreement, because Jesus is God. But that is what Luke is telling us. Jesus set aside all He knew as God and became a total man. The greatness of Jesus was not in His Divinity, but in the surrender of that Divinity in order that He might be a total man, and live in the promise of the Father. His entire life was a product of the Divine Activity Thing. The only explanation for all He was and did, is the wonder of the Father acting upon the stage of His life. Jesus simply responded to the action of the Father.

John the Baptist was also filled with the Holy Spirit (Luke 1:15). But we must understand this was not the same as the ***promise of the Father***. John was a part of the group of Old Testaments leaders who were selected to be filled with the Spirit for the purpose of leadership. This was a foretaste of the promise of the Father to come, but it was not the same kind of filling. There is a definite distinction between what takes place in Jesus and what takes place in John the Baptist. We need to discuss this difference carefully.

The Last – The First

John was the last in the long line of Old Testament prophets. He was the best the law could produce. He was a man of extreme discipline and commitment. You must remember, that according to Jesus, **"Assuredly, I say to you, among those born of women there has not risen one greater than John the Baptist;"** (Matthew 11:11). John is to be honored as the last of the Old Testament prophetic style.

But we enter a new realm with Jesus. He is the first of a new system or setup. He is to show us what a relationship with God is like. Jesus is the first who experienced the ***promise of the Father***. The Father is preparing for the sons of God, and Jesus is the first. He is the first to fulfill all God, the Father, wanted in the creation of Adam. Jesus made the way for many sons to follow in His footsteps and experience the promise of the Father.

John the Baptist was the last of the old dispensation. Jesus is the first of the new dispensation or covenant. So the baptism of the Holy Spirit fulfills the ***promise of the Father***. It is much more than an experience or an event. The baptism of the Spirit is entering into all Jesus is as the first. The Divine Activity Thing which acted through Jesus' life, now becomes ours. We experience the movement of God and respond moment by moment to that flow. We are brothers with Christ in this new dispensation. We can experience a new level of living.

This does not indicate that John the Baptist was wrong or even inferior. He was simply the one who stood on the very brink of the final hour of an old covenant and had the privilege of viewing the new, but did not get to experience it. He lived in a realm of doing the best he could do. His was of the "doing" dispensation. He was judged by his discipline and ability of action. He did well! But why would one want to even consider staying there when one can move into the dynamic of the ***promise of the Father***? Why would we choose to live in legalism when we can live in grace, in the presence of the Spirit? Why would anyone want to limp along, doing their best, when he can experience the best God can accomplish in his life? Why would anyone be satisfied with rules, when he can respond, moment by moment, to the leadership of Jesus from within?

The ***promise of the Father*** has come to fulfillment. We can now enter into all the Father has dreamed for us. We dare not let tradition and comfort hinder us when the new is now ours. What a great opportunity we have!

The Greatest – The Immersed

John Baptist was the greatest. Again remember these words of Jesus. *"Assuredly, I say to you, among those born of women there has not risen one greater than John the Baptist;"* (Matthew 11:11). The focus here is upon John and what he achieved. He is to be admired. In the midst of the sin of his day, he rose to the level of the greatest among those under the law. The Roman Empire was evil. There was much rebellion in the Jewish culture. The Pharisees experienced legal hardness. Yet, John the Baptist was able to see the truth. He recognized Jesus as the Messiah, and he committed himself to a revival in the law structure as God intended it. We must applaud the accomplishment of this great man.

But in comparison to the one we applaud, there is Christ. He receives no applause. He did not take a Nazirite vow for his entire life. Jesus said, *"For John came neither eating nor drinking, and they say, 'He has a demon.' The Son of Man came eating and drinking, and they say, 'Look, a gluttonous man and a winebibber, a friend of tax collectors and sinners!'"* (Matthew 11:18-19). From the testimony of Jesus and the Jewish leaders, we know there is a vast difference between the lifestyle of John and the lifestyle of Jesus. No one ever accused John the Baptist of breaking the laws of God, yet Jesus was constantly accused by the Pharisees for breaking their law. They wanted to kill Him. On the Sabbath day, Jesus healed a man with a withered hand (Luke 6:6-11). Jesus allowed his disciples to pluck grain on the Sabbath day and eat it (Luke 6:1-2). He healed a woman on the Sabbath day (Luke 13:10-15). Jesus even allowed his disciples to eat bread without washing their hands, which was a violation of the Jewish law (Matthew 15:1-9). Jesus was strangely different from John the Baptist.

Jesus refused to take credit for anything of which he was a part. He was constantly testifying that the Father was acting in and through His life. Before His crucifixion, while in the upper room, Jesus told His disciples, *"Do you not believe that I am in the Father, and the Father in Me? The words that I speak to you I do not speak on My own authority; but the Father who dwells in Me does the works,"* (John 14:10). To the leaders of Israel, He explained, *"Most assuredly, I say to you, the Son can do nothing of Himself,"* (John 5:19). John the Baptist never preached a message like this. Jesus did because He was walking in a new realm, the *promise of the Father*. Jesus was not living out of the law, or self-discipline. He was not "doing." He was living out of the Divine Activity Thing. He always responded to the action of God within His life. He was not responsible for what was taking place through Him, but was only responding to the movement of the Father.

Jesus turned to His disciples and said, *"for John truly baptized with water, but you shall be baptized with the Holy Spirit not many days from now,"* (Acts 1:5). The passive voice of the verb translated *be baptized* indicates the baptism by Jesus Christ with the Spirit is entirely a Divine Activity. The entire focus of the *promise of the Father* is on the action of God. It removes any part of the action coming from us and places the heart of the action within the Father. Every action is to be immersed in the Spirit until He is the total source of the action.

Why would anyone want to live out of themselves when they can live out of Divine Action? Why would anyone want to tolerate the failures, hatred, and bitterness of their own hearts, when they can have the very mind of Christ (His Spirit) within them? Why would anyone be satisfied to live with the best they can do, when they can live in the best the Father can do through them? It is a clear call to the *promise of the Father*.

But there is yet another distinction between John and Jesus which we need to understand.

The Least – The Normal

John the Baptist was the least in the Kingdom of God. Let me remind you again of what Jesus said. *"Assuredly, I say to you, among those born of women there has not risen one greater than John the Baptist; but he who is least in the Kingdom of heaven is greater than he,* (Matthew 11:11). While John was the greatest the old Testament law could produce, he is placed in comparison to the *promise of the Father*. Even the least in the Kingdom of heaven is greater than he. All that John did in "doing the law" could not come close to matching the beginning steps in the Kingdom of God.

It was the *promise of the Father* displayed in Jesus which is normal for the Kingdom of God. While John had been filled with the Spirit from his birth, it was a limited filling, designated for only a few for the purpose of leadership and special service. But the promise of the Father was going to be for all who would be brothers with Christ in the new covenant. Christ displayed the full resource of God operating in and through Him. Now, all Christ demonstrated was going to take place in each one who was in the Kingdom. The fullness of the Spirit in Christ was going to be the norm for each member of the Kingdom. There will be no great or small; there would only be the body of Christ. No man will need to instruct another in knowing God, for each one will know God. The laws will not be written on tablets of stone, but will be stamped in the nature and heart of every man (Jeremiah 31:31-34).

Jesus was the only normal man. He lived in the normal way. The victory He had was normal. This is what God intended for everyone. He promised it to all. It is the *promise of the Father*. Why would anyone want to settle for struggling and trying in the abnormal world of the old covenant when he can be normal in Christ? Why would anyone cling to his pride and cover his failure, when he can be liberated in the fullness of the Father and be normal as Christ was normal? Why would anyone be satisfied with mere rules and religious ceremonies, when He can know God in Christ? It is the *promise of the Father*.

PRECEDING THE ASCENSION

Acts 1:6-26

LOOSE ENDS

In the Book of Revelation, Jesus gives distinct messages to seven different churches. Though these churches actually existed, they seem to represent particular sections of church history. If you analyze the communication to each church, the truth of each message becomes apparent, and you can apply it to your life and your corporate church. One of these churches was in the city of Sardis, and the city's long history greatly influenced the church.

Throughout history, the church seemed to maintain the expressed attitudes of the city. Jesus strongly advised the church to **"Be watchful, and strengthen the things which remain, that are ready to die, for I have not found your works perfect before God,"** (Revelation 3:2). The word, **perfect,** expresses the idea of complete. They had loose ends which needed to be tied down. This church had let some things slide. If they continued their lack of response, certain death would come to the church.

This is visible in the history of the city. Sardis occupied a large valley, which flowed into a great hill. The heart of the city was built on top of this hill for safety. The hill was steep on the south side, making it impossible to scale the great wall. The city was so well fortified, many people moved there for its safety, and it became the capital city of the area. Everyone felt secure behind its wall. They were so sure of their safety, they posted no guards on the southern wall.

Part Three: Preceding the Ascension

One day the enemy witnessed a soldier climbing down from the top of the city's wall. Having lost his helmet, he cut steps in the wall to help him get down to retrieve it. Later the enemy led a group of soldiers up the steps in the wall, and they were able to defeat the city. Though the city later regained its safety, they were complacent. They neither repaired the wall nor guarded it. It only took a handful of soldiers to creep in and overtake them the second time, all because this city had failed to tie up the loose ends.

Jesus confronts the church at Sardis for the same attitude. The church had let important things slide. They failed to tie up the loose ends. He said, ***"For I have not found your works perfect*** (complete) ***before God,"*** (Revelation 3:2). This is a valuable message to the church and to us.

The same kind of message seems to come from the first chapter of the Book of Acts. As you view this chapter, everything taking place is prior to the great outpouring of the Holy Spirit. In the first chapter, Luke tells how the apostles take steps and make preparations which pave the way for this great spiritual event. Without the Day of Pentecost the church would not have grown, and we could not realize the power of God in our lives. The early disciples had to get ready, tying up the loose ends in order to receive all God wanted to do in and through them.

Is this the need of our lives? Perhaps we need to deal with our loose ends. The church seems to lack belief in the power of God which is available to us in this day. Church people seem to have a swelling hunger and desire to realize His presence. God is certainly anxious to give us all that we need to fulfill His dreams for this age. Why are we patiently going to our Sunday services wondering when God is going to bring the Day of Pentecost for our time? Could it be we have failed to respond to His prompting to tie up the loose ends? In response to the leadership of the Spirit of God, we need to deal with some key issues which are hindering the unleashing of all we know is available to us.

In the first chapter of Acts there are three events which God did not accidentally place here. These events all transpire prior to the fulfillment of the ***Promise of the Father*** (Acts 1:4). These were necessary things which the early disciples accepted, and this acceptance made them receptive to what God wanted to do through them. Luke does not list these events just to fill space or give historical facts. Let us hear the message. "Tie up the loose ends!" We will look at these three events in reverse order of Luke's record.

Corporate
Acts 1:15-26

This section gives us insight into the inner action of the group of believers before the Day of Pentecost. They recognized their corporate body was incomplete. There was "a loose end" with which they must deal. The basis of this is established by Peter himself as he quotes from the Old Testament. He stood before the body of believers. (Luke is very specific in the number being one hundred and twenty.) Peter boldly quotes the Scriptures as a basis for what he is proposing.

He begins with: ***Let his dwelling place be desolate, And let no one live in it,*** (Acts 1:20).

This is a quotation of the prayer of David, (Psalm 69:25). David cries out to God in regard to his enemies. He wants their homes to be desolate.

Peter continues by saying: ***Let another take his office,*** (Acts 1:20).

This is a quotation of another prayer of David (Psalm 109:8). He prays his enemy will die prematurely and his position be replaced by someone else. This was fulfilled in the life of Judas.

Part Three: Preceding the Ascension

Notice how Luke states the words of the prayer of the one hundred and twenty before they cast lots on the two disciples who were qualified for this position. *And they prayed and said, "You, O Lord, who know the hearts of all, show which of these two You have chosen to take part in this ministry and apostleship from which Judas by transgression fell, that he might go to his own place,"* (Acts 1:24-25). They are speaking of the apostleship and ministry as a position or thing, in and of itself. It is the ground or a place which a person occupies, but when that person is not there, the ground is still in place. It is as if it has a life of its own which is shaped by the person who is involved.

Before they can continue, they need to reckon with what has happened in that position, and they need someone to fill the vacant position left in the corporate body. They could not repent for Judas or make right what he did, but in a sense the corporate body had to make right what had gone wrong. It was not an individual sin only, it was a corporate sin. Individually we disobey God, but as a corporate church we can also deeply grieve the Holy Spirit. Before God could give the disciples the Promise of the Father, they needed to tie up the loose ends.

Is our church's leadership ready to lead in this area? People have hurt other people; they have made decisions which affected others in a negative way; they have carried out their selfish desires within the body. So many churches with past problems say, "We are in a time of healing." It is my fear, however, that healing is not taking place at all, because these churches have not recognized their corporate sin. It is far more likely they are only allowing time to pass so they can forget what happened in their midst. We have had people leave our fellowship, but the problem is only out of sight, not reconciled. It does not heal because we have not tied up the loose ends.

In my personal life, Christ takes me back to those broken relationships, those unforgiven things. He forces me to return to the hurts I have buried. Is it any different with the corporate church? Can a church body know the power of the Spirit while broken relationships have not been mended? Does a church need to repent of wrong attitudes and wrong decisions? It is easy to excuse ourselves by saying, "I was not here when all those things took place." But we are not speaking of repenting for the individuals who were involved, but for the office or position from which it came. It is a loose end which we must tie up!

Completion
Acts 1:12-14

These verses present to us a second loose end, which we need to tie tightly. ***Then they returned to Jerusalem...**** (Acts 1:12). The disciples have come from the Mount of Olives which was a Sabbath Day's journey from Jerusalem. This would be the distance a person was allowed to travel on the Sabbath Day. The Old Testament tabernacle was always in the middle of the encampment, and the furthest tent from the tabernacle was about one half to three quarters of a mile away. That is how the Jews determined the Sabbath Day's journey. The disciples entered the upper room (Acts 1:13), which probably was the same one used for the last supper with Jesus. This became their base of operation as they ***were continually in the temple praising and blessing God,*** (Luke 24:53). They spent a period of ten days in this location as they followed Jesus' instructions to "tie up the loose ends."

These eleven disciples were from Galilee, which was eighty to one hundred miles away. They were fishermen, not city dwellers. Jerusalem was not their kind of environment. They did not feel comfortable here in these surroundings. Jerusalem was the center of their disappointment. They had accomplished great ministry until they came to Jerusalem. It was here Jesus was crucified, and the threat of the same thing happening to them was present. The most natural thing in the world was to leave Jerusalem and go back to familiar territory. They had no reason to stay in Jerusalem. Why were they here?

This was the instruction of the resurrected Christ. ***And being assembled together with them, He commanded them not to depart from Jerusalem, but to wait for the Promise of the Father, "which," He said, "you have heard from Me;"*** (Acts 1:4). They were responding to Jesus by remaining in Jerusalem. They would not find the Promise of the Father by running away. In the middle of the threat, discomfort and unrest, they would experience all God had for them. So they obeyed the prompting of Jesus and stayed in Jerusalem. If they left, they would not experience the Day of Pentecost.

Are you feeling the prompting of the resurrected Christ within you? Will you respond? The loose end must be tied down if we are to experience all God wants to do in our lives. We can never advance beyond the most recent instruction of Christ in our lives. You cannot pick and choose which directions of the Holy Spirit you will follow. He does not give you a variety of guidelines and you can respond to the ones you especially like. God has a significant plan; every Holy Spirit prompting is of extreme importance. There is no way to go beyond the latest prompting of the Holy Spirit.

They did not come into Jerusalem, or pass through Jerusalem on their way. It was not a token response to the prompting of Jesus. ***These all continued with one accord in prayer and supplication,*** (Acts 1:14). The disciples have come to Jerusalem to remain until they experience the Promise of the Father. Nothing else will be sufficient. They have no deadline. They operate according to His time table. It is the same for us. We must respond with our whole hearts, which prepares us to experience the Promise of the Father. We must face our situation and tie up the loose ends.

Concentration
Acts 1:6-11

Luke begins this section with the word, **Therefore,** (Acts 1:6). This signals us that what he is going to say now is based upon what he told us in the preceding section. The disciples have been with Jesus. He has commanded them to wait in Jerusalem for the Promise of the Father. He spoke to them about the Promise of the Father previously. He described it as *you shall be baptized with the Holy Spirit not many days from now,* (Acts 1:5).

The disciples were stimulated by the idea of the Promise of the Father. They asked Jesus, *"Lord, will You at this time restore the kingdom to Israel?"* (Acts 1:6). They again misunderstood the focus and establishment of the Kingdom of God. After His resurrection, and during the forty days Jesus spent with them, He spoke *of the things pertaining to the kingdom of God,* (Acts 1:3). They had the right information, but they were concentrating on the wrong thing.

They continued to think on an earthly kingdom in which they would be rulers. It was their last flickering desire for political power. They were still focused on overthrowing Rome and establishing their own rule. This focus would fade from their thinking as they became aware of a new concentration. Soon they would receive power and be anointed by the Holy Spirit to become the expression of who Jesus is to the world. They would not just simply tell others about Jesus, or bear the news of His story, but they would actually be witnesses to His life by being that life in their world.

This was the reason Israel had been called by God in the first place.

"You are My witnesses," says the Lord,
And My servant whom I have chosen,

Part Three: Preceding the Ascension

> *That you may know and believe in Me,*
> *And understand that I am He.*
> *Before Me there was no God formed,*
> *Nor shall there be after Me, (Isaiah 43:10).*

But there is tragedy in the story because Israel failed to be this witness. Their obedience to the law was not a base by which this witness could come. Throughout the history of Israel, the people had responded exactly as the disciples were now responding. They concentrated on the wrong thing. They were always seeking selfish political power.

But the dream of God for a witness never faltered. Paul renewed this call upon the people of God by quoting Isaiah 49:6. He said,

> *"For so the Lord has commanded us:*
> *'I have set you as a light to the Gentiles,*
> *That you should be for salvation to the ends of the earth,'"*
> *(Acts 13:47).*

Now the disciples see the new vision in beginning form. God is calling upon them to be witnesses. **"But you shall receive power when the Holy Spirit has come upon you; and you shall be witnesses to Me in Jerusalem, and in all Judea and Samaria, and to the end of the earth,"** (Acts 1:8). They would become the life of Jesus displayed in their world. This was the new focus. But they had to be open to this new focus before the **Promise of the Father** could be theirs. It was a loose end.

Nothing blocks the flow of the Spirit of God through us like our lack of focus. Oh, it is not that we are not focused, but we are focused on the wrong thing. We cannot know the power of God among us when we are distracted. How can He come when the space is occupied with so many other things? Jesus commanded them to wait as a part of the process. They were not to do anything. They were not to form any new programs or put any new systems into place. They were to focus on Jesus and wait for what He wanted to do next.

The ***Promise of the Father*** is ours. None of us dispute the availability of the power of God for us. The consistent question is how can we get this power for our activity? Where is the power and how can we tap into it? Could it be it has everything to do with tying up the loose ends? We need a corporate repentance within the church body. The wrongs we have done need to be set straight. We need to concentrate on Jesus alone, instead of what has occupied our space. The power of God is available to us! Will we experience it?

Acts 1:6-11

A KINGDOM VIEW

The Kingdom of God was the central focus of Jesus' ministry from the very beginning. It was the watchword of all His preaching and teaching. The Kingdom of God was a comprehensive statement for the content of His messages. Matthew said of His beginning ministry, *And Jesus went about all Galilee, teaching in their synagogues, preaching the gospel of the kingdom, and healing all kinds of sickness and all kinds of disease among the people,* (Matthew 4:23). This theme seemed to be what attracted the disciples to Jesus. *Now it came to pass, afterward, that He went through every city and village, preaching and bringing the glad tidings of the kingdom of God. And the twelve were with Him,* (Luke 8:1).

Jesus soon found it necessary to expand His ministry. The disciples were ready to begin ministry as well, and the need was great. The purpose of their mission was simple. *He sent them to preach the kingdom of God and to heal the sick,* (Luke 9:2). When Jesus began telling parables in His preaching, the disciples were concerned and asked, *"Why do You speak to them in parables?" He answered and said to them, "Because it has been given to you to know the mysteries of the kingdom of heaven, but to them it has not been given,"* (Matthew 13:10-11). Jesus repeatedly introduced His parables with the words, *"The Kingdom of heaven is like … ."* (Matthew 13:24, 31, 33, 44, 45, 47).

The Kingdom of God was well known in Israel. When Jesus

introduced it to His world, it was not the first time it had been mentioned. Luke presents *a man in Jerusalem whose name was Simeon,* (Luke 2:25). Simeon had been looking and longing for the Kingdom of God. Anna joined him in this desire. When she learned of the birth of the Christ child, she went about telling all those of her group who had dreamed of His coming that He was here, (Luke 2:38). Luke also tells us of Nicodemus and Joseph of Arimathea, two men who were *also waiting for the kingdom of God,* (Luke 23:51).

The disciples were attracted to Jesus, because they believed He was the One who could fulfill their dreams concerning the Kingdom of God. Jesus spoke the Kingdom language, which excited them. He did the works of the Kingdom, which indicated to them He had the ability to bring about the Kingdom they desired. Everything was in place for the Kingdom to be established. But three years of ministry went by, and their dream was not fulfilled. What was taking Jesus so long? There seemed to be no reason for the delay.

In the meantime, the disciples worked to establish the Kingdom according to their own standards. Within their group they formed a political structure which would carry over into Jesus' Kingdom of God. *At that time the disciples came to Jesus, saying, "Who then is greatest in the kingdom of heaven?"* (Matthew 18:1). They worked from every angle and used every means possible to carry out their idea of the Kingdom. *Then the mother of Zebedee's sons came to Him with her sons, kneeling down and asking something from Him. And He said to her, "What do you wish?" She said to Him, "Grant that these two sons of mine may sit, one on Your right hand and the other on your left, in Your kingdom,"* (Matthew 20:20-21).

There was a huge difference between Jesus' concept of the Kingdom and the disciples' concept. This should have been obvious to the disciples, but it was not. It was not that the disciples did not believe in the Kingdom of God, but their focus

Part Three: Preceding the Ascension

was different. Their emphasis was upon "the kingdom," while Jesus emphasized "of God." The disciples envisioned rulerships and thrones. They limited their vision to this earth and the kind of rulership they had studied from history. They remembered the stories of David and Solomon, when Israel was in her glory. God gave victory after victory, and the borders of Israel were expanded. The descriptions of the courts of Solomon with all of its wealth, prosperity and glory was strong in their minds.

It was not hard for the disciples to picture themselves at the side of Jesus in this same kind of wealth and glory. Had not Jesus promised them this when he said, *"Assuredly I say to you, that in the regeneration, when the Son of Man sits on the throne of His glory, you who have followed Me will also sit on twelve thrones, judging the twelve tribes of Israel,"* (Matthew 19:28). And the disciples were not the only ones who had these kinds of visions. Jesus had just provided a great banquet for five thousand men, besides women and children. He had been performing many miracles among them, and this was like the ultimate climax in the minds of the multitude. The crowd rose to their feet and attempted to *take Him by force to make Him king,* (John 6:15). When Jesus had this kind of power, why should he not rule the world? Who could stop Him? It was not hard for the disciples to see Jerusalem as the world government, and Jesus as the Jewish King. Israel would have worldwide dominion, and they would be right by Jesus' side in the court of the Kingdom.

The disciples knew that this could never be with Rome in the way. If Israel was to rule, Rome would have to be expelled. How was Jesus going to overtake the Roman Empire? Would He conquer them with magic? Would He raise up an army and march in war? Perhaps the heavens would part in a single moment and the Kingdom of God would descend, settling everything (Luke 19:11). The disciples were not concerned as to how Jesus would do it, but their question was when would He bring it to pass.

The disciples had no difficulty in seeing Jesus in this role. That is what attracted them to Him. They believed in His message of the Kingdom of God. They knew He was the One to take the throne of David. He was the Messiah King. But then He ended up dead. The crucifixion was such a disappointment. How could it have happened? In His Gospel account, Luke writes of the Emmaus road. Two of the disciples were traveling along the road when a stranger drew near. In their minds, this stranger knew nothing of the events which had shaken their lives. They needed to tell someone their problem, so He became the listener to their woes. In the course of their conversation, they said, **"But we were hoping that it was He who was going to redeem Israel,"** (Luke 24:21). They shook their heads in sadness.

Then came the resurrection! They must have been startled by the realization their dearest friend was alive! When Jesus was resurrected, a new theology of the Kingdom developed in the minds and hearts of the disciples. God had restored their dream! What they thought was over, was now even more within their reach. Surely God would now establish His Kingdom and put Israel (meaning them) in charge.

In spite of all their moments of doubt, and three years of impatience on their part, it was all paying off now. Rulership was more of a possibility than ever before. God raised Jesus from the dead. The worst thing Rome could do to Him had been done, and He survived it all! Certainly all things would come under His control now. They spend forty days with Jesus discussing these very things (Acts 1:3). Jesus gave them new enlightenment of what He had spoken to them about prior to the crucifixion, only now they saw it with the eyes of the resurrection.

The disciples had no doubts about Jesus' resurrection. They were absolutely convinced He would establish the Kingdom of God. The issue for them was not "if," but "when." **Therefore, when they had come together, they asked Him, saying, "Lord, will You at this time restore the kingdom to Israel?"** (Acts 1:6).

Indeed, they had missed it again. Their focus was wrong, but it seemed they were coming closer. Jesus needed only to give them a mild correction, asking them to wait patiently for the Promise of the Father. Jesus was going to bring them to His focus. ***And He said to them, "It is not for you to know times or seasons which the Father has put in His own authority. But you shall receive power when the Holy Spirit has come upon you; and you shall be witnesses to Me in Jerusalem, and in all Judea and Samaria, and to the end of the earth,"*** (Acts 1:7-8).

In Luke's record of the account, this is the final statement of Jesus prior to His ascension. It is a summary statement; it shows His focus. He takes the heart of the kingdom and places it into an unforgettable slogan. The statement is powerful. All of our commentaries say this verse (verse eight) is the outline of the entire Book of Acts. This is the single ingredient in the mission of the Kingdom of God. It is the fiber which God weaves into the fabric of the structure of the Kingdom.

Present Kingdom

It is interesting to note the disciples were not the only ones who were concerned about the time the Kingdom of God would arrive. The Pharisees also engaged Jesus in a conversation, and asked **when the kingdom of God would come,** (Luke 17:20). Jesus knew what the Pharisees were thinking. His answer corrected them. He said, **"*The kingdom of God does not come with observation*";** (Luke 17:20). The word, **observation,** is an astronomical term. They were looking for some great upheaval and manifestation in the physical heavens that would constitute the Kingdom of God. Their questions concerned what they thought would be a highly visible event. But Jesus continued with these words, *"nor will they say, 'See here!' or 'See there!' For indeed, the kingdom of God is within you,"* (Luke 17:21).

The verb is present tense. The Kingdom of God is in their midst, at this very moment, and it is an internal reality.

Jesus knew the Kingdom of God had come. The crowds were impressed with the miracle involving demons. The possessed man was blind and mute. As the multitude began to raise the issue of Jesus being the Messiah, the Pharisees took opposition to that view. They said Jesus was doing this miracle by the power of **Beelzebub, the ruler of the demons,** (Matthew 12:24). When instructing the leaders of Israel, Jesus said, ***"But if I cast out demons by the Spirit of God, surely the kingdom of God has come upon you,"*** (Matthew 12:28). We can only conclude from this statement that God was presenting His Kingdom to the leaders of Israel at that very moment.

That is the very context of the *Promise of the Father* in the Book of Acts. While the verb tense of verse eight is future, and Jesus is proposing a great happening on the Day of Pentecost, it is only a continuation of what has already taken place in the life of Christ, as seen in *the former account.* The Kingdom of God as was present in Jesus was now going to continue on, and into, the disciples. Jesus saw the Kingdom as a present Kingdom.

Progressive Kingdom

The Kingdom of God was present tense in the life of Christ. In His view, the Kingdom of God had already begun and was progressing during His earthly ministry. Every miracle was an intrusion into the kingdom of Satan, and a conquering step of the Kingdom of God. Jesus taught this forcibly through the parables. *And He said, "The kingdom of God is as if a man should scatter seed on the ground, and should sleep by night and rise by day, and the seed should sprout and grow, he himself does not know how. For the earth yields crops by itself: first the blade, then the head, after that the full grain in the head. But when the grain ripens, immediately he puts in the sickle, because the harvest has come,"* (Mark 4:26-29).

Jesus used this picture repeatedly in the Parables of the Kingdom (Matthew 13:3ff, 13:24ff, 13:31ff). God had planted His Kingdom, and it was growing in full stature. It was like leaven (Matthew 13:33), hidden *in three measures of meal till it was all leavened.* The Kingdom is on the move and growing. What was about to happen in the lives of the disciples would be a vital step in that growth process.

Pluralistic Kingdom

The Kingdom of God was going to grow, permeate and dominate the entire world. But it was pluralistic, not nationalistic. I consulted the dictionary to make sure I was using the word, pluralistic, properly. It means, "a condition of society in which numerous distinct ethnic, religious, and cultural groups coexist within one nation."

The disciples, and all of Israel, considered the Kingdom of God as a nationalistic Kingdom. The manner in which the disciples ask their question indicates this. **They asked Him, saying, "Lord, will You at this time restore the Kingdom of Israel?"** (Acts 1:6). As all good Jews, they expect a national kingdom to be established on earth. **Restore** suggests a return to the national independence enjoyed under former kings. They reflected back on the days of David and Solomon. Central to the Old Testament faith, it was their conviction that God would, in the end time, fully restore His people to their inheritance in the land. Then they would live securely without foreign domination (Jeremiah 16:15; 23:8; 50:19; Hosea 11:11; Joel 3:17).

But the Kingdom of God would not belong to the Jewish nation. It would be pluralistic and include every ethnic and cultural group. Jesus impacted the world forever when He made this statement in the Parable of the Great Judgment. He said, ***"When the Son of Man comes in His glory, and all the holy angels with Him, then He will sit on the throne of His glory. All the nations will be gathered before Him ... ."*** (Matthew 25:31-32). The Kingdom of God is for whosoever will.

Political Kingdom

I have always had very negative feeling about politics. Politicians manipulate people in order to get position and power. But the dictionary states the primary meaning of the word, politics, is "of, relating to, or dealing with the structure or affairs of government." This applies to the Kingdom of God. There is a definite structure to the Kingdom of God. The politics of the Kingdom of God is spiritual in nature. The focus of this spiritual nature is the cross. Instead of seeking power, those in the Kingdom of God seek service. Position is not the goal of Kingdom people. Their goal is redemption.

This is precisely the answer Jesus gives the disciples when they ask Him "when" (Acts 1:6). He addresses the issue of the politics of the Kingdom. He speaks to the disciples about their focus. Their emphasis is on the establishment of an earthly political structure, a position for each of them. Jesus is interested in the power of the Holy Spirit, displaying the cross style life through them, which would reveal Jesus to the entire world.

The desire of Jesus is expressed in the word, ***witnesses*** (Acts 1:8). The root word for witness has to do with "to bear in mind," or "to be concerned." This is all about focus. The Greek word translated "witness" is our English word for "martyr." In the New Testament, the word is often used without any reference to giving up your life for your testimony. But in the days of the early church, the word was associated with dying, or at least the risking of your life. It meant more than simply bearing witness to facts. It pertained to an indwelling Christ who would change a world. Christ was being duplicated in His disciples until what He had done in one isolated setting would be done all over the world. Being a Christian is more than not listening to immoral jokes. It is more than just being able to quote the four spiritual laws with the correct Biblical passages. Being a Christian is about losing your life to the life of Christ. It is about being crucified, and allowing Christ to manifest His life within and through us. It is the heart and focus of the Kingdom of God.

Just maybe the problem the disciples had is our own personal problem as well. We see the Kingdom in terms of buildings, budgets and size. The measure of success is in how big is our church facility and how many people sit in our pews. Have we transformed the Kingdom of God into a political structure of an established earthly power? Has the important thing in our life become position, image and personal power? Is your energy spent in maintaining an organization, or it is the display of the life of Christ through your person? Perhaps we need the instructions of Jesus again! We need to experience the spiritual infilling of the Spirit of Jesus, then the display of the life of Christ will be seen through us.

Acts 1:7-8

TO BE WITNESSES

The disciples come to Jesus with this question. *"Lord, will You at this time restore the kingdom to Israel?"* (Acts 1:6). They insist upon an answer. The first part of the verse is, *Therefore, when they had come together, they asked Him, saying,* (Acts 1:6). The verb *asked* is in the imperfect tense, which denotes the disciples repeatedly asking the question and urging Jesus to give them the answer.

And He said to them, "It is not for you to know times or seasons which the Father has put in His own authority," (Acts 1:7). In a literal sense, Jesus is saying, "It is none of your business!" The question they ask is focused on the wrong subject. Their emphasis is on the time when this will happen, and it is to be of no concern to them. As I view my prayer life, I easily see this in the emphasis of my prayers. I may not be as specific as the disciples were, but I see it in the tone and desire of my prayers. This same tone permeates my relationship with Jesus. When will He heal my body? When will He solve my financial problems? When will He save my loved ones? When will He give me the new job? When will He come back the second time?

The disciples are somewhat severe in their question. *"Lord, will You at this time…"* Their question is not only "when," but they insist on it being "now." This is the constant emphasis in the lives of the disciples. They argued about who would be first in the Kingdom of God. They wanted Jesus to decide immediately,

(Matthew 18:1; 20:21). On the Mount of Transfiguration, Peter wanted to build three tabernacles and establish immediately (now) what he thought was the Kingdom of God, (Matthew 17:4). Here they come again, insisting on the time frame of now.

This is characteristic of our present generation. We have microwave ovens for instant food preparation, fast food restaurants for instant meals, and wedding chapels for instant marriages. We have instant experiences through the television, buy lottery tickets hoping for instant wealth, and we even have quick lubes for instant car care. We want the same in our spiritual experience with Christ. We do not want the worship service to go more than one hour. Keep the truth to a minimum. We do not want a long, drawn out investigation of the Word of God. Just tell us a story, please. Our devotional books are designed for a quick look at the Word of God, so it does not take much time. We want to be as spiritual as Jesus, but make it quick!

This is a demonic pattern. Do you remember the wilderness temptation of Jesus in Matthew 4:1-11? It begins in this manner. ***And when He had fasted forty days and forty nights, afterward He was hungry,*** (Matthew 4:2). This period of time is the Divine pattern. He was not in a hurry. This was not one or two hours spent at the church in prayer. Jesus was not focused on "now," but He was seeking the fellowship of the Father. The Devil's pattern is evident in his temptation of Jesus. Each temptation was focused on the immediate. If Jesus is hungry, He should simply ***command that these stones become bread,*** (Matthew 4:3). Do not wait, simply get it now. The second temptation was on the pinnacle of the temple. The Devil suggests that Jesus throw Himself down and let the angels save Him. This would prove He was the Son of God. He did not need to spend three years of ministry going through a cross to bring this to pass. One simple leap from the pinnacle would be adequate. Why wait? The third temptation was a view of all of the Kingdoms of earth, and an offer that they could all be His with a simple moment of Devil worship. The purpose for which He had come to earth could be fulfilled with a quick moment right now, rather than the pattern of the cross. This is the way the Devil thinks.

Jesus minces no words in telling the disciples their focus is wrong. The ***times or seasons*** are none of their business. These two words do not refer to the same thing. However, together they do cover the whole realm of what we would call prophecy. The Greek word translated ***times*** means periods of the same length. This is in reference to the great epochs of prophecies and the intervals between them. The Greek word translated ***seasons*** means the definite time for the occurrence of a predicted prophetic event. It is none of our business, and we should not be focused on the moment, particular time, or even upon the general time period.

Jesus is specific in telling the disciples this should not be their focus. He uses the words, **His own authority.** In the English, this is a simple possessive pronoun. But the words, **His own**, is one word in the Greek language. It is much stronger than a possessive pronoun. It is an adjective, which means "private" or "personal." This is something which really belongs to God. This information is completely out of your realm, and it will not be discovered by you regardless of how diligently you investigate it.

Jesus has established that some things are only in the realm of God's responsibility. What the disciples want to know is none of their business. He begins His next statement to them with the conjunction ***But***, (Acts 1:8). He wants to contrast what is none of their business with something that really pertains to them. He has completed a picture on one side, and now He portrays another picture on the other side. On one side is what the disciples cannot know, ***but*** the other side reveals what they can know. He says it very plainly. ***"But you shall receive power when the Holy Spirit has come upon you; and you shall be witnesses to Me in Jerusalem, and in all Judea and Samaria, and to the end of the earth,"*** (Acts 1:8).

I must admit to you I have struggled with this verse. It is easy to view the verse in the normal surface manner, and use its statement to introduce a class on witnessing. But this verse, seen in its context, introduces a depth which we must not miss. I am not sure I can communicate it, or even grasp it. Perhaps this verse needs to wear me as its garment for a few years.

Not One Aspect, But the Whole

It is very important that we see the verse as a whole. This is not one part of Christianity to be emphasized or highlighted. The entirety of this concept is Christianity. This is a summary of the throbbing heart and soul of the Gospel. Everything in this verse points to the concept of *you shall be witnesses.* The verse opens with a declaration of the power which will bring this to pass. Luke closes the verse telling us where this will be accomplished. So the entire verse brings us back to the central focus of *you shall be witnesses.*

We must not be fooled into thinking we are to *be witnesses* during special seasons of the Christian calendar. We are to highlight basic doctrinal truths and spiritual disciplines, such as tithing, Bible reading, prayer and witnessing. This might be true if you are presenting a watered down version of witnessing, but it is not Jesus' reference point in this verse.

Luke has a special usage for *witnesses,* which gives it unique importance. One must have been present with Jesus when certain things took place. A witness can tell what he knows because he was there. The gospel is a revelation in our history, and we know definite facts about it. But the witness must be to facts which have become truth within the witness. Anyone can memorize these academic facts. Anyone can learn the four spiritual laws and quote the specific Scriptures. But this does not constitute the witness Luke describes.

Luke describes these facts becoming the experience of the believer until they become truth within him. There are facts about Jesus which everyone can know, but when those facts become truth, we have embraced Jesus, for He is the Truth. Jesus tells us the great facts of the gospel, but when, by faith, we take hold of the facts, it becomes Him embracing us. Jesus becomes the focus. In Luke's concept, it is impossible to experience the facts without being gripped with the person of Christ, and to be focused on His person is to be a witness.

Luke forcibly plants this in the verse. He reminds us this will take place because the Holy Spirit (the Spirit of Jesus) will come upon us. The Holy Spirit will be the power for the witnessing. The actual idea is that of enabling or resourcing. The very Spirit of Jesus will enable the disciples to be the demonstration of the life of Jesus in their world.

This should not surprise us. We understand the theme of Acts (volume two) and the Gospel according to Luke (volume one) to be a Divine Activity Thing. As the Holy Spirit worked in and through Jesus to produce the demonstration of the Father, so the Spirit of Jesus will work through us to demonstrate the life of Jesus to our world. We are not eye witnesses to His resurrection, or crucifixion, but we are the flesh in which His person has come to demonstrate all He is! This is the witness. It is the demonstration of His life.

Not Doing, But Being

The verse says, *"But you shall receive...; and you shall be..."* (Acts 1:8). Could anyone who understands the Book of Acts dispute this? Repeatedly, when the power of witnessing took place, the person was ***filled with the Holy Spirit,*** (Acts 4:8). Everyone knows this book is not really entitled "The Acts of the Apostles," but it is "The Acts of the Holy Spirit." Were the disciples involved? Did they do something? Certainly they participated, but they were being resourced. This is not about the disciples and their talents or abilities, but it is about Jesus and His greatness. He demonstrated Himself through the individuals who became filled with Him.

There is a vast difference between doing a witness and being a witness. The one is about my actions, and the other is about how I am being acted upon. One is about what I proclaim, while the other is about what is being declared through me. One is about the facts I speak, and the other is about the truth being seen through my life. One can be explained in terms of training, ability, personality, or talent, while the other is all about Jesus being seen in me. One is speaking about Jesus, and the other is about Jesus being seen because He is living through me. One is about effort, and the other is about relaxing and surrendering. One is about trying and duty, while the other is His love, passion and life flowing through me.

In seventy years, the early disciples won their entire world to Christ. They did not do it by memorized phrases or communication skills. They did not do it by educational achievements, (Acts 4:13). It was accomplished by an indwelt Life, which became their living. They were being acted upon, and they responded to that action. It was about being, not about doing!

Henry Stanley, a reporter, went to spend time in Central Africa with the great missionary, David Livingston. He came back with this report. "If I had been with him any longer, I would have been compelled to be a Christian, and he never spoke to me about it at all."

But we have this understanding from the very theme of these two great volumes, The Book of Acts and the Gospel According to Luke. It is all about the Divine Activity Thing. It is about the second member of the Trinity giving up all He had as God to become a man surrendered to God. God, through this man, Jesus, demonstrated who He was and is. It was not about what Jesus did, for He consistently said that He could do nothing. His life was a response to the action of the Father, through the Holy Spirit. This same dynamic took place in the lives of the disciples. They were filled with the Spirit of Jesus, who was the source of their living. They were witnesses. They were a complete demonstration of Jesus to their world.

Not Partial, But Complete

Jesus is very specific in this verse. He says, "... *in Jerusalem, and in all Judea and Samaria, and to the end of the earth,*" (Acts 1:8). If Jesus had only pointed *to the end of the earth,* the disciples would have focused on the remote regions, and lost sight of their neighbors. If He had said only *in Jerusalem*, they would have stayed in their Jewish organizational structure and settled to be a sect. But it was clearly a call to demonstrate the life of Jesus to the entire world. It included the religious organization which had forty days earlier crucified Jesus. It reached out and engulfed the Samaritans, which certainly removed any racial barriers to the demonstration. This was to be a complete demonstration of the life of Jesus all the time, to everyone.

There were to be no limits to the demonstration of the life of Christ through the disciples. It was definitely fulfilled in the Book of Acts. The disciples demonstrated the life and power of Christ to the crippled beggar (Acts 3:6), and to the rulers, elders, and scribes (Acts 4:5). It took place through Philip for a man from Ethiopia (Acts 8:27), and it took place in those who persecuted the disciples of the Lord (Acts 22:20). There seemed to be no limits on the demonstration of Jesus through the lives of the disciples.

But when you understand the theme of this great book (volumes one and two), this is no surprise. The Divine Activity

Part Three: Preceding the Ascension

Thing is to flow through lives to our world. When do I have the right to turn it off? When do the circumstances become such that I have an excuse for not showing Him? When does the other person say the words or do the thing which exempts me from giving them Christ? When does the other person have the color of skin, or economic status, which is too big a barrier to allow Christ to be seen in me? If you can turn the demonstration on or off, then you have ample evidence to know it is not His demonstration, but your own! Certainly He is not in control.

    I am brought again to my knees in absolute submission to Him. Oh, for my life to be a demonstration of His person, because He has come to live through me. Oh, for this demonstration to be so consistent, it will cover my entire world at all times. This is my prayer.

Acts 1:8

THE UNASKED QUESTION

The disciples are excited about the Kingdom of God being restored to Israel. They come to Jesus, asking Him when this will take place. At the time of Jesus' crucifixion, they were convinced the Kingdom of God would never be restored to Israel. All their hope was gone. But now, Jesus is resurrected from the dead, and He spends forty days with them, *speaking of the things pertaining to the kingdom of God,* (Acts 1:3). They are pressing Him for an answer to their question. They do not ask it once or twice, but repeatedly. *"Lord, will You at this time restore the kingdom to Israel?"* (Acts 1:6).

We have looked at Jesus' answer to the disciples (Acts 1:7-8), but the depth of that answer requires more investigation. This verse (Acts 1:8) is very important to the entire Book of Acts. It is the outline for all Luke is going to use in the following pages. This verse is a summary of the message. It is the heart of the *Promise of the Father,* (Acts 1:4).

The Divine Activity Thing is presented by Luke as the proposition of all he wants to highlight. It is the thrust of the Gospel of Luke (volume one) and the Book of Acts (volume two). It is the extreme focus in this passage. Luke magnifies it in such a way as to leave no room for adjustment or compromise. There is no way anyone can reduce the Gospel to legalism or doing.

Luke's idea is to allow us to see the gigantic shift the disciples make from their physical view of the Spirit of Jesus to the spiritual view. They move from doing to being! Self-initiated activity ceases and God-initiation flows. They stop their straining, struggling and trying, and they begin to relax, lean and depend. Luke's emphasis is upon the disciples' effortless reliance upon the Spirit of Jesus. The focus is upon what the Spirit of Jesus doing in them. The action takes place **in Jerusalem, and in all Judea and Samaria, and to the end of the earth,** (Acts 1:8). It is directed and enabled by the Spirit of Jesus. These disciples are to say nothing. When the Spirit of Jesus comes, something takes place which is beyond man's ability to speak. Jesus enables them to speak in adequate ways, which is symbolized by the fact they **began to speak with other tongues, as the Spirit gave them utterance,** (Acts 2:4). They do not strive to be anything. It is impossible for them to shape themselves into what they should be. They no longer have the need to seek position or glory for accomplishment. The Spirit of Jesus enables them to **be witnesses,** (Acts 1:8). Jesus does not call upon the disciples to do anything. They do not have to get organized. Church structures are not their issue. Numbers, buildings and budgets are of no consequence to them. All accomplishments are the result of the Spirit of Jesus. He does the miracles, multiplies the church, and establishes the witness (Acts 2:47).

We can clearly see this in Luke's opening conjunction. Jesus is speaking to the disciples. He is responding to their question. **"But..."** (Acts 1:8) is a conjunction of distinction, which marks a contrast. We are to see verse seven contrasted with verse eight. Jesus is contrasting what is not within the knowledge of the disciples with what they will know and experience now. He says, **"It is not for you to know..."** (Acts 1:7). The verb, **know,** is in the active voice which means the subject is responsible for the action of the verb. The subject is relating to the disciples who are responsible for the action of knowing. But notice the word, **not,** places this fact in the negative. The disciples are not going to be responsible for knowing. The **times or seasons which the**

Father has put in His own authority are not under their control.

Now Jesus gives them the realm of their focus (Acts 1:8). Here is what they will experience! It will be accomplished through the Spirit of Jesus. What they have been, and what they will be, will be altered by the Spirit of Jesus. What they have said, and what they will say, will now be changed by the Spirit of Jesus. What they have done, and what they will do, will now be enabled by the Spirit of Jesus. It is a new day! But you must catch the key phrase in the verse. Jesus says, ***"You shall receive…"*** Then He goes on to say, ***"You shall be…"*** But what is most important are the words sandwiched between these truths. Jesus says, ***"… when the Holy Spirit has come upon you";*** (Acts 1:8). Everything that takes place will be because of the Spirit of Jesus.

"But you shall receive power…" is the opening statement of Jesus. This is a powerful statement of promise given by Jesus. ***You shall receive*** is one word in the original Greek language of the New Testament. It is a verb which is in the future indicative. This means Jesus is speaking of something which will take place, and it is a simple statement of fact. There can be no argument or debate over the issue. He makes no attempt to explain or convince them. It is simply the truth! It is a sure thing!

The same is true of the ***Promise of the Father,*** (Acts 1:4). The statement, ***you shall receive power*** is an extension of this ***promise.*** The word ***promise*** has the idea of freely given. The Father did not make the promise under obligation. It flowed directly from His heart, which is filled with grace. This promise is God-initiated. He does not fulfill this promise because of peer pressure, duty, or guilt. He freely gave this promise, and He freely fulfills it. This promise is backed by the loving heart of God. It is a sure thing. ***You shall receive!***

The focus of what ***you shall receive*** is ***power.*** It is easy for us to misunderstand this focus because of our worldly framework. This world is twisted with self-centeredness, and that shapes our view of power. From the world view, power translates into position and personal gain or fulfillment. But Jesus speaks the opposite of the world's view. The Promise of the Father is that we will receive the Spirit of Jesus. Jesus says it clearly in the verse of this study (Acts 1:8), ***the Holy Spirit has come upon you.*** He equates the power with the Spirit of Jesus. In this Spirit there is no selfishness. This power is filled with servanthood in the style of the cross. The Spirit of Jesus will empower and enhance our lives, so all we might label as power is a reflection of the Spirit. He does not give power, but we derive power from His person. Thus, every demonstration of the power is a reflection of Him. How will this power be viewed? It will look like Jesus.

The actual Greek word for ***power*** is the basis for our English word dynamite. It is a measurable power, for it shows itself in physical activities. It is explosive in nature, and it often disrupts everything. As it is used in the Gospel accounts, it is most often translated ***mighty deeds.*** It is a great word to describe the movement of the Spirit of Jesus throughout the account of the Book of Acts.

The very essence of this word bespeaks the intimacy between the demonstration through the believer and the Spirit of Jesus. The Greek word has to do with the inherent power residing in a thing by virtue of its nature. This power is not from an instrument the Spirit of Jesus gives to me. It is not like a gun in my hand, which could give me the power to rob a bank. But the power which ***you shall receive*** will come from the nature which resides within you. The nature of the Spirit of Jesus will so interweave itself in your personhood, it will be who you are. It is not something you have, but rather He has you. Because of who you are in Him, you have this power, which demonstrates the Spirit of Jesus within you.

Paul expressed it in these words. ***But we have this treasure in earthen vessels, that the excellence of the power may be of God and not of us,*** (2 Corinthians 4:7). We cannot learn this in seminars, because it is not the power of knowledge. We do not develop this in training sessions, for it is not the result of skill. We do not practice improving on this, for it is not the increase of our ability. This is of God. The power resides within the Spirit of Jesus. He demonstrates Himself through us. It is as if the power and the Spirit of Jesus are the same. Just as water and wet are synonymous, so the Spirit of Jesus and power are synonymous. One bespeaks the other. To think of being filled with the nature of God and not live in His power would be absurd.

Now we come to the parallel statement, **you shall be witnesses to Me,** (Acts 1:8). As in the former phrase, the verb **shall be** is in the future indicative. It is a definite statement of fact. There is no need to defend it or argue the fact. This is simply the way it is. As certain as **you shall receive power,** so **you shall be witnesses to Me.**

The focus is not on doing, but it is upon being. The same basic Greek root word, which presents the **I AMS** of Jesus (John 6:48; 14:6), is used here in reference to us. It has to do with existence, not performance. It is nature, not activity. It is the fiber and substance of the person, not their accomplishments. The focus is on who we are, not on what we are doing! This is our own personal "I AM!"

What is it that "I AM?" **You shall be witnesses to Me,"** (Acts 1:8). The etymology of the word **witness** seems to find its beginning in the root word, which means "to bear in mind" or "to be concerned." The witness would then be one who remembers and can tell about something. From the perspective of Judaism (especially during the time of Christ), the meaning of witness was almost always surrounded by suffering. This became true as the word was used in Christianity. The Greek word translated into witness is the word "martyr."

In Luke's writing, witness must also be combined with the truth. He makes a distinction between fact and truth. To be a witness, one does not simply repeat the facts, but he must be gripped by the truth. It goes back to the apostles, and the

Part Three: Preceding the Ascension

fact they had to be eyewitnesses. As the early disciples came to replace Judas, they realized his replacement must be *of these men who have accompanied us all the time that the Lord Jesus went in and out among us, beginning from the baptism of John to that day when He was taken up from us, one of these must become a witness with us of His resurrection,* (Acts 1:21-22). To be a witness of the resurrection of Christ, the replacement had to have experienced more than just seeing the resurrected Jesus. He must have been gripped with the teaching, moved by the miracles, crushed by the crucifixion, and experienced the joy of knowing Christ is alive. This is more than facts. This is truth which has become passion. It involved who the person is!

The witness to which Jesus is calling us is not to be one who has attended the witnessing seminar and received a certificate. He is one who has experienced the deep awareness of his sin and been crushed by its consequences. He has become aware that the cross is the only way to deliverance, and not a piece of gold we wear on a chain. The witness must embrace a living Christ and become alive in Him. He cannot possibly keep from witnessing, because He is a witness.

This is the desire of my heart! This is what I want to receive and what I want to be. When will this finally take place in my life, allowing me to boldly declare, "I am a witness!"? Perhaps a better question would be, "How shall this happen to me?" Remember the special structure of the verse (Acts 1:8). Jesus begins with *you shall receive power,* and He ends with *you shall be witnesses to Me.* But in-between these two statements is sandwiched the resource to the reality. It is the answer to when and how!

Jesus says, *"… when the Holy Spirit has come upon you;"* (Acts 1:8). This is His explanation. The answer to "when" is at the moment the Spirit of Jesus resources you. This brings us back to a total focus on the person of Jesus Christ. The in-filling of His Spirit in me produces the linkage of facts with truth, which produces passion. It is the reality that He is the Truth.

This is the basic theme of Luke's writing, both in volume one and in volume two. The Divine Activity Thing is the source for all that takes place. The Spirit in Jesus, as demonstrated in the Gospel account, became the Spirit indwelling the disciples in the Book of Acts. Everything that takes place in and through their lives is a demonstration of the empowering and enhancing of this Divine Spirit.

Did you notice the emphasis ... *has come upon* ...? Jesus stresses the idea of **upon.** The preposition "upon" is included in the Greek verb, and then "upon" is repeated again at the end of the phrase. It is given twice. A literal translation would be, **"... when the Holy Spirit has come upon upon you."** The entire phrase is called a genitive absolute, which expresses time, cause, or condition. So this phrase, **"... when the Holy Spirit has come upon you;"** is the condition, or cause, of the preceding phrase, **"But you shall receive power ..."**

You will not have power, and you will never be a witness unless the Spirit of Jesus has come to produce this within you! There is nothing said here about personality types, talents, experiences or training. Everything is focused on the Spirit of Jesus. Would you not conclude that when the Holy Spirit fills you, you cannot help but be a witness? When the Holy Spirit does not fill you, it is impossible to be a witness. Would you not conclude when you are being a witness, the Holy Spirit is empowering you, and when you are not being a witness, you lack His empowering? It is impossible to be filled with Jesus and not be a witness, and it is impossible to be a witness without being filled with Jesus.

To fulfill the Biblical mandate, we must be stripped of all self-initiated living. No other source can be present. There must not be a mixing of resources, some of Jesus and some of me. He may use me, but I am not the source of the use. He is empowering and enhancing our lives, and ... **you shall be witnesses to Me in Jerusalem, and in all Judea and Samaria, and to the end of the earth,"** (Acts 1:8).

Acts 1:9-11

THE ASCENDED LORD

The subject of the ascension is extremely important. It is much weightier than I ever dreamed. It will take many studies to scratch the surface of its expanse. My fear at the outset is we will lose sight of the exposition of the Word of God. Our primary goal is to examine closely and in great detail, these verses from the pen of Luke (Acts 1:9-11). These words have application to our personal lives in very practical ways. But in order to get to the exposure of the Word, we must know the context from which Luke is writing. We must understand the spiritual realities which surround the ascension of Jesus. At first this may appear we are venturing afar from the main purpose of expositional Bible study, but it is all for the purpose of adequately understanding the text.

Do you understand what we mean when we talk about your framework? Your framework is created by the surroundings and people present in the area and time in which you live. We live in the twenty-first century, and our present framework is one of computers and the internet. Our framework is very different from that of the disciples. The call of the ascension was a call for the disciples to shift from their framework to a spiritual framework. When we know how different our framework is from theirs, we can understand how difficult it was for the disciples to shift from their framework. Then we can begin to relate to them in our own struggle with the framework of God.

The disciples lived in the framework of their Jewish culture

The Ascended Lord | **Acts 1:9-11**

with its many traditions. What the disciples had been taught through life shaped their concept of the coming Kingdom of God into a focus on the physical. They dreamed of a military Messiah, who would be the Deliverer from Roman domination. Jesus had the ability to accomplish the task, but He simply would not do it. The disciples had waited for three years, both patiently and impatiently. Then Jesus was crucified on a cross. This event ended their hopes and dreams for the future. Can you imagine their excitement when they discover the truth of the resurrection? If they had any hope before the crucifixion, they certainly have absolute confidence now. What could stop Jesus from fulfilling their dream? Rome could not touch Him since He had already experienced death!

Following His resurrection, Jesus spent forty days ***speaking of the things pertaining to the kingdom of God,*** (Acts 1:3). Luke says they pestered Him with the question of "when?" They repeatedly asked, **"Lord, will You at this time restore the Kingdom of Israel?"** (Acts 1:6). They visualized a physical Kingdom. They viewed it as a reestablishment of the great days of Solomon and all of his glory. It was a time when the surrounding nations were frightened of Israel and her power. In their mind's eye, the disciples could see Jesus sitting on the throne of David, and they would occupy the twelve thrones over the twelve tribes of Israel, just as Jesus had promised (Matthew 19:28). What a glorious day that would be!

When their enthusiasm is at its peak, and the disciples are absolutely sure Jesus is going to establish the Kingdom of God on earth, He ascends into heaven. They surely stood with their eyes and mouths wide open as they watched Him physically ascend from their sight (Acts 1:9). They could not believe what they were seeing. Just when everything was in place for their wildest dream to be fulfilled, He was leaving.

The ascension is a clear call to shift in framework. The disciples clearly did not have the concept of the Kingdom of God which Jesus had displayed from the beginning. They watched

Part Three: Preceding the Ascension

Him for three years, but they still did not grasp the reality. This Kingdom of God was not a doing away with the present world, only what this world had become. There is no elimination of the physical. Christ would never adhere to any movement which would propose the idea of flesh and bones being evil within themselves. Both the resurrection and the ascension events contain a strong reference to maintaining the physical. God raised Jesus physically from the dead. He appeared in a new physical body. He said to His disciples, **"Behold My hands and My feet, that it is I Myself. Handle Me and see, for a spirit does not have flesh and bones as you see I have,"** (Luke 24:39).

As Luke paints the picture of Jesus physically ascending into heaven, he does so with a special emphasis. He uses four different Greek words in this passage to describe how the disciples watched, saw, looked and gazed. He uses four different Greek words to describe how Jesus was taken up, received, went up, and ascended. He describes it in many different ways in an attempt to be sure we do not miss it. Jesus physically ascended from this physical earth.

Luke further emphasizes the physical aspect by relating the message of the angels to the disciples (Acts 1:11). The angels impact the disciples with the message that this same physical Jesus will return in the same physical form. The indication is He has maintained this physical appearance all the time He is gone. His physical condition is not a suit He wears and will discard after He disappears from their sight. It is not a costume He wears for our benefit. The physical is an essential part of who Jesus is. It reveals the truth that He has really joined with us. He has become one with us, and He will never be anything else.

Paul described it like this. **Behold, I tell you a mystery: We shall not all sleep, but we shall all be changed - in a moment, in the twinkling of an eye, at the last trumpet. For the trumpet will sound, and the dead will be raised incorruptible, and we shall be changed. For this corruptible has put on incorruption, and this mortal has put on immortality,** (1 Corinthians 15:51-54).

This also describes what will take place in our lives in the final hour of this world. The same change which took place in the flesh of Christ in the resurrection will also take place in us. The words of Paul are very specific. The word, *corruptible,* means to decay or perish. It is a description of what is happening to our flesh in this present world. The word, *mortal,* means to die. We are in the process of dying from the day we are born. But a change will take place in us. It will happen *in the twinkling of an eye, at the last trumpet.* We will be changed to the *incorruptible,* which is non-decaying and non-perishing. We will experience the *immortal,* which is eternal and never dying. It is still our flesh, but it has been changed from dying to non-dying, from temporal to eternal. Paul says we are going to *put on* this new change. The Greek word literally means "to sink into a garment." Our spirits will wear a new set of clothes, which are eternal.

There is an obvious shift we need to make in this new framework of the ascension, and it is to stop thinking in the temporal and gain an eternal perspective. Can you imagine the newness of this kind of perspective? This will bring a radical change to every aspect of living. It will be a radical shift from the now, or immediacy, to the long range, or the forever. This will change our stresses, our concerns and our anxieties. The things which seem to be so big at the moment will shrink in size when we see in the light of forever. It will change the way we respond to our circumstances and our surroundings!

However, we must understand that living forever is not the issue. It is the quality of life which we will have forever. People who go to heaven, and people who go to hell, are all going to live forever. The difference has to do with the quality of life. The quality of life we have forever is an enhancement of the quality of life we have now. Death is not a magic wand. The inward feelings you have now are the ones you will have forever. It is a scary thought! You must realize the quality of life is very bad for many people, and the number of those who take their

Part Three: Preceding the Ascension

lives annually is very high. Please understand that eternity is an extension of what you already have and are now. Can you imagine living forever in the state of the situation which caused you to take your own life?

The Kingdom of God established by Jesus is forever. The quality of life in the forever Kingdom is what He describes to His disciples during the forty days. It has to do with the ***Promise of the Father.*** The life of the Father is the eternal life of the Kingdom. It is the nature of God with its resource empowering and enhancing us forever. Everything the Father demonstrated through the life of Jesus, from His security to the peace beyond understanding, all describe the eternal life we can have in the Father. It is yours now. Let this be the quality of your life now and forever. Seek Him! Do not allow any temporary physical stuff keep you from experiencing the quality of the life of God.

The most important aspect of the eternal quality of life is relationship. If your idea of Christianity is ceremony, law, theology or doctrine, this scene of the ascension should clarify that forever. There is no discussion of such things taking place here. The entire focus is on relationship.

We see this clearly in the context of the ascension as seen in volume one (the Gospel according to Luke). The ascension is the culmination of the relationship between Jesus and the Father. This ascension is the ultimate embrace as the Father takes Jesus to Himself! The Father and Son come into a new aspect, level or expansion of relationship. Who can describe it, for who knows the details of this relationship?

We can see this clearly in the ascension itself. We will only touch on it at this time, because it really needs a complete and detailed analysis. As Luke is introducing the ascension, he writes, ***Now when He had spoken these things, while they watched, He was taken up, and a cloud received Him out of their sight,*** (Acts 1:9). We must pay close attention to the fact ***a cloud received Him.*** It is a most intriguing statement.

The Greek word translated, *received,* is only used five times in the New Testament. Twice it is translated, *suppose* (Luke 7:43; Acts 2:15). One time it is translated, *answering* (Luke 10:30). The remaining two times it is translated, *receive* (Acts 1:9, John 8). Each time it is translated it carries the picture of intimacy and close involvement. It is not the idea of receiving a payment for a debt, or a teacher receiving an assignment which needs to be graded. This Greek word carries the picture of intimacy in the act of receiving. When it is translated, *suppose*, it has the idea of taking up in one's mind.

It is very intimate to assume or accept into your mind what is being said. When it is translated, *answering*, you are taking it up in your speech. You are entering into a conversation and sharing ideas. When you are *receiving* it, it carries the idea of taking up in welcome. If you are receiving the idea of another, you are inviting them in and embracing them.

In the same manner, you can see this concept in the **cloud** (Acts 1:9). A vapor mist in the sky did not receive Jesus. That is impersonal. The very person of the Father descended in this same form in the Mount of Transfiguration (Luke 9:34). The Father's presence is depicted in the Old Testament in this manner repeatedly. He appears in a pillar of cloud by day and a pillar of fire by night (Exodus 14:19). God appeared on Mount Sinai in this same form (Exodus 24:15-16).

Can you visualize this? God, the Father, is embracing Jesus, the Son, to Himself in the moment of the ascension. It is relationship. This is a part of the eternal focus of the ascension. The heart of God is all about embracing. This is the framework of eternity. You must protect, guard, and build your relationships. In the eternal view, nothing matters but relationship. Whatever you have to do to maintain relationship, do it!

In light of the focus on eternal relationships, there is another part of this shift in framework which we need to propose. It has to do with Jesus reigning as King. What the disciples desired all

Part Three: Preceding the Ascension

the time is actually taking place, but in an eternal realm. Jesus is ascending to the right hand of the Father to reign as King over the eternal Kingdom.

We will need to make a major shift in our framework. All of the time the disciples have been planning the Kingdom on this earth, in their time bracket, now they must begin to think about the Kingdom of Heaven of which they will forever be a part. They have been focused on the physical as if this world is an end in itself. Now they must focus on the spiritual realities with a new end. It is a difficult shift to make.

Our Christianity seems to operate in the framework of this world. We constantly want to use the power of God for the improvement and betterment of our conditions. We seem to want to build something for this world. Every time we seek position here on earth, we are declaring we have missed the greatness of what Christ has brought us into. The Christ who indwells us is also sitting on the throne of the heavenlies, and He is operating a spiritual Kingdom beyond what we are able to comprehend. We should operate within that framework. We seek to get men saved so they can join our church, when our concern should be to get them into this new Kingdom. We seek to build a great church in our town when we should seek to bring every man and every woman into the Kingdom of which Jesus is King.

The ascension is a call to a new framework. It takes a Divine action within us to bring such an alteration. I am seeking Him for the new view.

THE ASCENSION

Acts 1:9-11

THE ASCENSION'S BLESSING

Luke wrote the two volumes which make up the Gospel of Luke and the Book of Acts. He begins volume two (The Book of Acts) with a definite reference to the Gospel according to Luke (volume one). ***The former account I made, O Theophilus, of all that Jesus began to do and teach,*** (Acts 1:1). He gives something of a summary of the closing issues of ***The former account.*** His focus is on the resurrection appearances of Jesus Christ, and he relates the activities of the forty days of Jesus' visitation with His disciples (Acts 1:3). Luke writes about the content of the discussion during those forty days as ***speaking of the things pertaining to the kingdom of God.***

Then Luke moves us into the final moments of Jesus' time on this earth. Jesus gives His disciples last minute instructions ***to wait for the Promise of the Father,*** (Acts 1:4). He describes it as ***you shall be baptized with the Holy Spirit,*** (Acts 1:5) and ***you shall receive power when the Holy Spirit has come upon you;*** (Acts 1:8).

As Jesus was speaking these instructions, He ascended to the Father. These words tell us what was most important in the mind of Christ. He sets the tone for everything He wants His disciples to have and be. Every event of Jesus' time on earth has built to this climax. Everything He will accomplish in the ascension will further complete the disciples. His work is not over! It will continue in a different context.

Part Four: The Ascension

What is this new context? We can see it clearly in the bigger view of the ascension. Luke gives us more details in volume two concerning the ascension (Acts 1:9-11). He writes of the two angels in volume two, and the promise of Jesus' return in the same manner is given through them. But the way Luke introduces the ascension in His Gospel account is significant. Before he gets into the details (Acts 1:9-11), he gives the larger view of what Jesus is doing, and is going to do, through the ascension (Luke 24:50-51). *And He led them out as far as Bethany, and He lifted up His hands and blessed them. Now it came to pass, while He blessed them, that He was parted from them and carried up into heaven,* (Luke 24:50-51).

Luke sets up the ascension in the context of a blessing. He is writing to the Jewish culture, and Jesus' actions come from the Old Testament tradition. There are many examples in the Old Testament of the priests and prophets blessing the people. One such occasion is the original consecration of the priests in the days of Moses and Aaron. *Then Aaron lifted his hand toward the people, blessed them, and came down from offering the sin offering, the burnt offering, and peace offerings,* (Leviticus 9:22). Balaam, the Old Testament prophet, was called upon by Balak, King of the Moabites, to come and curse the children of Israel (Numbers 22). He had heard about the great power in the blessings and cursings of the prophets of God.

What Jesus was doing with the disciples in the moment of the ascension was in the Old Testament tradition. But there was certainly more going on here than simply following a tradition. The Father had blessed Jesus, and then He was passing what the Father had bestowed upon Him onto His disciples. Luke emphasized this in *the former account,* and it is important to recognize it here in volume two. That which was taking place in Jesus was so He could impart it to us. The Father was working dynamically through Jesus, and the ultimate purpose of this work would be done by Jesus through us. The power the Father wants to work in our lives can only be accomplished in us by His Son. Jesus is not just our example for living, He is the means by which we will live. Jesus is not just the prototype, He is the source of our production. Jesus is not just the first one, He is the material and substance for all that is to follow.

The New Testament frames this condition and position in the "blessing." The ascension was a necessary part of the continuation of this "blessing." The ascension takes place as Jesus gives the "blessing." This "blessing" continues through the ascension and is extended into the exaltation of Christ as He is seated at the right hand of the Father.

We see this clearly through Paul's teaching in his Epistle to the Ephesians (1:3-6). ***Blessed be the God and Father of our Lord Jesus Christ, who has blessed us with every spiritual blessing in the heavenly places in Christ,*** (Ephesians 1:3). In this verse, Paul refers to both the earthly ministry of Jesus as well as His heavenly ascended ministry. He ties the two aspects together as if they are a continuation of the same plan. He wants us to know that God, the Father, has one desire. He wants to bless ***us with every spiritual blessing.*** In order to accomplish this He became the ***Father of our Lord Jesus Christ,*** and the incarnation took place. The second member of the Trinity leaped off His throne and became the Son. He joined us in our humanity and received the blessing from the Father to bring about the blessing for us. He became the instrument through which the Father can fulfill the "blessing plan." But it does not stop there, for the ascension takes place and the blessing becomes a part of the eternal heavenly realms. God did not dare limit the blessing to this time zone; He had to make it eternal, and His instrument was the ascended Lord.

The verse (Ephesians 1:3) is simply the beginning of a sentence which continues into verse six! Verses three through six are one great statement, and the heart of the statement is verse three. The additional verses modify the content of the opening statement. Paul gives us insight into the content of the blessing in Christ. It has to do with the fact that *He chose us in Him before the foundation of the world,* (Ephesians 1:4). God chose us with great purpose. He chose us *that we should be holy and without blame before Him in love,* (Ephesians 1:4). He has *predestined us to adoption as sons by Jesus Christ to Himself,* (Ephesians 1:5). And if that were not enough, *He made us accepted in the Beloved,* (Ephesians 1:6). Intimate relationship is the focus of the Father. The key words are *chose, predestined, adoption,* and *accepted.* Everything is relational. The blessing is being His!

The word, blessed, is used three different times in three different forms in this verse. Each time it is used, it is the same Greek word in three different grammar forms. The first usage opens the sentence with a focus on God, the Father. *Blessed be the God and Father of our Lord Jesus Christ, ...* (Ephesians 1:3). The word, *Blessed,* is used as an adjective which describes God. This form of the word is used only eight times in the New Testament, and it is used exclusively for God, the Father. You will recognize the Greek word for it as the word, eulogy. It is two words combined. There is "eu" which means well or good, and "logos" which means word. This word has to do with the goodness of the person being declared.

At first glance, you might think Paul is indicating that God receives praise and worship (good words) from His people. That is true and should be. However, there is something beyond that here. It has to do with praise, glory, and worship coming from God, Himself. It is the atmosphere in which God lives. Praise and worship flow from His being. He produces it!

We must not view praise and worship as something we do, or create, to honor God. Rather, we gather together in a worship service in openness to the presence of God. When He comes upon us, we begin to worship. This enables Him to give us a greater sense of His presence. From where does this worship

The Ascension's Blessing | **Acts 1:9-11**

come? It comes from God. The word, **Blessed,** means the blessing is flowing from God, through us, back to Him. He is the source of it all. This means the heart of worship is surrender. This is not emotional hype or the beat of the music. Worship is an expression of your personal relationship and intimacy with God. To worship you must lose yourself in Him. If you are living out of yourself, you cannot truly worship, for you cannot produce it. Worship is contained in God alone!

Paul paints a tremendous picture of God sitting on His throne. He is surrounded by the mist of His own greatness. Coming from His very person is glory, praise, honor and majesty. He does not strain to bring it to pass. It simply is His natural atmosphere, produced from His heart. He lives in this state at all times.

Paul has opened this sentence with a focus on God in the majesty of His own blessedness. In the second usage of this word, He says, **who has blessed us,** (Ephesians 1:3). He uses the word as a verb. It is in the form of a participle, which acts as an adverb in describing the main verb. If you look closely at this verse in the Greek language, there is no verb given; it is assumed. In the English translations, we have inserted the verb "be" as this assumed main verb. It is as close as we can come to it in our language, for Paul is referring to a state of being, which is contained within God. But we dare not miss the fact that this state of being is not content without action. God, in the state of His own glory and blessedness, had to act on our behalf. He was driven to it by His heart, or being. The good word (blessing) which flows from the person of God, comes from who He is! God takes what He is, and imputes or imparts it upon us through His Word.

When God speaks, things happen! The creation of the world is explained in the speaking of God (Genesis 1). God's speaking contains a creative quality. Paul paints an awesome picture for us. God sits on His throne in the midst of His glory and honor (blessedness). He opens His mouth and speaks all of this same glory and honor (blessedness) into being for us. It flows from Him to us. We lack nothing that He is. He brings all He is to us in this blessing.

It is a picture of surrender and resting. Why would we not allow our lives to be engulfed with this great blessing? Why would we not relax in Jesus and allow this intimate relationship of His presence to flow from Him to us? Why would we not rely on and cling to this resource? The heart of the blessing is about **chose, predestined, adoption** and **accepted.** This blessing is about His intimate embrace.

It is important to understand the grammar of this participle (verb), **has blessed,** is in the aorist tense. It indicates a complete and finished action. Paul goes on to tell us Christ is the completed and finished blessing. God has dreamed about and spoken of good things concerning us, and He has completed us in Christ. It is the same Jesus who ministered on this earth for three years. He refers to Jesus as the One who died upon the cross and God resurrected from the dead. But in this particular verse, Paul refers to the Christ who has ascended into the heavenly realms. He goes on to tell us Christ is **seated ... at His right hand in the heavenly places, far above all principality and power and might and dominion, and every name that is named, not only in this age but also in that which is to come,** (Ephesians 1:20-21). God completes the blessing in the ascension.

The third usage of this same Greek word, "blessed," is in this verse too. **Blessed be the God and Father of our Lord Jesus Christ, who has blessed us with every spiritual blessing in the heavenly places in Christ,** (Ephesians 1:3). It is a noun in this third usage. It is **every spiritual blessing.** Paul's description of this blessing as **spiritual** is of great interest to me. This word is always used in connection with the presence and work of the Holy Spirit. The focus of this idea is not on the content of the blessing, but on the source of the blessing. The blessing is not necessarily immaterial or mystical. Paul does not contrast a material blessing over and against an immaterial blessing. He focuses on the source of the blessing as the Spirit of Jesus.

As you view the blessing as singular, it becomes even clearer. There may be a variety of aspects to this blessing as is described in the rest of the sentence (Ephesians 1:4-6). But these manifestations are only of a single blessing. Paul further emphasizes this truth by placing all of this spiritual blessing *in Christ*. It is not in Christ as in a storage unit, but it is in Christ through relationship. All the aspects of the blessing listed flow from the intimate relationship with the person of Christ. Think of the awesomeness of it! The creative speaking of God is bringing about this great blessing, and the blessing is contained in the One who is called the Word of God (John 1:1).

We can only find what we need in the ascended Lord, through the Spirit of Jesus. We need not look anywhere else. We do not need to experiment with any other means. All God has purposed for us is found in Jesus. We must surrender to Him. He must be our single source of living. There is nothing for me but Jesus!

Acts 1:9-11

IN THE ASCENSION

The ascension of Jesus Christ is of vital importance to the total aspect of Christian life. You could not have come this far in our study and not be convinced of this. The crucifixion and the resurrection events are complete, and their accomplishment has great significance in our lives. The results of Jesus' death and resurrection continue to work in our behalf. The ascension of Jesus continues to work in our lives in an even greater way. God has turned the ascension into exaltation. Jesus is ministering in our behalf in an exalted state. God has extended the ascension.

Luke closes his gospel account (volume one) with the record of the ascension. As he begins to write the Book of Acts (volume two), he opens with the ascension to give definite details of the event. He highlights the forty days of Jesus' ministry in His resurrection form, and then he focuses on the final moments and the conversation just prior to His departure.

Jesus was only concerned about one thing at the time of His departing. It was the Promise of the Father (Acts 1:4). He explained it in the terms of ***but you shall be baptized with the Holy Spirit not many days from now,*** (Acts 1:5). When the disciples were sidetracked by their surroundings and circumstances, Jesus brought them back into this focus. They wanted to know if He would ***at this time restore the kingdom of Israel?*** (Acts 1:6). Jesus' answer was forceful and direct. In essence, He told them it was none of their business, and they should not think about it any longer (Acts 1:7). The focus of the disciples was to be on *you shall receive power when the Holy Spirit has come upon you,* (Acts 1:8).

Luke highlights this theme from the beginning. What happened in the life of Jesus was to now happen in the lives of His disciples, and so to us. Jesus imparted the fullness of the Holy Spirit, which He had received from His Father, to His disciples. He focused His entire ministry on this. It was the climax of the dreams of God for mankind.

The ascension takes place within this framework. In the closing of volume one (The Gospel of Luke), Luke labels this truth the **blessing.** He stresses the usage of this word. *And He led them out as far as Bethany, and He lifted up His hands and blessed them. Now it came to pass, while He blessed them, that He was parted from them and carried up into heaven,* (Luke 24:50-51). The blessing which Jesus received, and experienced from His Father during His three years of ministry, He would now bestow on the disciples. It is in this framework the ascension takes place. Jesus ascended *while He blessed them.*

We must pay careful attention to the word, **while.** We have no literal translation for this word. There are two Greek words which the translators have placed in this one word. The two Greek words are "in" and "the." The word, **blessed,** is a verb in the present tense. It is in the infinitive mood, which creates the idea of "to bless." This tells us Jesus was in the blessing as He ascended. God was blessing Jesus, and Jesus was bestowing the blessing on the disciples as the ascension took place. The framework of this great event is the blessing.

Paul speaks of this same concept in his epistle to the Ephesians. *Blessed be the God and Father of our Lord Jesus Christ, who has blessed us with every spiritual blessing in the heavenly places in Christ,* (Ephesians 1:3). In this verse, Paul connects the earthly ministry of Jesus with the heavenly ministry. He highlights the earthly ministry of Jesus as he writes, *Blessed be the God and Father of our Lord Jesus Christ.* Paul moves from

Part Four: The Ascension

there into ***the heavenly places in Christ,*** and the ascension is the bridge between the earthly and heavenly ministry of Jesus. This ministry is one plan, one action, and one dream from the heart of God. God frames it in the idea of ***blessing.***

The Greek word, which is translated "in," is presented to us three times in this verse. Jesus was "in the blessing" as He ascended (Luke 24:51). Paul uses three prepositional phrases beginning with "in" to describe the blessing. They are ***in every spiritual blessing, in the heavenly places,*** and ***in Christ.*** Regardless of what your translation reads, each phrase begins with the same Greek word, and its primary translation is "in."

If we are to understand this in light of the ascension, we must thoroughly comprehend this word, ***in,*** which plays such an important role in the verse. Whatever you say about this word, it is the complete opposite of doing or performance. You and I do nothing to bring this about, and we can do nothing to add to it. The focus is in "being." A blessed God has creatively spoken His total provision into the blessing. God lives in a state of blessedness. He produces it from His nature. He desperately wants us to live in this state with Him. His very nature compels Him to act, and the action is creative speech. This blessing is ours, and we need only to respond by surrender, relaxation, dependence and submission. We are to have the attitude of abiding. The blessing will source and initiate everything we require to live in His presence. In this state of being we will find all holiness, purity and the fulfillment of the law and justice. It is a product of God alone.

The preposition "in" can have a variety of meanings as it is used in the New Testament. There are three basic usages for the word. It can mean place or location. Luke describes a wicked woman who comes to anoint the feet of Jesus while He is at a Pharisee's home. Luke writes, ***And behold, a woman in the city who was a sinner…*** (Luke 7:37). He is telling us the location of the woman.

"In" is used to indicate an instrument or means by which something is done. It is often translated "by" or "with." In speaking of Jesus' ability to redeem us, John writes, **This is He who came by water and blood - Jesus Christ; not only by water, but by water and blood,** (1 John 5:6).

John tells us Jesus redeems us with the instrument of His blood.

The third usage of the word "in" denotes time, either a definite time or a period of time. The Pharisees were consistently disturbed by the actions of Jesus and His disciples on the Sabbath Day. On one occasion they said, **"Look, Your disciples are doing what is not lawful to do on the Sabbath!"** (Matthew 12:2). The word, **on,** is a translation of the same Greek word which indicates a particular day.

The interesting thing about Paul's Ephesians passage is he uses all three of these meanings in this writing (Ephesians 1:3). He does not use one definition each time, but he uses all three definitions in each usage of this Greek word. Look carefully at this statement, **Blessed be the God and Father of our Lord Jesus Christ, who has blessed us with every spiritual blessing in the heavenly places in Christ,** (Ephesians 1:3). God, the Father, is sitting on His throne in the midst of His own blessedness. The essence of His blessedness is always redemption. He produces it from His heart. Therefore, He is speaking into existence blessedness for us.

Where is the blessing located? It is found *in every spiritual blessing!* It is located *in the heavenly places!* We can only experience it *in Christ!* By what instrument or means will we experience this blessedness? The instrument, means or substance is *every spiritual blessing!* The means is *the heavenly places!* Certainly the instrument is *Christ* alone! Is there a definite moment or period of time? The time is only when you are *in every spiritual blessing!* It is while you dwell *in the heavenly places!* It is when you are *in Christ!* Paul gives us the location, the means or instrument, and the time period for the blessing God has for us!

To erase any doubts you might have about the above statements, let's look at each statement carefully. Paul writes, **Blessed be the God and Father of our Lord Jesus Christ, who has blessed us with every spiritual blessing...** (Ephesians 1:3). As we noted in another study, the adjective, *spiritual,* is the idea of source. It is always used in relationship to the work of the Holy Spirit. Paul does not attempt to make a distinction between material and immaterial, but He wants us to focus on the Spirit of Jesus as the single source of the "blessing."

The word, *blessing,* is in the noun form. However, it is interesting to note the word appears in the feminine gender while the other two usages are in the masculine gender. When the masculine gender is used, it refers to concrete things, while the feminine usage refers to things more abstract. Therefore, the indication is **with every spiritual blessing** is abstract in its concept. Personally, I react negatively to this shift. I would rather have the concrete rather than the abstract. The concrete is measurable and solid. I can examine it easily while I handle it. It is easier to define, and therefore to figure out and explain. Abstract is illusive and difficult to communicate.

When I get honest, I know the most valuable things in my life have to do with the abstract. The things which I cherish, and want to last forever, are not in the realm of the concrete. The difference between the two is not real or unreal. Love is abstract. How do you measure that which takes place between husband and wife? How can we describe it? The question asked by young people is, "How do I know when I am really in love?" Who has ever adequately answered this question? It is abstract, but I do not want to live without love.

If you and I are going to be *in every spiritual blessing,* which God is speaking into existence for us, we must yield to what we cannot adequately describe, explain or understand.

We must go beyond the realm of our own thinking and ability. We must not limit ourselves to what we can do. Performance must not be the measuring rod of our lives. We need to come in surrender and submission to what God has already done for us.

Now we move onto the second prepositional phrase. ***Blessed be the God and Father of our Lord Jesus Christ, who has blessed us with every spiritual blessing in the heavenly places...*** (Ephesians 1:3). Our minds automatically move to the location of the blessing, and that is certainly involved. The ***heavenly place*** is where we experience the spiritual blessing. The word, ***places,*** is not really there in the original language, but it is inserted for the sake of translation. The word, ***heavenly,*** is an adjective, not a noun. What is the noun which the word, ***heavenly,*** describes? There is no noun present. The author is not describing a place or a location as much as an atmosphere. It is a condition, attitude or dimension rather than a location.

The Greek word, translated ***heavenly,*** is made up of two words. There is the basic word which is "heaven" and a prefix which is "in." Thus, it relates to the idea of "in heaven" or those things which pertain to heaven. Here in Ephesians, Paul does not refer to heaven as a place far above us where God dwells. He describes the atmosphere around us. It is pushing in upon us, surrounding us every moment, and influencing our lives constantly. In this atmosphere are principalities, powers, the rulers of the darkness of this age, and spiritual hosts of wickedness (Ephesians 6:12). But also, in this ***heavenly*** are the angelic hosts who are the counter parts to this evil force, ***which He worked in Christ when He raised Him from the dead and seated Him at His right hand in the heavenly places,*** (Ephesians 1:20).

If ***every spiritual blessing*** is found ***in the heavenly places,*** one must ask what have I done to bring this into existence? The answer is nothing! While this ***heavenly*** is in the atmosphere all around us, and is pressing in upon us, we do nothing to contribute to it or take from it. It is strictly "beyond us." Therefore,

Part Four: The Ascension

this is both the location, the means, and the time of our spiritual experience. It is at the end of ourselves, our ability, our thought process, our effort, our wisdom and our self discipline that God has placed what we need. It is there that He has spoken into existence His power, His might, His thought process, His effort, His wisdom and His discipline. When we come to our end in total surrender and submission, we experience "the blessing" of His complete provision.

Blessed be the God and Father of our Lord Jesus Christ, who has blessed us with every spiritual blessing in the heavenly places in Christ, (Ephesians 1:3). This is the final prepositional phrase. The focus of the blessing is Christ. He is the location, the instrument or means, and the time of all God dreams for you. You can only find the blessing in Him. Jesus is the Word of God (1John 1:1). The speaking of God is so powerful it has its own personality, and it is Christ. He is the living Word of God, and He is the means by which we experience everything God has designed for us.

Many look at Christianity and ask, "How can I do this? How can I live in this victory?" You cannot find it in your doing. It is just beyond all you can do, and it is only found in Christ. We derive everything we are from Jesus. Therefore, we do not need what we desire, we only need Him. Intimacy with Jesus should be our only focus. Night and day, moment by moment, give yourself entirely to this passion. Strive to know Jesus. Anything other than that is religion with religious activities.

The "blessing" is fulfilled in the ascension. What Jesus experienced as blessed by the Father, He now gives to us. We find all we need in only Him. "O, I want to know Him more. Deep within my soul, I want to know Him."

Acts 1:9-11

THE ASCENSION OF THE ATONEMENT

Words are intriguing. Though we have many other means of communication, such as body language, facial expressions, wordless utterances, and even silence, words make the strongest impact. To bring clarity of thought in Bible study, words are very significant, and they produce a study all on their own.

In the closing verses of Luke's Gospel Account (24:50-51), and in the summary Luke gives in the beginning of Acts (1:9-11), he uses six different Greek words to highlight the ascension. Each word is in the action form, painting a unique picture of what is happening. These words appear in four simple verses without duplication. Luke carefully planned this with the inspiration of the Holy Spirit. He attempts to relate the large picture of Jesus' ascension to us, and gives us the key role it plays in the continued redemption we experience in Him.

We need to list these words so we can have them in our minds. As Luke closes his Gospel account, he focuses on the ascension. ***Now it came to pass, while He blessed them, that He was parted from them and carried up into heaven,*** (Luke 24:51). Here we find the first two Greek words Luke uses to describe the ascension. The first is ***diestee,*** which is translated, ***He was parted.*** The action of this word is one of separating from something. It is used three times in the New Testament, and only by Luke.

Part Four: The Ascension

The second word is ***anefereto,*** which is translated, ***carried up.*** The action of this word shows sacrificial offering. This word is used ten times in the New Testament, and seven of those times it relates to offering up a sacrifice.

The remaining four words are found in the Book of Acts. ***Now when He had spoken these things, while they watched, He was taken up, and a cloud received Him out of their sight,*** (Acts 1:9). The first one is ***epeerthee,*** which is translated, ***He was taken up.*** This word describes the act of lifting up, as in hoisting a sail (Acts 27:40). The second word is ***hupelaben,*** and it is translated, ***received.*** At the heart of this word is the action of relationship. It paints the picture of interaction and intimacy taking place.

This brings us to the last two words. One is found in verse ten. ***And while they looked steadfastly toward heaven as He went up, behold two men stood by them in white apparel,*** (Acts 1:10). The action word is ***poreuomenou,*** which is translated, ***as He went up.*** It describes the continuation of a journey or mission. The final word is found in, ***who also said, "Men of Galilee why do you stand gazing up into heaven? This same Jesus, who was taken up from you into heaven, will so come in like manner as you saw Him go into heaven,*** (Acts 1:11). The Greek word is ***analeemftheis,*** and it is translated, ***is taken up.*** It is used thirteen times in the New Testament and five of those relate to the ascension. It paints the picture of being received.

These six words relate to each other, which makes them significant. The total message of the ascension is presented in the relationship of each word to the others. They give us the full view of the ascension and its impact as each word ceases to be distinct by itself and becomes connected to the others.

Continued Response
Luke 24:51 & Acts 1:10

As Luke paints the first picture for us, he puts great emphasis on things that are continuing. What the disciples thought was over is not over at all. The ascension seems to take what is in the resurrection and places it in a new context, on a different plain. We have been aware of this before in our study. What was true for Jesus will be much more true in our lives and our future ascension.

Surrender, submission, and dependency are not temporary as related to life on this earth. In the theology of my upbringing, I have been left with the implication that the fullness of the Holy Spirit, and my surrender to Him, are only necessary in the trials of my life. As we all know, when we get to heaven there will be no more sorrow, no tears, no death, no trials and no problems. So why will we need the Spirit of Jesus flowing through our lives?

Death to self-centered carnality is necessary here on this earth. After all, it is the plague of our lives. Carnality is woven into the structure of our culture, and we do battle with it every day we live in this world. Jesus may have delivered us from within, but carnality constantly presses upon us from without, forming a multitude of temptations for our lives. Therefore, we need to die to ourselves and live in total dependency upon the Spirit of Jesus, who indwells us.

But I was taught when we get to heaven, this will all change. We will live in an environment totally free from such evil. Jesus will not only deliver us from the source of sin within, but also without. There will be no more sin. Here on earth we have a desperate need for Christ to live through us, but that need ceases when we pass from this world. Submission, surrender, dependency and daily crucifixion are needed here to maintain redemption, but when we pass from this earthly world, the

Part Four: The Ascension

redemption Jesus established moves us beyond such things.

In the ascension of Jesus, Luke disputes such thinking! In His resurrection state, Jesus is in submission to the Father. What took place in Jesus' relationship with His Father on this earth, continued in the ascension and its ministry to come.

At the close of his Gospel account, Luke writes, ***Now it came to pass, while He blessed them, that He was parted from them and carried up into heaven,*** (Luke 24:51). The Greek word, ***epeerthee,*** is translated, ***He was parted.*** It is used only three times in the New Testament, and only by Luke. He only uses it once in connection with the ascension. He paints the picture of parting or separating from something. The context of the verse tells us Jesus was separated from the disciples. Jesus had a tremendous love for His disciples. He remained forty days with them following His resurrection. He poured His life into them for three years of ministry, and all He knew on earth He was now putting aside.

The verb is in the active voice, which tells us God did not force this upon Him. Jesus, the subject, is responsible for the action. Luke wants us to know that Jesus is actively involved in the ascension. He responds to the Father by releasing Himself from all that would hold Him to this earth. He submits and surrenders to His Father as He has always done. The event of the ascension demonstrates the submission of Jesus at its heart!

Luke carries this same emphasis into the Book of Acts. ***And while they looked steadfastly toward heaven as He went up, behold, two men stood by them in white apparel,*** (Acts 1:10). The Greek word, ***poreuomenou,*** is translated, ***He went up.*** Luke paints the picture of one who is continuing a journey, or is traveling. In the Gospel of John, Lazarus died. When Jesus became aware of this fact, He said to His disciples, ***"Our friend Lazarus sleeps, but I go that I may wake him up,*** (John 11:11). John uses the same Greek word used by Luke to suggest Jesus is going somewhere to accomplish a task. This word is often used to express the mission of Jesus (Luke 4:42).

In the ascension, through this word, we view Jesus to be on a journey. He will continue His ministry in the heavenly realm. Luke uses this participle in the middle voice, which is something like the active voice. The subject is responsible for the action taking place. Luke emphasizes again Jesus' involvement in the ascension. Jesus responds and surrenders to the Father, consenting and committing to the Father's will.

Dependency on the life of the Spirit is an eternal thing. It is not a tool for us to use in the troubled times of life. Dependency is the very nature and heart beat of what we are as citizens of the Kingdom of God. We must never think that surrender, submission, dependency and yieldedness are temporary actions connected to this world. They are eternal. This earthly experience is the training ground for having the continual power of the Spirit in eternity. This is the very make up and nature of the Kingdom life!

Continued Relationship
Acts 1:9-11

This brings us to the second picture Luke presents for us. It is the picture of positive response. A relationship never plateaus, it is either growing or dying. The key to any relationship is positive response, which enables the relationship to continue and grow. The relationship between God and man must constantly grow and change, and the determining factor is response.

We see this clearly in the relationship between Jesus and His Father. The ascension is a continuation of what had been growing and deepening between the two. Luke makes it plain that Jesus had been growing in His spiritual relationship with His Father. This does not mean He was moving from rebellion to submission or from disobedience to complete obedience. He was actively expanding in the surrender and submission He already had.

Luke finalizes his insight in the childhood and teenage stage of Jesus' life with these words. ***And Jesus increased in wisdom and stature, and in favor with God and men,*** (Luke 2:52). You might dismiss this as something Jesus needed for His childhood days, but it was unnecessary in His manhood. The author of Hebrews would not agree. He writes, ***though He was a Son, yet He learned obedience by the things which He suffered,*** (Hebrews 5:8).

Now Luke moves us to insight for the relationships of eternity. In a previous study we discussed the word, ***hupelaben.*** It is translated ***received*** in Luke's opening statement of the ascension in the Book of Acts. ***Now when He had spoken these things, while they watched, He was taken up, and a cloud received Him out of their sight,*** (Acts 1:9). This Greek word is only used five times in the New Testament. Twice it is translated, ***suppose,*** (Luke 7:43; Acts 2:15). Once it is translated as ***answering,*** (Luke 10:30), and twice it is translated ***received,*** (Acts 1:9; 3 John 8).

The word this picture paints is far different from the way we would define the word receive. It is not that of a bill collector receiving payment. Luke wants us to see something more than the disciples not being able to view Jesus any longer. This word gives us the picture of intimacy in relationship. When you suppose something, you receive it to yourself. You embrace it as true. It becomes a part of you! Answering means you have been in conversation with someone. You have taken in what that person has said, and you come back to them with further information. This Greek word tells us the cloud brought Jesus into itself in the same manner.

The cloud is used repeatedly in a description of the Father (Exodus 13:21-22; 40:38; Leviticus 16:2; 1 Kings 8:10; Luke 9:34). The ascension is the embrace of the Father in a new and continuing way. The word, ***received,*** is in the active tense, which means the Father is doing the receiving. The relationship Jesus had with His Father while on earth will be expanded into the kind of continual relationship we will have with God in eternity.

Luke uses two other words for the ascension which point to this same truth. *Who also said, "Men of Galilee why do you stand gazing up into heaven? This same Jesus, who was taken up from you into heaven, will so come in like manner as you saw Him go into heaven,"* (Acts 1:11). The Greek word is analeemftheis, and it is translated, *was taken up.* It is in the passive form, which means Jesus is being acted upon by the Father. *Now when He had spoken these things, while they watched, He was taken up, and a cloud received Him out of their sight,* (Acts 1:9). The Greek word, *epeerthee,* is translated, *was taken up.* It is in the passive form, which tells us Jesus is being acted upon by the Father.

The ascension is a continued response of Jesus to His Father. God is embracing Jesus in a new way for His continued ministry in the eternal realm. This experience of Jesus is the pattern for us. What an exciting time awaits us in the future!

Continued Redemption
Luke 24:51

Now we come to the third picture Luke paints with words. The heart of the relationship is always response. Relationships are always expanding, but they also have a great purpose. Those involved in the relationship set the direction it is to go from their character and strength. In the relationship between the Father and the Son, the hearts of the Father and the Son embrace on a new level, and there is an explosion of purpose and destiny. The purpose does not change from what it has always been. It is intensified.

The purpose of the relationship between the Father and the

Part Four: The Ascension

Son is the redemption of the world! The ascension ministry will be one of continued and intensified redemption. Luke introduces this concept to us at the close of volume one (The Gospel of Luke). ***Now it came to pass, while He blessed them, that He was parted from them and carried up into heaven,*** (Luke 24:51). The Greek word is ***anefereto,*** which is translated, ***carried up.*** It is used ten times in the New Testament, and seven of those times it refers to the offering of a sacrifice.

One of the most significant places this word is used is in the Book of the Hebrews. The author relates an entire treatise on Jesus as the High Priest. He writes, ***Who does not need daily, as those high priests, to offer up sacrifices, first for His own sins and then for the people's, for this He did once for all when He offered up Himself,*** (Hebrews 7:27). The Greek word under discussion is translated, ***offer up,*** and is used twice in this one verse to refer to the redemptive sacrifice of Jesus Christ. It paints the picture of offering up oneself.

The Hebrew author continues to use this word when he writes, ***so Christ was offered once to bear the sins of many. To those who eagerly wait for Him He will appear a second time, apart from sin, for salvation,*** (Hebrews 9:28). This time the Greek word is translated ***bear.*** It has the idea of taking a burden upon oneself.

Luke then paints the most awesome picture for us with the word, ***anefereto.*** It is important to note that he uses the word in reference to the ascension, and it is in the perfect tense. This indicates there is a continual action taking place. The redemption, which finds its heart beat in the cross is continuing in the action of the ascension. Redemption is the flow of the crucifixion, resurrection and ascension. This Greek word is also in the passive form, which tells us Jesus is being acted upon by the Father in this continued ministry of redemption, which is forever.

The ascension of Jesus gives us tremendous insight into

our own futures. Surrender and submission to His full working through us is an eternal experience. In the eternal realm, our relationship with Jesus is going to expand and be raised to new levels beyond our imagination, and it will be all for redemptive ministry. The cross style is the style of the eternal Kingdom. This earthly life is the training ground for such an everlasting experience. How are you "being" in the process?

Acts 1:9-11

THE ASCENSION MINISTRY

Now it came to pass, while He blessed them, that He was parted from them and carried up into heaven, (Luke 24:51). Luke mentions the ascension for the first time at the close of this Gospel account. In this presentation of Jesus' ascension, he establishes the strong foundation of the ministry involved in this event. The Greek word translated, **carried up,** is too startling to ignore. We have noted in our previous studies that Luke paints a beautiful picture of Jesus being offered up. It is used ten times in the New Testament, and seven of those usages refer directly to a sacrificial offering. It is not difficult to see the picture Luke paints. The word he uses is in the imperfect tense, which gives us the idea of continuous action. Thus, the ascension is the continuous action of the cross carried up into the heavens.

Another Greek word which gives added support to this concept is translated, **He went up.** Luke puts a strong focus on the continued redemptive ministry of Jesus in the ascension. *And while they looked steadfastly toward heaven as He went up, behold, two men stood by them in white apparel,* (Acts 1:10). This Greek word paints the picture of the continuation of a journey or mission. It is used often in the Gospel accounts for the ministry of Jesus. Luke paints the picture again of the continuation of the ministry of Jesus. The cross, the resurrection and the ascension are all one flowing ministry of redemption. The ascension is not the end of redemption, but a continuation.

As you begin to investigate the ascension ministry, there is a special word which starts to appear! It is the word, **MEDIATOR**. It is used six times in the New Testament, and each time it refers to Jesus. This is a powerful verse. *For there is one God and one Mediator between God and men, the Man Christ Jesus,* (1 Timothy 2:5). Three times this word is used in the Book of Hebrews. *But now He has obtained a more excellent ministry, inasmuch as He is also Mediator of a better covenant, which was established on better promises,* (Hebrews 8:6). *And for this reason He is the Mediator of the new covenant, by means of death, for the redemption of the transgressions under the first covenant, that those who are called may receive the promise of the eternal inheritance,* (Hebrews 9:15). *But you have come... to Jesus the Mediator of the new covenant, and to the blood of sprinkling that speaks better than that of Abel,* (Hebrews 12:24).

A mediator is one who intervenes between two people, to either make or restore peace and friendship, or to form a compact, or for ratifying a covenant. It is one who is a medium of communication or an arbitrator. This seems to be at the very heart of the ministry of Jesus! The ascension is a key element in the continuation of this mediation. Luke makes a definite reference to this ministry as he describes the ascension. What a ministry it is! It tells us the very nature of the redemption itself. It is a ministry of reconciliation. Paul wrote, *For it pleased the Father that in Him all the fullness should dwell, and by Him to reconcile all things to Himself, by Him, whether things on earth or things in heaven, having made peace through the blood of His cross,* (Colossians 1:19-20). The ministry of redemption is not just to save us, but to reconcile us to God. It is relational in its nature.

As Mediator, Jesus represents God to man. Is He not a demonstration of the Father to us? Do we not look into His face and see the Father? It is not because He is the Father, but He is filled with the Father. As He constantly responds to the Father, Jesus enables the Father to act through Him, bringing a visualization of the invisible God to our lives. Jesus tells us the truth about God.

As Mediator, Jesus represents man to God. Is He not a demonstration of how a man should live, in intimacy and dependence upon the Father? Do we not look into His face and see exactly what we are to be? As Jesus responds to the Father, we discover what intimate relationship with the Father should produce in our lives. Jesus tells us the truth about man! Jesus tells us the truth about God, because He is the truth about man. This is the destiny of who we are as Kingdom people. We are a demonstration of the truth about God.

This is the heart of the ascension ministry. If your reaction is like mine, there is a cry for more detail than Luke gives us. While he suggests this continued ascension ministry, he does not describe it. There is, however, a fitting description found in the Book of Hebrews. The author lays the foundation in the beginning chapters of what he wants to say. As he comes to chapter eight, he writes, **Now this is the main point of the things we are saying: We have such a High Priest, who is seated at the right hand of the throne of the Majesty in the heavens,** (Hebrews 8:1). The theme of the book is that of Jesus as the High Priest in the ascension ministry.

The author of Hebrews writes, **But now He has obtained a more excellent ministry,** (Hebrews 8:6). As the ascended High Priest, Jesus is far superior to all other High Priests. His ministry in the ascension surpasses anything ever accomplished up to this time. The author continues by stating five major reasons why His ministry is superior.

Better Covenant
Hebrews 8:6

But now He has obtained a more excellent ministry, inasmuch as He is also Mediator of a better covenant, which was established on better promises, (Hebrews 8:6). The promises of this new covenant are far beyond any prior covenant between God and man. They are certainly superior to the covenant of the law, which is doing. The Promise of the Father is the context of the ascension. Jesus has been with His disciples for forty days, instructing them *of the things pertaining to the Kingdom of God,* (Acts 1:3). At the close of the forty days He gathers them close for their final instructions. He gives them the Promise of the Father. He describes it as *you shall be baptized with the Holy Spirit not many days from now,* (Acts 1:5). As he speaks these words, He ascends!

The Hebrew author expands on this promise. Obviously, the first covenant was not adequate. If it had been, *then no place would have been sought for a second,* (Hebrews 8:7). But because the law (doing) was inadequate, God promised a new covenant based upon superior promises of which the law (doing) could not imagine! God promised, *I will put My laws in their mind and write them on their hearts; and I will be their God, and they shall be My people. None of them shall teach his neighbor, and none his brother, saying, "Know the Lord," for all shall know Me, from the least of them to the greatest of them. For I will be merciful to their unrighteousness, and their sins and their lawless deeds I will remember no more,* (Hebrews 8:10-12).

This is a detailed description of exactly what Jesus' ascension was meant to bring to pass for us. He is mediating this new covenant in our behalf. The Promise of the Father is being received by us at this moment because of the ascension ministry. We can now experience the indwelling of the Holy Spirit in our lives, just as Jesus knew it. Peter spoke of it in his Pentecost sermon. *Therefore being exalted to the right hand of God, and having received from the Father the promise of the Holy Spirit, He poured out this which you now see and hear,* (Acts 2:33).

Better Continuation
Hebrews 9:11

This news takes us to a new realm! *But Christ came as High Priest of the good things to come, with the greater and more perfect tabernacle not made with hands, that is, not of this creation,* (Hebrews 9:11). We know *of this creation* as decaying and dying, but this new ministry in this new place is non-decaying and non-dying. He goes on to emphasize this by using the word, *eternal,* three times. *Not with the blood of goats and calves, but with His own blood He entered the Most Holy Place once for all, having obtained ETERNAL redemption,* (Hebrews 9:12). The author contrasts the blood of Christ with the blood of bulls and goats, showing the basis of the eternal quality of this redemption. He also highlights how the sacrifice was offered as he says, *who through the ETERNAL Spirit offered Himself without spot to God,* (Hebrews 9:14). This is the basis of all Jesus has to grant to us. *And for this reason He is the Mediator of the new covenant, by means of death, for the redemption of the transgressions under the first covenant, that those who are called may receive the promise of the ETERNAL inheritance,* (Hebrews 9:15).

The Greek word translated, *eternal*, is an adjective, and it means unceasing. The Hebrews author is repeatedly making this contrast throughout the book. The sacrifice of the old covenant (doing) was offered every year. The sacrifice of the new covenant is once and for all, unceasing in its effect, (Hebrews 9:25).

But this word, *eternal,* has a startling undercurrent to it. It speaks not of simple duration of life as related to redemption, but quality. The law (doing) became obsolete (Hebrews 8:13), while the fullness of the Spirit living through us (being) is a quality of life worthy of being called *eternal redemption.* This eternal redemption is produced by the *eternal Spirit,* (Hebrews 9:14), while the law (doing) is produced by mortal and corruptible self-effort. The quality of life in redemption is an *eternal inheritance,* (Hebrews 9:15), which man does not have to produce. In the old covenant (doing), man had to focus on constantly renewing.

Better Content
Hebrews 9:13-14

The formula for each covenant is vastly different. *For if the blood of bulls and goats and the ashes of a heifer, sprinkling the unclean, sanctifies for the purifying of the flesh, how much more shall the blood of Christ, who through the eternal Spirit offered Himself without spot to God, cleanse your conscience from dead works to serve the living God?* (Hebrews 9:13-14). The content of the old covenant (doing) is the inferior blood of animals and substitute blood, which is focused on purifying the flesh in terms of its defilement. It was a correction for the exterior. Man had to focus on doing the right thing.

But the blood of Christ is a focus on internal matters. The *blood of Christ* is not significant simply from the physical aspect. Behind the sacrifice of Christ was the motive and personal quality of His life. He was empowered, enhanced and charged with the principle of Divine life within Him *(eternal Spirit).* He responded to the life of God. The sacrifice was the offering of His deepest self, His innermost personhood. This was a sacrifice which went beyond time to before *the foundation of the world,* (Hebrews 9:26), for He was always responding this way.

Did you notice that this sacrifice will *cleanse your conscience from dead works to serve the living God,* (Hebrews 9:14)? He is not going to save us from works, but from **dead works!** And what are dead works? We must include self-initiated doing, duty, law, obligation, or have to works. The works are going to be transformed into service for the living God, because they will be empowered and enhanced by Him (being.) It is a new level of living in response to the Spirit who is living in and through us! F.F. Bruce says that "the severest test of Christ's power to redeem is his ability to loose the bonds springing out of a legal religion, by which many are bound who have escaped the dominion of gross, sinful habits."

Better Consecration
Hebrews 10:12

The sacrifice of Christ was complete. The Hebrew author consistently contrasts this with *every priest stands ministering daily and offering repeatedly the same sacrifices, which can never take away sins,* (Hebrews 10:11). *But this Man, after He had offered one sacrifice for sins forever, sat down at the right hand of God,* (Hebrews 10:12). The sacrifice Christ made was complete in its content and its duration. It was not a substitute sacrifice for a temporary appeasement. Where is there another priest who offers himself? Where is there another priest who is without sin who can offer himself?

Throughout the years there were hundreds of priests who did their duty and performed their priestly functions, but there was none who gave themselves like Christ. He totally and absolutely abandoned all He was in order to not only offer the sacrifice as the High Priest, but to also be the Sacrifice! There is no other sacrifice which surpasses the consecration of Christ. He totally surrendered all He was as God to become the worst humanity can produce. It was an all surpassing consecration.

Better Context
Hebrews 9:24

The Hebrew author presents to us the place in which the High Priest is serving. We see the startling reality when we read, *For Christ has not entered the holy places made with hands, which are copies of the true, but into heaven itself, now to appear in the presence of God for us,* (Hebrews 9:24). This author gives a description of the *earthly sanctuary* (Hebrews 9:1). It was divided into two parts with all of the furniture and sacred items necessary for the priests to perform their services (Hebrews 9:1-9). He reminds us of the focus of this earthly place and service was *concerned only with foods and drinks, various washings, and fleshly ordinances imposed until the time of redemption,* (Hebrews 9:10).

But Christ came as High Priest of the good things to come, with the greater and more perfect tabernacle not made with hands, that is, not of this creation, (Hebrews 9:11). Christ, in His ascension ministry, went to a superior place. He took the sacrifice (Himself) and went into the Holy of Holies in the heavenly realm, and He offered this sacrifice to God once and for all. Due to this ministry, He released the Promise of the Father and ratified the new covenant. Everything God dreamed for us is in place. We are reconciled to Him. The first covenant (doing) is now obsolete and the new covenant (being) can now be experienced. How ridiculous for us to even attempt to reestablish the old, obsolete covenant of doing, performance, self-sourced living, when we can live in His fullness. We can be produced by His Spirit.

Acts 1:9-11

THE ASCENSION PLAN

For as long as I can remember, I have always had a passion to be a Biblical preacher. I am not sure I always understood what this meant, but God is faithful to teach those who have a sincere heart. One of the things which emerged from this training was the Bible study principle called **SATURATION.** This simply means the message preached must come from the source of the Word of God, not my own personal reservoir of information or learning. In other words, you must spend time in the Word of God until the Author of the Book begins to reveal the truth of the passage. It is not an intellectual process, but a spiritual process. God becomes the resource for the message.

I must confess I have not always adequately saturated in the Word. It took some time during my early preaching experience to come to this principle. I would often find myself pressed for a Sunday morning sermon and would simply preach a sermon written by someone else. Everything I said was the truth, but it was not truth God revealed to me from His Word. I found the message in a sermon book or heard it on a cassette tape.

The reason I explain this to you is to let you know I am doing that very thing with this sermon. I want to investigate a sermon which is not mine, but was written by someone else. It is not that I did not have time to prepare, but I have a strong desire to go back as close to the ascension as we can. The first report of the ascension by the disciples is the first sermon

The Ascension Plan | Acts 1:9-11

preached after the ascension. It is Peter's sermon, which he preached on Pentecost. It was not a sermon produced by study, but a spontaneous message spilling forth from the Holy Spirit on the Day of Pentecost.

Peter was just seven days (maybe ten) from the experience of the ascension. He can still remember the look on Jesus' face as He told them of the Promise of the Father. He can still hear the excitement in the voice of the ascending Lord as He told them of the baptism of the Holy Spirit. Now it has all taken place, and Peter attempts to update a group of people concerning this event. He addresses them, saying, *"Men of Judea and all who dwell in Jerusalem..."* (Acts 2:14). It must have been a massive crowd, for three thousand people responded to his message (Acts 2:41). They seemed to have come from all over the world (Acts 1:9-11).

This is a common sermon, preached repeatedly. It has been translated into thousands of languages. The message is nearly two thousand years old. And most significantly, it has become a part of the sacred writings of the Word of God, inspired by the Holy Spirit. We investigate it because of the insight it gives us into the ascension of Jesus.

The message begins with **Peter, standing up with the eleven, raised his voice and said to them,** (Acts 2:14). He states his proposition for the sermon (Acts 2:14-21), and he reads the passage from which it comes. Having accomplished this, he addresses them again, *"Men of Israel, hear these words:"* (Acts 2:22). He begins to trace the movement of God, through Jesus, from His earthly ministry, through the cross, and into the resurrection (Acts 2:22-24). As he prepares to present the ascension of Jesus, he quotes King David (Acts 2:25-28). He assures us King David, *"is both dead and buried, and his tomb is with us to this day,"* (Acts 2:29).

However, *"This Jesus God raised up, of which we are all witnesses. Therefore being exalted to the right hand of God, and having received from the Father the promise of the Holy Spirit,*

Part Four: The Ascension

He poured out this which you now see and hear, (Acts 2:32-33). The insight Peter shares with us is the fact of the intimate tie between the ascension and the outpouring of the Holy Spirit. Pentecost came because Jesus ascended. It was the promise of Jesus to His disciples. *"Nevertheless I tell you the truth. It is to your advantage that I go away; for if I do not go away, the Helper will not come to you; but if I depart, I will send Him to you,"* (John 16:7). A part of the ascension ministry was the sending of the Holy Spirit to us! What Jesus had within Himself, He wanted us to experience also. We want to look at the details of Peter's message.

God Has A Plan

The Jews to whom Peter was preaching knew that God had a plan. A part of that plan was the Feast of the Passover, and a multitude of people had gathered in Jerusalem to celebrate this occasion. Because they believed God had a plan, they were faithful to observe and maintain their traditions. Their history was a constant unfolding of God's plan. The education of their children contained the marvelous acts of God fulfilling His plan. Every time they offered a sacrifice, it was a statement about the plan of God and its fulfillment.

In this sermon, Peter brings the people up to date concerning the plan of God. There is a strong focus on the movement of God. One walks away from hearing this message with an overwhelming awareness that God has initiated it all. God has a plan.

Peter begins with the fact that "God Proved." *"Men of Israel, hear these words: Jesus of Nazareth, a Man attested by God to you by miracles, wonders, and signs..."* (Acts 2:22). The Greek word, translated *attested,* has the idea of proving. It has the emphasis of showing off. God is no longer hiding in concealment.

The Ascension Plan | Acts 1:9-11

In the fullness of time, God decided to step out and show off who He is (Galatians 4:4).

Peter proceeds with the fact that "God Poieo." *"Jesus of Nazareth, a Man attested by God to you by miracles, wonders, and signs which God did through Him in your midst, as you yourselves also know - "* (Acts 2:22). What is it exactly that God is showing off? The idea of the Greek word, *poieo,* is creative nature. It paints the picture of something flowing from the heart of the individual who produces and brings something into existence, such as a work of art or a score of music. It is contrasted with duty and obligation, like that of a required job. The same word is used in connection with the creation event in the Greek translation of the Old Testament. God has shown off His creative nature before mankind. It is unlike any other revelation we have ever experienced from God. Obviously the plan of God has to do with this direct revelation of Himself. This revelation took place in the middle of those Peter was addressing, so they knew what he was proposing.

The next thing Peter speaks of is "God Purposed." *"Him, being delivered by the determined purpose and foreknowledge of God,"* (Acts 2:23). This has the idea of having been designated. It was on purpose and came from the foreknowledge of God, who desired it. This statement carries with it the concept of a decree. In His sovereignty, God has decreed this great plan.

It is not surprising to know that the next step is "God Produced." God has thrown all of His energy and effort into the accomplishment of the plan. Peter preaches, *"whom God raised up, having loosed the pains of death, because it was not possible that He should be held by it,"* (Acts 2:24). The production of God was done through an untying. God simply untied the cords of death that had bound Jesus, which produced the resurrection.

What is the basis of all this action of God? It is simply "God Promised." The promise was actually given to King David.

Part Four: The Ascension

"Therefore, being a prophet, and knowing that God has sworn with an oath to him that of the fruit of his body, according to the flesh, He would raise up the Christ to sit on his throne," (Acts 2:30). God always keeps His promises.

Do you see the strong emphasis on God having a plan? God proved (Acts 2:22), God poieo (Acts 2:22), God purposed (Acts 2:23), God produced (Acts 2:24), and God promised (Acts 2:30). God has a plan!

Jesus Is The Plan

The Jews had come by the hundreds to Jerusalem for the religious holiday. Peter addresses them, and his message assumes they know the details concerning the life of Jesus Christ. Evidently this was talked widely among the Jewish population. In fact, in his message, Peter says, *"as you yourselves also know,"* (Acts 2:22). Could it be there was controversy over the life of Jesus and His ministry? Certainly there was much discussion by everyone concerning His death and possible resurrection!

Peter does not hesitate to address the issue. He uses blunt confrontation. His message is plainly that "Jesus is the plan of God." Peter highlights the "Plan of God in the Earthly Ministry of Jesus" when he says, *"Men of Israel, hear these words: Jesus of Nazareth, a Man attested by God to you by miracles, wonders, and signs which God did through Him in your midst, as you yourselves also know - "* (Acts 2:22). Jesus was a Man possessed by the Spirit of God. God proving and showing off through this Man, by miracles, signs, and wonders. The creative Spirit of God dwelt in Jesus, and He was manifesting God's heart in the midst of the world. This was not only the plan for Jesus, but the plan for all mankind. Jesus was the beginning of a new breed of man, being the demonstration of the heart of God. It was the new covenant provided by the new promises based on the new and superior sacrifice. Jesus is the focus of this plan!

Now Peter moves to relate the "Plan of God in the Crucifixion of Jesus." He makes this most intriguing statement. ***"Him, being delivered by the determined purpose and foreknowledge of God, you have taken by lawless hands, have crucified, and put to death;"*** (Acts 2:23). The absolute fact is that God, the Father, delivered Jesus to the cross. It was His plan. He manipulated the histories of the world to time the event. God, in His sovereignty, calculated into His plan the **lawless hands** of men. Men were strutting around as if they were in charge of plotting the crucifixion, when they were simply falling into the plan of God. God's plot was much bigger than theirs. It is an awesome thought to realize the sovereign God and lawless men worked together to fulfill the plan, which is Jesus crucified for the redemption of the world.

But the plan of God did not end here. It also included the "Resurrection of Jesus." Peter continued in his speaking with the words, ***"whom God raised up, having loosed the pains of death, because it was not possible that He should be held by it,"*** (Acts 2:24). The resurrection of Christ was a result of the sovereign God's plan. He untied the painful cords of death and released Jesus.

David prophesied of this in the Old Testament (Acts 2:25-28). As Peter speaks to the Jewish crowd, he purposely shows Jesus as far superior to their **patriarch David,** (Acts 2:29). He reminds the listeners ***"that he is both dead and buried, and his tomb is with us to this day,"*** (Acts 2:29). The fulfillment of the plan of God is not David, but Jesus. David is only significant because of the role he played in the plan of God, and the plan is Jesus.

The "Plan of God in the Ascension of Jesus" is also highlighted by Peter. ***"Therefore being exalted to the right hand of God, ..."*** (Acts 2:33). The plan of God is for Jesus to sit at **the right hand of God** and rule over the Kingdom. It is the fulfillment of the promise of King David ***that of the fruit of his***

body, according to the flesh, He would raise up the Christ to sit on his throne, (Acts 2:30). Jesus ascended to this position, having established the Kingdom according to the plan of God. God has an amazing plan, and it is Jesus!

The Spirit of Jesus Is the Climax of the Plan

Remember that Peter is giving the Jews an up date on the plan of God. They have just witnessed Pentecost, the outpouring of the Holy Spirit. He reminds them that God has a significant plan, and the plan is Jesus. We see it in His earthly ministry as God works through Him. The plan of God is fulfilled in the crucifixion, the resurrection, and now the ascension.

As Peter comes to the ascension ministry of Jesus, he gives tremendous insight into the climax of the plan of God. Everything God has been doing through the ages has been focused on, and pointing to, this single thing. Think of the energy God has expended in order to bring about this one dream. As the ascension takes place, God's heart must be beating fast in anticipation of the fulfillment of His desire. This is what He has wanted all along. This is His purpose for giving the law. The sacrificial lambs and all the temple ceremonies were to prepare for this one thing. This is what it is all about!

Jesus ascends to the right hand of the Father (Acts 2:33). The Kingdom of God is now complete with Jesus as the proper King. His first official act in the ascension ministry is to receive the promise from the Father. Jesus instructed His disciples concerning this promise. He called it, ***the Promise of the Father,*** (Acts 1:4). Those who heard this sermon were asking, *"Men and brethren, what shall we do?"* (Acts 2:37). Peter gave them good instruction, and then encouraged them by saying, ***"For the promise is to you and to your children, and to all who are afar off, as many as the Lord our God will call,"*** (Acts 2:39).

This is the grand moment when God fulfills His dream for mankind. All He wants to do within the life of man He now pours out. We can experience the Promise of the Father. Peter states it this way in his sermon, *"Therefore being exalted to the right hand of God, and having received from the Father the promise of the Holy Spirit, He poured out this which you now see and hear,"* (Acts 2:33).

The structure of this verse is very important. The main verb is **poured out.** The One who is doing the action is Jesus. He has just received the promise from the Father. It is Jesus in His ascension ministry who is giving the fullness of the Holy Spirit to us! The verb is in the aorist active indicative. This means it has a sense of completion about it (aorist). The subject is responsible for the action of the verb (active). It is a simple statement of fact (indicative). The Greek word, translated **poured out**, paints a picture far beyond simply giving. It has the idea of abundance or gushing. It is used in connection with the pouring out of the blood of Christ. In the same exact lavish manner, Jesus offers Himself as the sacrifice, so now He abundantly gushes forth the fullness of His Spirit. He is not stingy in bestowing His Spirit upon us. He wants us to have the fullness.

The rest of the verse is basically made up of participles. These participles act as adverbs and give content to the main verb. **Being exalted** is one of them. **Having received** is another. Peter tells us the lavish outpouring of the Holy Spirit is a direct result of the ascension and exaltation of Christ. All He experiences in oneness with the Father, Jesus wants us to have. As He lives by the power of the Holy Spirit, He is anxious for us to experience the same. This is not a side benefit or a minor issue. This is the heart of what God purposes and determines for the new covenant in Christ. It is intimacy with Him in a new way.

Have you experienced the lavish, abundant outpouring of the Spirit of Jesus in your life?

PREPARING FOR PENTECOST

Acts 1:11-14

RETURNING TO JERUSALEM

If we are ever to understand the Scriptures, there is much we need to know about the culture of the day in which it was written. In each particular scene, the people have a mind set, a way of doing things. We must place ourselves in the middle of the action, striving to understand and experience the cultural surroundings of those about whom we are reading. Think of what the disciples have had thrust upon them. They were now in fear of their own lives. They had given themselves completely to Jesus, and His death was a major blow to them. How will they ever recover from this? Can they ever believe in another who proposes to be the Messiah? If Jesus was not the Messiah, will there ever really be one?

Now they are impacted by Jesus' resurrection from the dead. It is not just an event in their lives, but it becomes a continual flow of life as they spend forty days with the resurrected Lord (Acts 1:3). The instruction and insight of Jesus concerning the Kingdom of God changes them forever. He clears up all questions in their minds about His redemptive ability, and they now understand His call upon their lives. This is not a side issue to them, and it is not a portion of their lives. They are absolutely consumed with Christ. Can you feel this within them?

Think of the schedule of events they have experienced. The crucifixion took place on the Feast of the Passover. From that day to the Feast of Pentecost was a period of fifty days. Three

Part Five: Preparing For Pentecost

of those days were occupied with the crucifixion and burial of Christ. Forty days were spent in the resurrection appearances and the ascension of Christ (Acts 1:9-11). Only one week, seven days, remains before the day of Pentecost. Jesus is gone from their presence. They return to Jerusalem. They feel alone and without adequate leadership. What are they going to do during these seven days? What atmosphere surrounds the group? Who is actually present? What attitude do they have, and what is their perspective on things? These are the questions Luke seems to be dealing with in this paragraph.

As we view this passage (Acts 1:12-14), the element of obedience seems to stand forth. We see it in the heart of the passage as well as the flow of the context. Just before Jesus ascends to the Father, He gives the disciples instructions on what they are to do during the seven days remaining before Pentecost. In this paragraph we see them take the beginning steps to obey those instructions.

But as we have consistently discovered, obedience may not be what we have always thought it to be. There is a Biblical view of obedience which gives a different perspective. We can best express it in the word "response." Obedience is far above the accomplishment of certain tasks or actions. Obedience is located in the inner attitude of the disciples. It is not centered on their actions, but in their responses. It is their motive and heart passion! It is difficult for us to grasp because we have been trained that obedience is carrying out someone's demands. We pass the test of obedience if we accomplish what is demanded of us. What other kind of obedience could there be?

The New Testament presents us with a new picture of obedience. Christian obedience flows from relationship. It is not our action as much as our heart motive. It is not contained within the act of doing, but rather in the heart of responding. It is a call to shift in source from self-initiated action to God-initiated action. The obedience of response has a different focus!

Response
Acts 1:12

In describing the action of the disciples after the ascension of Christ, Luke is very selective in the word he chooses. ***Then they returned to Jerusalem from the mount called Olivet, which is near Jerusalem, a Sabbath day's journey*** (Acts 1:12). Luke plants the disciple's actions of the next seven days leading into Pentecost in the phrase, ***Then they returned.*** The Greek word he uses gives a much stronger picture than a physical movement or change of location. A physical action is present in what Luke says, however, he tells us something which is beyond this. He wants us to know the inner heart of the disciples. What are they feeling?

This same Greek word is used in Peter's writings to speak of turning back from belief. Peter paints a strong picture which warns us not to waver. He urges us to not turn back to the unrighteousness we once knew. What is there to go back to? ***For it would have been better for them not to have known the way of righteousness, than having known it, to turn from the holy commandment delivered to them. But it has happened to them according to the true proverb: "A dog returns to his own vomit," and, "a sow, having washed, to her wallowing in the mire,"*** (2 Peter 2:21-24).

What the disciples are doing in this word parallels the concept of repentance. They make a complete about face. It is the positive use of the word, while Peter uses it in the negative way. They are restored and see again the wonder of the Gospel. The disciples had lost all hope in Jerusalem. They feared for their lives in Jerusalem; now they rejoice and praise God in the Jerusalem temple. They lost the vision of redemption in Jerusalem; now they turn to the vision and purpose of life in Jerusalem. They are admitting they have been wrong. They experience a dramatic shift in their attitudes.

Part Five: Preparing For Pentecost

Their response is incredible! Though they are active, their response is not to do something. They respond in surrender that God might do something in and through them. Their response is not to do something, but to wait on Him. They return to Jerusalem in response to what Jesus instructed them before He ascended. He told them ***not to depart from Jerusalem, but to wait for the Promise of the Father,*** (Acts 1:4). Their waiting is not from laziness or inactivity. They are about to be more involved in ministry than they have ever been. Again the waiting is a call to an attitude which will possess them for the rest of their lives. They have an attitude of response. They no longer source themselves, but the Spirit of Jesus is their source. They consistently look to Him; He is the stimulus which will move them in ministry. They live responding.

Luke highlights the Mount of Olives in this verse. That is very significant. ***Then they returned to Jerusalem from the mount called Olivet, which is near Jerusalem, a Sabbath day's journey,*** (Acts 1:12). The Mount of Olives is a limestone ridge which runs north and south, covering the eastern side of the city of Jerusalem. It is slightly more than a mile in length. There have been several explanations for this emphasis. Perhaps Luke was giving this information to his Gentile reader, Theophilus, (Acts 1:1). Any Jewish reader would already have this knowledge. Perhaps it was a sentimental memory of events gone by which slipped into his writings.

But you need to go beyond this kind of thinking and remember what the Mount of Olives was to Jesus. It was a retreat center on several occasions, but especially during the Passion Week. He would go to the Mount of Olives at night. After preaching His last public message, which followed a pressure filled day when the leaders of Israel questioned Him (Tuesday), He went to the Mount of Olives with His disciples (Matthew 24:3). The Mount of Olives was also a training center for Jesus. He gave the parables of judgment in response to the disciples questioning (Matthew 24:3).

Returning to Jerusalem | **Acts 1:11-14**

It was also a prayer center for Jesus. The Garden of Gethsemane was located on the Mount of Olives, and this is where Jesus took His disciples to pray. They followed this practice when they were in the area. It was a small private garden surrounded by a fence and a locked gate. Jesus had been given a key by the owner for His own personal use. The Mount of Olives marked a place where great events took place. At this point in the time of our study, the disciples had just experienced the ascension of Jesus in this place.

In comparison to what Jesus feels about this area, think of what Jerusalem is to the disciples. It became the center of conflict for them. Every time they ventured into Jerusalem with Jesus, the conflict increased, finally climaxing in His death. Now Jerusalem contained nothing but a threat to their personal safety. They knew the leaders of Israel would stop at nothing to eliminate the continuation of the ministry of Christ. Every one of these disciples was from Galilee, which was eighty to one hundred miles north of Jerusalem. It was an entirely different place with a different environment. It was country atmosphere instead of the city pressure of Jerusalem. Galilee lacked the scholarship and refinement, while Jerusalem prided itself in those things. Everything which produced discomfort for the disciples was found in Jerusalem. No doubt their very hearts cry out to escape back to Galilee where they can find safety and comfort.

But they are responding to Jesus. They are not responding to accomplish a task and then they can leave. They are not on an errand which will last several days, and then they will be free to do as they desire. They do not slip into Jerusalem from the Mount of Olives in the night and run back to safety in the morning. They surrender completely to the action and planning which is going to take place in and through them. Their response is to wait on Him. This will be the tone of all Christian experience from now on. It is our call as well. We have been focused on doing and accomplishment instead of waiting on His sourcing. We have become self-sourced instead of God-sourced. We have moved with what seems to be good in our minds instead of responding to His mind. Perhaps we too need to return to God's original plan for us. We need to respond to Him.

Response in Detail

The disciples did not just decide to return to Jerusalem. They responded directly to the instructions of Christ. Jesus was with them for forty days in His resurrection presence. On the final day, just before He ascended, He gave them a focus for the next seven days. Let's review those instructions. ***And being assembled together with them, He commanded them not to depart from Jerusalem, but to wait for the Promise of the Father,*** "*which,*" He said, "*you have heard from Me:*" (Acts 1:4).

The Greek word translated, ***being assembled together with them,*** gives us a clue to the intensity of the atmosphere. It is one which is really close, united, and filled with His presence. The actual word means "gathered together," however, there is a prefix added to this word as used in this verse. It is the prefix "together." Thus, a literal translation is "together gathered together." Luke intensifies the idea of the closeness of the fellowship and the concentration upon each other. Be sure and keep this tight focus as we view the rest of the instruction.

He commanded them is the bold statement of the verse (Acts 1:4). This Greek word is very specific. It does not refer to a list of orders or duties. Jesus did not give them distinct tasks to perform while waiting in Jerusalem the last seven days before Pentecost. If He had, we would have taken the list and made it a requirement for all who wanted to experience the Promise of the Father. This Greek word has to do with "enjoined." It is about a focus, a direction, or an emphasis. It is a military term which pictures the commanding officer coming along side his men, giving them instruction and encouragement. Jesus focuses them on the **Promise of the Father** (Acts 1:4), being **baptized with the Holy Spirit** (Acts 1:5), and being sourced by God **when the Holy Spirit has come upon you** (Acts 1:8).

Now Jesus gives them an atmosphere in which they are to maintain this focus. **He commanded them not to depart from Jerusalem, but to wait for the Promise of the Father** (Acts 1:4). The Greek word translated *wait* has to do with anticipation, or eagerly, excitedly, expectantly. They were not to bear the load and do their duty. They were to respond with great joy to the focus of the Promise of the Father. This is exactly what they did. They did not hide in an upper room but **were continually in the temple praising and blessing God** (Luke 24:53). The focus was upon what Jesus had done and what He was going to do in and through them.

Response of Faith

The disciples are not meeting in an upper room, holding evangelism seminars on winning the world. They are not entering into special educational classes for development of leadership. They are simply responding to Christ in faith. What He said will be true, and they are waiting with great expectation. They know it will be true because they have experienced His resurrection. They have absolute faith in Him.

The disciples are not meeting in an upper room, holding evangelism seminars on winning the world. They are not entering into special educational classes for development of leadership. They are simply responding to Christ in faith. What He said will be true, and they are waiting with great expectation. They know it will be true because they have experienced His resurrection. They have absolute faith in Him.

Response is always based on faith in God. Self-sourcing results from faith in oneself. Doing is an act of faith also, but it

Part Five: Preparing For Pentecost

is a faith in self. It is ironic how we state our faith in Christ and then do everything we can to accomplish it on our own. It is so hard to die to self-sourcing. But there will be no Pentecost without it. The Promise of the Father always comes when we are in a position of response. It will be the explanation for the rest of the Book of Acts. It will not be the Acts of the Apostles, but the Acts of the Holy Spirit. The disciples were definitely involved. They participated intimately in all that took place. But they were not the source. They were responding.

We must return to this simple truth. The Gospel is not a challenge to Do, but to RESPOND.

Acts 1:14

ONE ACCORD

Most of us have studied the lives of the disciples enough to feel like we know them. Through Bible reading, Sunday school, and church, we have become very familiar with them. This sometimes causes us to take them for granted. We know their faults and their shortcomings. If you are like me, you tend to look over most of their foibles because you identify with such things in your life.

One of the visible faults of the twelve apostles during their three years with Jesus is division. They are always in a struggle to establish power and position. It is the way they approach the Kingdom of God. They expect a military move from Jesus. Rome must be eliminated if Jesus is to establish the Kingdom of God and rule the world. They ask the question, "What will be our role in this coming Kingdom?" After all, as disciples of Jesus, they should have responsible positions of influence in the coming Kingdom. They see great importance in Jesus deciding this before He establishes the Kingdom.

The disciples were constantly exploding within their group. One time they came to Jesus after long hours of debate and argument. They demand that Christ settle the issue at hand. What is distressing them? *At that time the disciples came to Jesus, saying, "Who then is greatest in the kingdom of heaven?"* (Matthew 18:1). They want Him to establish the pecking order of their group. It is not the only time they request such a thing.

Part Five: Preparing For Pentecost

James and John got their mother to come and ask Jesus if they could have the right-hand and left-hand positions in the coming Kingdom (Matthew 20:20-21). How did their request affect the other disciples? ***And when the ten heard it, they were greatly displeased with the two brothers*** (Matthew 20:24).

When the Rich Young Ruler rejected the call of Christ, Jesus gave the disciples a discourse on the danger of riches. Peter responded with the question, ***"See, we have left all and followed You. Therefore what shall we have?"*** (Matthew 19:27). It is the kind of attitude which created the division among the group.

At this time in our study Jesus has been with the disciples for forty days of resurrection appearances. He has now ascended (Acts 1:9-11). Only seven days remain until "The Promise of the Father." They do not know the time frame, but they do know Jesus' instruction was simply to ***wait for the Promise of the Father*** (Acts 1:4). The group is no longer just the twelve minus Judas. Their number has grown to one hundred and twenty (Acts 1:15).

The group is waiting in an atmosphere of expectancy and anticipation. They are on the very brink of seeing the Kingdom of God fulfilled as Jesus promised. But He did not give them orders of authority or leadership. He left them no flow chart of the organizational structure, spelling out who would fill what positions. He is now gone. More people have rushed in to threaten the security of the key positions the disciples have coveted.

Luke makes a point to stress the fact of the presence of the brothers of Christ in this waiting period of seven days. ***These all continued with one accord in prayer, with the women and Mary the mother of Jesus, and with His brothers*** (Acts 1:14). One of these brothers was James, the writer of one of the books of the New Testament. He seems to be the leader in the early organization of the church (Acts 1:5). Can you hear the eleven apostles talking among themselves in the corner of the upper

One Accord | **Acts 1:14**

room? They may be looking at the brothers of Christ with scorn. After all, they were not followers of Christ during His three years of ministry. They had even come to take Jesus home at one point because they thought he was mentally unstable (Matthew 12:46). Jesus' brothers did not become believers in Him until the crucifixion. It would not surprise us to have heard Peter say something like, "I suppose they think because of their family relationship with Jesus they can march in here and take over! Well, it is not going to happen!" With the growth of any group comes the threat to the leadership position. Division is inevitable in this group!

Look carefully at the list of the eleven disciples (Acts 1:13). It is the same as is written in the previous gospel accounts with the exception of Judas, the betrayer (Matthew 10:3; Mark 3:18; Luke 6:14). They are divided into three groups of four each. (With Judas gone, there are only three listed in the last group.) Peter is always listed at the beginning of the first group. Philip heads the second group, and James, the son of Alphaeus, seems to be the leader of the third group. Thus, the division spreads from individuals who seek position to groups who are jealous and want control. The upper room is filled with political groups, all looking for opportunities to advance to the top place of authority.

To add to the mix, there are women present. Each woman has her own opinion and will want to express it. Mary, the mother of Jesus is there. Does she think she will have a special right to oversee the operation of this group? Jesus gave these women liberation, and they will no doubt wish to express it to these men. Division is surely inevitable in this group.

This gathering of people has no idea their waiting period is only seven days. If we base this group's reaction on their past record of disharmony, we cannot see them making it through the week. They are waiting. Doesn't patience always wear thin when we have to wait? They are anxious about the promise coming to pass. They may expect it to happen on their first

Part Five: Preparing For Pentecost

day back in Jerusalem, which was probably a Thursday. They come to the end of the day with some disappointment, but console themselves that it is only the first day after all. The voice of Jesus is still fresh in their memories. Then Friday and Saturday pass. Did any of them question that they were wasting their time? How long will this go on? Surely Sunday, the first day of the week will be the day. That would be perfect for it is the day of the resurrection from the dead celebration. It would be the ideal time for the promise to be fulfilled. But Sunday comes and goes.

Do you think they discussed among themselves what they were waiting for? They knew they were waiting on the Promise of the Father, but what exactly did that mean? They had not experienced this in reality. It was only a concept and teaching of Jesus at this point. Monday and Tuesday are filled with more prayer and praise at the temple, but no answer comes. You can see how nerves would begin to wear thin. Certainly doubts would arise and someone was bound to question how long they were to maintain this period of waiting. When might they draw the line and quit? How long do they want to give to this waiting? If there was ever a set up for division, this was surely it. Division is inevitable in this group, don't you think?

The waiting gave great opportunity for theological division. Jesus gave special instructions, but did they all hear and understand it the same way? Were all of them there all of the time? Can you hear the differences of opinion as each tries to quote what Jesus actually said? Knowing this group as we do, we can hear the raised voices and the debates rise in strength. They were famous for making a mess of Jesus' teachings. Even after the Mount of Transfiguration, Jesus told them to, *"tell the vision to no one..."* (Matthew 17:9). He knew their confusion would cause them to misinterpret the wonder of the occasion. Only three of the disciples were present then. Now there are one hundred and twenty, each with their own viewpoint of what Jesus said.

One Accord | **Acts 1:14**

Division is inevitable in this group.

Surely the best thing to do is to allow the three groups of disciples to separate. Peter is the head of one group. He and his group can go to another section of Jerusalem and wait there, or better yet, they can demand to stay in the upper room and have the other groups leave. Peter can call his denomination "The Church of the Rock," because Jesus gave him that title (Matthew 16:18). Philip, as head of the second denomination, can go to the east side of town. They can call their group "The Miracle Church," because Philip is the one who really headed up the feeding of the five thousand (John 6:3). Compassionate ministry can be their focus. James, the son of Alphaeus, will lead the smallest group or denomination, and this makes sense because he is called, "The Less." They can call their group "The True Way," since Jesus preached, *"Because narrow is the gate and difficult is the way which leads to life, and there are few who find it,"* (Matthew 7:14). We grow through dividing, so this is really a good thing. Division is inevitable in this group.

With all of these excuses, we are startled by this statement. *These all continued with one accord in prayer, with the women and Mary the mother of Jesus, and with His brothers* (Acts 1:14). How can they possibly be in one accord? What exactly does that mean? Can we duplicate it in the church today? Is this what allows the Spirit of God to do His fullest and finest purpose through the body of Christ?

Let us focus on the phrase *one accord.* This is a translation of one Greek word. It is used eleven times in the New Testament, and ten of those are found in the Book of Acts. The Amplified New Testament translates it, *with their minds in full agreement.* Many other translations say it is simply *one mind.* This Greek word seems to be designed to help us understand the uniqueness of the Christian community. The Greek word is actually two words which have been combined. They mean "rushing away" and "in unison." The Greek language paints

Part Five: Preparing For Pentecost

a picture. In this case it is the picture of an orchestra. This large group of musicians plays together on various instruments, strings, brass, woodwinds, and percussion. As they play the same musical notes, the different sounds harmonize in pitch and tone. All of the musicians with their various instruments are under the direction of a concert master, and together they make beautiful music.

There is another important aspect of this Greek word which adds description to the picture. The word denotes the inner unity of the group as the people are engaged in an externally similar action. This term does not denote the personal sympathy of these participants, but points to the harmony through a material interest in a specific action. This material interest is not based on a similarity of inclination or disposition, but upon an event which comes on a group from without and provokes a common reaction.

This group of one hundred and twenty individuals has just come through fifty days of intense study on the Kingdom of God (Acts 1:3), and it has drawn them together. They have experienced the Resurrected Lord during these forty days. The ascension astounded them. It took them beyond their concept of a military Kingdom of God. In light of all they experienced, what could the **Promise of the Father** have in store for them? The resurrected Lord's call for them to go into the all world is linked with this promise. THIS has become the captivating focus in their lives. It pushes aside all of their personal preferences and desires. Can it now be summarized in WHO IS HE? They have become so enthralled in who He is nothing else seems to matter. They have been captured by His person, and they have lost sight of everything else. Christ became so important to them, everything else was secondary. *These all continued with one accord...* (Acts 1:14).

Focus

Whatever the external activity of interest is that unites a group, it is the supreme and most significant thing to each of its individual members. The thing that unites them is their focus. When all the members of the group began to focus on the same thing they became of *one accord.* The disciples in Matthew's account are focused on the same thing. They have the same passionate desire. It is the Kingdom of God and their position in the Kingdom. This unites them! But wait, it did not unite them; it divided them. They came arguing about who was going to be number one in the coming Kingdom (Matthew 18:1). So when they were focused on position and organizational structure, they were divided.

The leaders of Israel were focused on the preservation and protection of Israel as a nation. This included the temple building with its ceremonies, laws and traditions. This united them! But wait, it did not unite them. It divided them. The Pharisees could not stand the Sadducees. The scribes were trying to dominate both groups. They were definitely separated from the Gentiles and would not embrace Jesus and His disciples. Division was strong among them. So when the leaders of Israel focused on their personal doctrine, ceremonies, and positions, they were divided.

The same thing is true in our families. Both husband and wife are focused on having a happy home. However, this does not unite them; it divides them. The husband is interested in maintaining control as head of the house. The wife feels threatened and attempts to bring equality into the relationship. She feels disharmony and arguments are the result of this external focus.

When a group focuses on an external activity with their entire beings, will this bring unity? Isn't it obvious this proposition is not true? But wait! What if they focus on the person of Christ?

Suppose they spend forty days with His resurrected person and are totally enthralled with who He is? What if they seek His will with passionate commitment? All they desire is for Him to live His life through them in the Promise of the Father. Will this bring them into *one accord*? If we focus on tradition, ceremony, position, or control, division is inevitable. But when we seek Him and Him alone, we find unity which allows His Spirit to work through us.

Force

The external activity of a group unites them, becoming the force of the group. The common interest which drives and motivates the action of the group is the desire for the fulfillment of this activity. What unified the disciples was their desire to see the military Kingdom of God in their day. They long to be a part of the establishment of that Kingdom, which will give them the right to positions of influence. But wait, this does not unite them; it divides them. The leaders of Israel are driven by one motivation. They want to see a strong Kingdom of Israel. This factor divides them among themselves, as well as from the Gentiles and from their own Messiah. Our families are united because we have one drive and motivation to establish a home and relationships. But wait, this does not unite us. It divides us. Who is going to control this relationship? What role will I get to play, and will my needs be met?

The proposition that a group motivated by a single force is united is not true. Though the motivation may be single, the perspective of each person in the group is varied. The only driving force which will not divide is Jesus. If we had spent the forty days with Jesus, experiencing His resurrection and hearing His instructions, we would be captivated and motivated by His person. Just as the disciples, there would be nothing else of importance in our lives? This would bring us to *one accord*, just as it had for those gathered in the upper room. Every other motivation, even religious, divides, but Jesus unites.

Familiarity

When an external activity unites a group, that activity is the one thing they know, study and discuss. It occupies their minds and dominates their conversations. This activity strongly influences every thing they do, and they are united. The disciples are absolutely determined to have positions and authority in the coming Kingdom. They are always discussing it within their group and with Jesus. But wait! They argue over the pecking order of the organizational structure of the coming Kingdom. It does not unite them; it divides them.

As for the leaders of Israel, their occupation is the importance of the law. It has become their tradition. They spend long hours discussing it, and they develop its application to their lives. Thus, they are united. But wait! They spend their days debating its application and judge each other repeatedly. It does not unite them; it divides them.

The same thing applies to our families and relationships with each other. Even though we study, discuss, and know about a single subject, it does not unite us. But what would happen if we had just spent forty days with the resurrected Christ? Our inner spirits would be utterly captivated by Him. We would not be able to talk about anything else. Everything that happened to us, we would see in the context of His reality. We would be united, not divided. The only possibility of being in *one accord* is Jesus. Outside of Him is nothing but disharmony.

Acts 1:14

LET'S PRAY

The disciples are preparing for Pentecost. All creation anticipates the moment when the Spirit of God will be outpoured. This anticipation has been building since the first sin of man (Genesis 3). God has been moving man from the absolute disaster and devastation of relationship to the reconciliation and restoration of Pentecost. He is going to fulfill His dreams and plans for man. At this point in time He will accomplish the single purpose for which He made man. Man will become the flesh through which God can live. What happened in the life of Christ can now happen in whosoever will.

In our study thus far, we uncovered the elements which seem to be present as the final seven days of preparation are fulfilled. One such element is "repentance," **Then they returned to Jerusalem...** (Acts 1:12). It is the concept of returning back to what they had lost. In the instructions of Jesus, it was ***wait*** (Acts 1:4). They are not to wait as one waiting for an event. They are not to simply spend time. They are to rest, yield and depend upon God, and come out of themselves. It is not to be a waiting for the seven days, but it is to be a permanent attitude they will maintain as the Spirit acts in and through them.

Secondly, there is the element of ***one accord.*** It is the extreme focus on the person of Christ. He is superior above everything else. All of the other things have not changed or been eliminated, but Jesus has become the only thing they see.

The issues over which they once argued and were divided are still present, but they have set them aside. Someone much bigger has captivated them, and they have lost interest in what they once thought important. They have just spent forty days with the resurrected Lord. He has absolutely consumed them.

The third element is perseverance, which we will discuss in the next chapter of our study. Our focus at this time will be on the element of prayer.

These elements are more than simply preparatory issues. None of these things disappear when the Promise of the Father is given. The Greek word for **one accord** is used eleven times in the New Testament, and ten of those times are in the Book of Acts. This was not only a characteristic of the disciples in preparation for the coming of the Holy Spirit, but they maintained it as the Spirit moved through them into their world. Their focus on Jesus was what enabled them to come in **one accord**. This was evident in them throughout the Book of Acts. Paul declared this to be the subject of his preaching. **For I determined not to know anything among you except Jesus Christ and Him crucified** (1 Corinthians 2:2).

The same is true with the element of prayer. The Greek word translated **prayer** in Acts 1:4 is in the noun form. It is used thirty-seven times in the New Testament, and nine of those times are found in the Book of Acts. The verb form of this same word is used sixteen times in the Book of Acts. As you go through this book it appears they are always in a state of prayer.

The elements necessary for the coming of the Holy Spirit are the same elements necessary for living in the Holy Spirit. The disciples' response during these seven days of waiting will be the same response they will maintain in the ministry of the Holy Spirit. Any lack of these elements in our lives will hinder us from knowing the fullness of the Spirit of Jesus.

Let us focus our attention on the element of prayer. Our verse says, **These all continued with one accord in prayer, with**

Part Five: Preparing For Pentecost

the women and Mary the mother of Jesus, and with His brothers (Acts 1:14). This Greek word translated *in prayer* is a noun and is used thirty-seven times in the New Testament. Only eight of those usages are found in the Gospel accounts. If you look carefully at those Scriptures you will discover they are always related to Jesus. Even more amazing, the verb form of this word is used forty-seven times in the Gospel accounts. Every time it refers to what Jesus does or is used in the words of Jesus. The disciples are never seen in the action of this word.

If that is true, the disciples enter into a new experience in this verse (Acts 1:14). For the first time they participate in what Jesus has taught them. He ascended to the right hand of the Father, and they are now praying in His name. Opening before them is a new era of interaction between God and man. Were they aware as they prayed that He had gone behind the veil for them in the Holy tabernacle not made by hands? Jesus, at that moment, was making intercession for them (Hebrews 7:23). Not one of the one hundred and twenty stopped and cried out, "Let us ask the Father in His name." (John 16:23-24).

Can you imagine the amazement of the angels? They had rejoiced often over the prayers of a repenting sinner, but now, for the first time ever, they can hear the prayers authorized and accredited by the name of the only begotten of the Father. They were prayers based on the name which just recently became *a name which is above every name* (Philippians 2:9). Can you imagine the joy of that first hour of praying in the name of Christ? Something new is taking place! There is a new access and interaction between heaven and earth. Something is happening which was not possible before the new High Priest arrived.

How do you suppose the disciples are reacting? It is certainly not business as usual. They surely felt and sensed the newness of the activity of prayer. The ritual and chants before this time now turn into power and life. What a privilege it is to enter into a discourse with the heavenly realm. Now they can pray as they observed Jesus pray.

What exactly was this prayer in which they participated? How long did it take? What sacrifices did they make to do it? How vital is it to the experience for which God was preparing them? Let us begin by looking at the three basic words for prayer as they are listed by Timothy. This will give us the best picture of the distinction between the ideas suggested in the three words. ***Therefore, I exhort first of all that supplications, prayers, intercession, and giving of thanks be made for all men*** (1 Timothy 2:1). ***Supplications*** is a word which focuses on the expression of a need. It is the statement of a petition. It is possible for this word not only to be used in relationship to God, but also your fellow man. ***Prayers*** is the word in our study of Acts. It is used exclusively toward God and no one or anything else. It is a word of sacred character. It has the idea of devotion and fellowship. Then the word ***intercessions*** expresses childlike confidence as man expresses his heart to God.

The focus on the group's activity during these seven days of preparation is not intercessions or supplications, but it is on prayer. We gain understanding of the word's usage here (Acts 1:14), when we view the other places in the Scriptures where this word is used. Matthew quotes Jesus as saying, ***"It is written, 'My house shall be called a house of prayer,' but you have made it a 'den of thieves,'"*** (Matthew 21:13). The temple was not called a house of "intercession," nor was it called a house of "supplication." It is a house of prayer, which means far more than just a place to ask for something. It is a place of sacrificial offering, of worship, of cleansing, of fulfillment of activities related to relationship with God. It would be like calling your home a house of marriage. It means that everything connected with marriage is contained within that house. Eating, crying, laughing, resting, planning, dreaming, and loving are all a part of what takes place in this house. It is a place where two lives intersect.

Part Five: Preparing For Pentecost

This is the picture of prayer used in relationship to the one hundred and twenty. It is not a picture of being on your knees, yelling at the top of your lungs. It is the activities and aspects which pertain to intimacy with God. It is conversations about Him and with Him. It has to do with worship and singing. It is eating and knowing He provided the food for you. We have labeled this interaction "practicing His presence."

The last verse in volume one (The Gospel according to Luke), gives a description of the activities of the disciples during this seven-day period. Luke writes, *And they worshiped Him, and returned to Jerusalem with great joy, and were continually in the temple praising and blessing God, Amen* (Luke 24:52-53). This gives us the context of what is taking place in prayer. The prayer is an active participation in worship, singing, and speaking about Jesus. They are testifying and focusing on Christ. It encompasses the expression of Paul as he encouraged us to *pray without ceasing* (1 Thessalonians 5:17). This is a translation of the verb form of the Greek word Luke uses in Acts.

"What did you do today?"

"I spent the whole day in prayer."

"You mean you did not go to your job?"

"Oh, no, I went to work, picked the children up from school and ate supper with my family. All of that was prayer. In all of it there was an interaction with Jesus. A focus was happening between Jesus and me which could not be broken. I felt and experienced His influence constantly. I found myself in constant worship, which makes up fellowship and interaction on a moment by moment basis."

"Well, that sounds really spiritual, but I am not sure it is very practical. How can you possibly do that? How can you maintain such strong discipline? Even when I get down on my knees and pray, and I am not doing anything else, my mind wanders. If I cannot concentrate on Him when I have my eyes closed and my head bowed, how can I possibly focus on Him when there are activities rushing around me? I just get distracted. How can I do this kind of prayer you are talking about?"

"You have asked the wrong question."

Luke explains in Acts 1:14, why this question does not address the issue at hand. ***These all continued with one accord in prayer, with the women and Mary the mother of Jesus, and with His brothers*** (Acts 1:14). The subject of the sentence is two fold. ***These*** is the nominative case, which names it as the subject. But ***all*** is also in the nominative case, which names it as the subject. The main verb in the above translation appears to be ***continued***, but this is not true. There is a verb in the Greek writing of this verse which was not translated. It is the verb "am." We have discussed this verb several times in previous studies. It is a state of being, not action. This verb is in the third person, plural, imperfect tense, which causes us to translate it ***were.*** So the statement is actually, ***These all were…***

The Greek word translated ***continued*** is a verb in the form of a participle. It acts as an adverb, giving content to the state of being word ***were,*** so we would translate this as, ***These were continually…*** The New American Standard Version gives this translation. The main verb being in the imperfect tense gives you the sense of a continuous state of being. This is now doubly emphasized with the adverb ***continually***. Luke wants to be sure you are aware of the consistent flow of this state of being among these disciples.

The phrase, ***with one accord,*** is actually a translation of only one Greek word. It is an adverb which again gives content and modifies the main verb. The state of being which must be consistently maintained has a single mind and focus. So let us add this to our translation, ***These all in one accord were continually…***

Now we come to the point which frustrates all English professors. I spoke personally with an English teacher who was not able to reconcile what Luke does in this sentence. He gives

Part Five: Preparing For Pentecost

us the Greek word, a noun in the dative case, which is translated *in prayer*. There is no dative English grammar. In Greek grammar, there are four different kinds of dative. As Luke writes this dative, it serves as an indirect object. Prayer is the thing to which something is done or given. But this is impossible in the English for two reasons. First, there is no direct object, so there can be no indirect object. Secondly, there can be no direct object for a verb of being; it must be an action verb.

Our translation thus far is, **These all in one accord were continually...** Without trying to reconcile the fact that a verb of being cannot have a direct object, is not the direct object assumed? The one who is receiving the action of the state of being, or the focus, or the concentration of the state of being is Jesus. The disciples have just finished forty days of being in His personal presence. They are absolutely consumed with Him. This is the infallible proofs of His resurrection. They cannot think about anything else. Their entire conversation is about Him. Their praise and worship are all focused on Him. What they have become in their state of being is all acting on Him.

Prayer became the indirect object of the state of being. It is the thing to which their focus and conversation are done and given. The action of the verb of being is on Jesus, and they are given to the state of prayer. I am sure English teachers will have problems discussing this, but we are attempting to get at what Luke is saying. The disciples are worshiping, praying, blessing God, having fellowship, eating together, and discussing what is happening to them. It is all in the context of a state of being called prayer, because Jesus is the object of it all.

Prayer in this case ceases to be an activity or something you do and becomes who you are. When it is something you do, it creates guilt. How many hours should you pray? Is one hour a day enough to dedicate to the Christ who died for you? No wonder we feel guilty when we only pray an hour or less each day. Would two hours relieve that guilt? After all, think of all

He has done for us. Would three hours be enough? Do I have to devote all of my time to prayer? How can I do that? It is time to experience what the disciples experienced, and "be" prayer. We are to be so consumed with Jesus that nothing takes place that does not include Him. But you say, "My mind wanders and I get distracted." It does not matter if you allow Jesus to be in the middle of your distraction. The issue is Him.

Acts 1:14

PERSEVERANCE

Perseverance in the life of the Christian has been a debated subject throughout history. Two theological camps have arisen out of controversy. None of us are exempt from the division of these two theological views. Augustine, with his view of original sin, came to the conclusion that man is saved only and entirely through the actions of God. Free well, or choice, has absolutely nothing to do with it. God's Divine grace is operating within the life of the man who has been elected for salvation. In salvation, there is neither man's initiative nor response. The obvious conclusion to this is the enduring of the elect to the end. Thus, eternal security is granted to the elect by God regardless of human watchfulness, striving or endurance.

Arminius, along with John Wesley, considered perseverance from a different perspective. God's grace comes to every individual. This is an enabling grace, giving mankind the ability to respond. Perseverance is a much needed element in the heart of the believer, supplied by the grace of God. Endurance requires a response from man to the grace of God. There is no reason or necessity for man to lose his salvation. God has enabled man to respond and persevere, if he so desires.

One of the strongest words in the New Testament for endurance or perseverance is found in Hebrews. ***Therefore we also, since we are surrounded by so great a cloud of witnesses, let us lay aside every weight, and the sin which so easily ensnares*** *us, and let us run with endurance the race that is set before us* (Hebrews 12:1). Contained within that word *endurance* is the idea of energetic resistance, steadfastness under pressure, and endurance in the face of trials. It is used thirty-two times in the New Testament, and in the King James Version they are all translated *patience.*

However, this is a different word than we are considering in our passage. *These all continued with one accord in prayer, with the women and Mary the mother of Jesus, and His brothers* (Acts 1:14). The Greek word translated *continued* is a most amazing word. The root word which means "to stay by, to persist at, or to remain at" has a prefix. The prefix strengthens the meaning of the word. The prefix means "intense." Therefore, this word speaks of an intense persistence or intense remaining.

The two Greek words may have the same intensity and energy expressed, but they are somewhat different in their focus. The word Luke uses in Acts has a more positive thrust. There is even a joy and delight about it. It has an inward drawing or focus. It is the idea of giving yourself to, or attending to, or paying attention. It is a continuation in something. It is in light of this, we need to see this word in the context of the passage, and determine exactly what Luke is trying to communicate.

Concrete

The Greek word which is translated *continued* is in the masculine grammar, and it is in this gender every time it is used in the New Testament. It is contrasted in this verse with the word *prayer.* The Greek word for *prayer* is in the feminine gender, and it remains in that gender everywhere in the New Testament. You may remember this same concept in our study of the ascension of Jesus. The ascension ministry of Jesus provides

Part Five: Preparing For Pentecost

significant resource for us. Everything God wants us to have is in place in Christ in the heavenly realms. In Ephesians it is called ***every spiritual blessing*** (Ephesians 1:3). The word for ***blessing*** is in the feminine gender. It appears that all the things which are connected to intimate relationship with God are in the feminine gender.

Feminine is abstract. It is indefinable, without handles, and cannot be adequately analyzed. Feminine has to do with intangible things which are difficult to express or explain. Masculine is the opposite. It is concrete. A table is an example of something concrete. You can measure it, describe it, and touch it. Love is an example of the abstract, something difficult to explain and beyond our understanding.

An interaction is taking place between the one hundred and twenty and the ascended Lord. Throughout the Gospel accounts, the disciples have never entered into ***prayer***. Something new in relationship and experience has captured them. It is abstract. What they feel for each other as they come to ***one accord*** is abstract. There differences have always brought division. They have moved from the logical, to the concrete, to the greater realm of love in the abstract.

The idea of ***continued*** is masculine or concrete. The disciples cannot detect what God is going to do or how He is going to do it. The fullness of the Holy Spirit is indescribable in any sense. Who can adequately tell of the love and security in Christ? It is all abstract. But there is something of which you can get a hold. There is a concrete, measurable, nail it down element in this verse. It is the stay by it, persist at it, and remain with it, element of perseverance. You can measure this. God planted it in the realm of the concrete. Will you simply lock onto it and stay with it? Will you steadfastly give yourself to the abstract, which you cannot understand, but you can experience?

Construct

The Greek word which is translated *continued* is a verb in the participle form. This means it acts as an adverb and gives content to the main verb. Since it is a verb, it has "voice." It can have either a passive or active voice. In this verse it is in the active voice, which means the subject is responsible for the action of this verb *continued.* In this sentence the subject is the word *these,* which refers to the one hundred and twenty persons. This group is responsible for the action of *continued.*

This could be a bit misleading since the main verb in this sentence is the verb of being *were.* The action of the verb in this sentence is bringing about the *continued.* A verb of being does not have action, so perhaps it would be better for us to use the word influence. *Continued* is flowing out of the state of being in which the one hundred and twenty are abiding. The "am" of the subject is responsible for producing the *continued.* The *continued* is not producing the state of being.

The hundred and twenty do not discipline themselves in this intense focus. It is not because they have come to a common agreement of personal gain, or because they have removed all the differences they have with one another. The reason they are able to maintain this intense focus is because of the state of being they are experiencing.

A major question in the minds of many people is, "How can I maintain a consistent Christian walk?" They want to know how it is possible to leave church on Sunday morning, having experienced the presence of God, and maintain the awareness of that presence throughout the week. The world is constantly bombarding our lives. There is distraction after distraction in our pathway. The enemy, who would want to lead us astray, is on the prowl. How can a person intensely persist, stay at, and remain in this focus?

Part Five: Preparing For Pentecost

The answer comes back to us! It is not a special formula or series of steps. It is not found in a spiritual ceremony. It is found in the state of being. We must come to this state! What is the state of being? Where do we find it? Let us move on to that answer.

Concentrate

The structure of the sentence in this verse is an English teacher's nightmare. *These all continue with one accord in prayer, with the women and Mary the mother of Jesus, and His brothers* (Acts 1:14). In a previous study we discovered the grammar of the sentence. *These* is the subject of the sentence. The verb, which does not appear in most English translations, is the being verb *were.* There is no direct object stated in the sentence. The reference to *one accord* is an adverb which describes the state of being. The statement, *in prayer,* seems to be the grammar problem. It is in the dative case. In this verse it is the pure dative, which is the indirect object. How can there be an indirect object when there is no direct object? How can there be an indirect object when the main verb is *were,* a non-action word? These are problems in the English language, but Luke was writing in the Greek language.

One of the problems is solved with the idea of the assumed direct object. This idea gives us clarity on the concept of *continued.* The direct object, which is receiving the action or influence of the state of being is Jesus. The disciples have just spent forty days with the resurrected Christ. It has been the most incredible experience of their lives. They have witnessed the *infallible proofs* of His resurrection. They are absolutely consumed by Him. They cannot talk about anything else. He has become the center point of their lives. They are focused on His person. Everything which approaches their lives appears in the shadow of His presence. Their direction for the future is determined by Him. Resistance is gone and division has ceased. It is all about Him!

There may be other things which produce a state of being, but the only explanation for this group is their focus on Christ. He is the source of the object of their state of being. These two things are interrelated. True love is an example of this. The young man sees the young lady of his dreams, and he falls in love. He does not love her before he sees her. Upon seeing her and interacting with her, he falls in love. It is the state of being in love which causes him to focus on her, yet, as he focuses on her, something about her continually creates the state of being in love. There is an interaction between the two.

The disciples are in a state of being, which is totally focused on the resurrected Christ. They are entirely consumed with Him. This concentration produces the state of being, which turns its entire state on Him. He is producing this state of being and at the same time is the recipient of it. The idea of the word **continued** acts like an adverb describing and giving content to this state of being. It tells you of the intense nature of the interaction between Christ and this state of being.

The secret of perseverance is not found in "doing" but in "being." It is not discovered in setting things aside, or retreating to a monastery. You experience it in the middle of the circumstances of your world. You will know it as He captures your life. If you see Him as He is, you cannot help but persevere. The answer is found in Him. Will you stop where you are? Will you open yourself to Him? Will you allow Him to reveal Himself to you as He did to His disciples? He is standing in your pathway with a passionate desire to make Himself known to you. You do not have to convince Him! Just respond to Him and see what He does in you. He will reveal Himself in such a powerful way that you will be drawn in concentration. The more you communicate on Him the more you will be drawn to Him. You will persevere!

Acts 1:15-26

MUST

The early disciples seemed to be motivated and controlled by a compulsion. Something amazing has happened to them. They had choices to make about many things, but they did not appear to have a choice in submitting to this inward compulsion. The resurrection of Jesus and the fulfillment of the Promise of the Father affected them beyond words. Whatever happened to them put them over the edge.

It seems to have been connected with the ***infallible proofs*** of Jesus' resurrection presence. They spent forty days with Him (Acts 1:13). My heart longs to understand what took place during those days. Something compelling happened between the resurrected Christ and His disciples, and they were forever changed. They had a constant direction and purpose. They did not waiver. I stand back and view it with awe and wonder. If I, as an individual, could experience Him in such a manner, would things not be easier for me? Oh, if we, as a church, could grasp His presence and experience the same results, how could we not be different?

This compulsion even appears in their business meetings. It was their reason for meeting. There is a word which appears throughout this section (Acts 1:15-26), and it is translated in various ways with the different versions of the Scriptures. The English word "must" seems to be an adequate translation. Peter speaks to the disciples and says, ***"Men and brethren,*** *this Scripture* (must) ***had to be fulfilled,*** ... (Acts 1:16). The word could also be translated ***must need.*** He continues in his message to them by quoting Scriptures from the Book of Psalms. He suggests they select two men for the purpose of ***one of these must become a witness with us of His resurrection*** (Acts 1:22).

The word has a necessity about it. More properly, we call it an absolute necessity. As the Greek word is used throughout the New Testament, it presents us with five different yet overlapping pictures. Luke attempts to pinpoint the foundation of the "must." We want to discuss the aspects of the necessity in this passage.

First, there is a necessity which lies in the nature of the case. John the Baptist was settling a dispute which arose between his disciples and a group of Jews. He boldly proposed the reason for his existence. He proclaims that, ***"A man can receive nothing unless it has been given to him from heaven,"*** (John 3:27). He reminds them he has told them many times he is not the Messiah, but what he has received from heaven is the privilege of being ***sent before Him*** (John 3:28). He parallels his position with the best friend of the bridegroom. The bridegroom receives the bride, and the best man rejoices with the bridegroom. This is the reason his joy is full. Then John the Baptist turns and boldly says, ***"He must increase, but I must decrease,"*** (John 3:30). Why is this a necessity? It is simply the nature of the case. There is a compulsion deep within the forerunner that everyone must focus on the One he came to announce.

The same applies to the group who is waiting for the Promise of the Father. The very nature of the case they are experiencing demands their present compulsion. It lies within the nature of the Scriptures that it must be fulfilled. The very nature of the expression of Jesus' total ministry, as His disciples experienced it, needs an adequate witness. This is not far from where we abide! The nature of what God has presented to us carries a great necessity with it. The revelation of truth from the Scriptures, and the experience of His resurrection presence within, creates an unprecedented *must.*

A second foundation point for the existence of the necessity comes trough circumstances or by the conduct of others. Jesus has a conversation with Peter before the Garden of Gethsemane when He reveals his upcoming denial. Peter is very strong in rejecting such an event. Jesus tells Peter how he will not only deny once, but three times. Peter's bold reply is, ***"Even if I*** (must) ***have to die with You, I will not deny You!"*** (Matthew 26:25). Peter uses the Greek word translated "must." He exclaims that death may be brought upon him by circumstances which are beyond his control, but he has a choice in denying.

You can clearly see how this necessity is included in the "must" of this early group who are waiting on the Promise of the Father. Their lives have been affected by circumstances completely beyond their control. Each one of them can look back and see how God has put together circumstances which have brought them to this point of necessity. Oh, they had choices in all of these circumstances, and yet, within the situation there seemed to be only one thing which they could do. The circumstance demanded it! The resurrected Christ gave them infallible proofs which demanded belief. To deny Him would be to deny the reality of truth. Not to respond to the compelling presence of the Holy Spirit would be unthinkable. The compulsion rests within the things which are happening to them.

A third basis for the necessity is in what is required to attain a specific end. Peter expresses it clearly in his opening statement. ***"Men and brethren, this Scripture*** (must) ***had to be fulfilled...*** (Acts 1:16). The necessity was that the plan of redemption and the Promise of the Father be fulfilled. Then these things could come to pass. The Scriptures must be true. Something bigger is going on here. It is more than the disciples ever dreamed, and they must express their awareness of it. There is an end, and God intends to accomplish it. He is playing it out in the lives of the believers. We must yield, submit, and surrender to God's intended end. In light of His dream for us, He compels us to do so.

The fourth emphasis of this necessity is the law and command. It has to do with duty. The servant was forgiven what he could not possibly pay, yet he refused to forgive his fellow servant a small amount which could have been paid. The master was ugly with the forgiven servant. He said, "(Must) **Should you not also have had compassion on your fellow servant, just as I had pity on you?**" (Matthew 18:33). Duty should have compelled the forgiven servant to pass on forgiveness to his brother.

Are we not duty bound? Because we have experienced the grace and greatness of God, we are to be witnesses of the resurrection. In light of all that has come to us, all we have experienced, all we have witnessed, MUST we not tell it? Is quietness an option in our lives? The words which were written on the breastplate of the high priest of the temple must not be a mere slogan. *"Zeal for Your house has eaten Me up,"* (John 2:17).

The last basis for this compulsion is the most pressing of all. The necessity is established by the counsel and decree of God. As the three disciples return with Jesus from the Mount of Transfiguration, they admit they are a bit confused. They present it in the form of a question. *"Why then do the scribes say that Elijah must come first?"* (Matthew 17:10). There seems to be a Divine decree established by the will of God, that before the Messiah can bring deliverance there must be One who comes to prepare the way. It is what Peter preached on the Day of Pentecost. *"Him,* (Christ) *being delivered by the determined purpose and foreknowledge of God, you have taken by lawless hands, have crucified, and put to death;"* (Acts 2:23).

A Divine decree echoes throughout the passage (Acts 1:15-26). God has willed it with a burning desire. *"Men and brethren, this*

Scripture (must) ***had to be fulfilled...*** (Acts 1:16). The sovereign will of God has declared it. A Divine choice is involved in the selection of a disciple to fill the office left by Judas. ***"One of these must become a witness with us of His resurrection."***

The reality of the situation in which the disciples found themselves is presently being replayed in our lives. All they experience in terms of the necessity and the burning compulsion is present now. If there was a Divine thumb in their backs, there is also one in ours! The basis of the ***must*** is the same for us as it was for them.

Record
Acts 1:16

*"**Men and brethren**, **this Scripture** (must) **had to be fulfilled, which the Holy Spirit spoke before by the mouth of David concerning Judas, which became a guide to those who arrested Jesus;"** (Acts 1:16). As we look at the original language of this verse, **Men** and **brethren** are two different Greek words. They are stated at the beginning of the sentence, and they are followed by the Greek word which can be translated **must needs**. This is followed by another Greek word which can be translated **have been fulfilled**. Peter addresses the disciple group with these words, **"Men and brethren, this Scripture** (must) **had to be fulfilled..."**

The Scripture was not a product of man. ***"Men and brethren, this Scripture had to be fulfilled, which the Holy Spirit spoke before by the mouth of David..."*** The Greek word which is translated ***by*** is a primary preposition denoting the channel or agent of an act. It is often translated "through." Peter is saying that the Psalms, which He is going to read to them, were the product of the Holy Spirit. It is God who took the mouth of David and spoke the desired words. David was intimately involved, and he expressed his personality, but as certainly as we acclaim these words to be spoken by David, so we can acclaim them as spoken by God.

There is a Divine necessity and compulsion in the fulfillment of the Scriptures. The Scriptures will be lived out in the daily activities of man. What would happen to the level of our living if we were keenly aware that God is living the Scriptures out in our lives? You are a channel through which God is fulfilling His plan. The conflicts, struggles, and even persecutions are all under the thumb of a sovereign God. He spoke it in the Scriptures, and He is fulfilling it in your life. Even the betrayer of a close associate is somehow tied to the fulfillment of God. Your life is a stage upon which God is acting out the fulfillment of His spoken Word.

This will bring you to a great sense of destiny. Each event of life will be seen as a piece of the puzzle fitting together to bring about the whole picture. The event would still be a puzzle, and the greater picture might still be unknown, but the reality of the knowledge of the Divine MUST will cause a completely different attitude toward the event. The event will no longer be good or bad, judged by our personal comfort, but we will use it as an instrument of God to effectively bring about His decree. Self-defense and resistance will disappear. Demanding attitudes will cease. We will live in response to the actions of God as the Scriptures are being fulfilled through our lives.

If this is true now, God is using your life as a stage upon which He fulfills the Scriptures. He is pulling off the great event of His Word for this hour and is depending upon your response. You must yield, submit and respond! It is the MUST of the Scriptures being fulfilled and lived out in the world. It will, however, happen with or without our submission. It is the Divine MUST. It will take place whether we resist or not. I want the will of God to be done because of me, not in spite of me.

Resurrection
Acts 1:22

Peter says, *"beginning from the baptism of John to that day when He was taken up from us, one of these must become a witness with us of His resurrection,"* (Acts 1:22). The focus of this complete action has to do with an adequate witness of the resurrection. There seems to be no other concern. This is played out in the action of the Book of Acts. All the sermons preached seem to center on the Christ, crucified and raised from the dead.

Peter feels compelled to call a meeting of the early one hundred and twenty disciples. The Scriptures compel them to replace Judas, filling the office he left. The driving MUST is that an adequate witness of the resurrection takes place in the world. Little do they know how tightly his witness is tied into the Promise of the Father.

Jesus told His disciples, *"But you shall receive power when the Holy Spirit has come upon you; and you shall be witnesses to Me in Jerusalem, and in all Judea and Samaria, and to the end of the earth,"* (Acts 1:8). The Divine nature He imparted to them will not only help them to say the right things at the right time, but they will be the living testimonies of the resurrection. The witness of the resurrection is not a "doing" but a "being" witness. The life of Jesus is going to be manifested in and out of them. This happens repeatedly in this great book. They speak great truth in witness, and God immediately displays, through the events which follow, a demonstration of great power. The resurrected Lord displays Himself among them. It takes a variety of forms, but it is always convincing and many are converted. The power of their preaching, coupled with the power of their living, is the witness that wins the world.

It was not programmed. It was not even planned. It all happened under the control of the compulsion, the MUST of what was happening within them. If it had been a result of their planning, they would have held seminars to teach their wise formulas for church growth. If it had been their program, they would have packaged their approach and sold it for profit. This was the Divine MUST burning within them, changing their lives, and winning their world. Dear Christ, do it again!

A GOD ORDAINED BOARD MEETING:
THE PROPOSITION

Acts 1:16

THE SETTING FOR PENTECOST

From the human perspective, one might be amazed by the material Luke places in the Book of Acts. We might think he chose between the events, including what was important and excluding what was insignificant. But we do not believe Luke made these decisions on his own. He was under the control of the Holy Spirit, and the truth flowed through him from the hand of God. Certainly, the resurrection/ascension was important (Acts 1:3, 9-11). And we understand the significance of the formation of the group as they gathered in Jerusalem. We need to know what they were doing and how they reacted to the events of that hour (Acts 1:12-14). But what about the recording of a business meeting? This raises many questions (Acts 1:15-26).

What does this business meeting have to do with the fulfillment of the Promise of the Father? The focus of this meeting is on the selection of an apostle to replace Judas. There are many Bible scholars who question whether or not this should have been done, confusing the issue more. Many of these scholars suggest the Apostle Paul was the real choice of God, and the disciples ran ahead of God's choosing.

Luke gives us sufficient material in these verses to clarify these questions. Peter reveals his concern for the vacancy of the office. There needs to be twelve apostles to fulfill the promises of Christ, not eleven. This is a significant issue. Jesus had given the disciples weighty instructions in regard to the structure of the Kingdom of God. When the Rich Young Ruler departed in rejection and sorrow, Peter asked Jesus, *"See, we have left all and followed You. Therefore what shall we have?"* (Matthew 19:27). Jesus highlights the structure of the Kingdom in his reply. *So Jesus said to them, "Assuredly I say to you, that in the regeneration, when the Son of Man sits on the throne of His glory, you who have followed Me will also sit on twelve thrones, judging the twelve tribes of Israel,"* (Matthew 19:28). The disciples did not take this kind of promise lightly.

The Apostle Paul does not meet the qualifications established for the newly appointed apostle (Acts 1:21-22). The group from which the selection is to be made is the *seventy others,* (Luke 10:1). Christ duplicated His ministry through them as He sent them out to minister two by two. From the details of the business meeting, we see clearly this is what they had to do to get ready to receive the Promise of the Father.

It will help us to follow an outline as we study this business meeting. We do not want to overlook any detail of truth which the Holy Spirit wants to give us.

I. SETTING - Acts 1:15
    A. This is the occasion from which the entire procedure flows.
    B. It provides an atmosphere and tone.

II. STORY - Acts 1:16-17
    A. No details are given for they were already known.
    B. Peter is sharing "concept."

III. SADNESS - Acts 1:18-19
    A. This is a parenthesis about the event associated with Judas and the awful consequences of his actions.
    B. It is a flashback.

IV. STATEMENTS - Acts 1:20
   A. This verse is connected to verse sixteen.
   B. Peter begins his remarks with a quote from the Book of Psalms.

V. STANDARD - Acts 1:21-22
   A. The disciples need to replace Judas.
   B. The replacement must meet certain qualifications.

VI. STRATEGY - Acts 1:23-25
   A. Peter gives the method they are to use to accomplish the selection.
   B. Prayer is a major factor.

VII. SOLUTION - Acts 1:26
   A. Matthias is selected by God.
   B. He was numbered with the eleven apostles.

We want to focus on the opening verse. ***And in those days Peter stood up in the midst of the disciples (altogether the number of names was about a hundred and twenty), and said,*** (Acts 1:15). To understand this passage, we need to understand the three natural elements which this verse contains.

The Sequence

This business meeting sets the tone for the preparation of Pentecost. Even though we have already studied this, we need the reminder. This meeting took place ***in those days.*** Luke attempts to enlighten us with the information that this happened sometime between the ascension and the Day of Pentecost. This was a period of seven to ten days, depending on how you interpret the number of days. It seems logical to assume it was not on the first or second day, but it was a result of their time together

Part Six: A God Ordained Board Meeting: The Proposition

under the Holy Spirit's direction.

The united disciples saturated these days with prayer (Acts 1:14). They were greatly impacted by the experience of the ascension. They had experienced the significant forty days of Christ's resurrection appearance. They were overwhelmed with the imprint of the resurrected Lord upon their lives. It utterly changed the focus and attitude of the group. They were enthralled with Jesus. They became so focused on Him, there was nothing else. With the coming of the indwelt Spirit of Jesus, there was nothing that could distract them. The responsibility of the Holy Spirit is to glorify Jesus. Jesus told the disciples, **"He will glorify Me, for He will take of what is Mine and declare it to you,"** (John 16:14). Jesus became the determining factor in the lives of the disciples. He created within them a hunger and a seeking for all that had been promised through the Father.

Jesus spent forty days *speaking of the things pertaining to the kingdom of God,* (Acts 1:3). The Kingdom of God is Christ Himself. Each disciple was focused on the indwelling of the Spirit of Jesus, reigning and enhancing their lives. It was about the Promise of the Father. The wonder of the possibility absolutely overwhelmed them. God was about to fulfill all the dreams of the Old Testament. The disciples felt it!

A sense of persistence was present during these days. Remember how Luke described it in the closing verse of the first volume, *and were continually in the temple praising and blessing God. Amen,* (Luke 24:53). Luke expands this insight in his second volume. *These all continued with one accord in prayer...* (Acts 1:14). The disciples were focused now, and they each had an attitude of openness, a pressing desire to see all that Jesus wanted to do. They had given up hidden agendas, and they were overcome with a new compulsion. They seemed to be driven by one desire.

This is the great need in our lives. We need this same openness and desire, forming an atmosphere in which the Holy Spirit can come. Only when we have this kind of hunger can we find intimacy with God and discover a new depth of relationship with Him. Doing our duty, keeping the rules, and abiding by our traditions only create walls which block His coming. We need to be gripped by desperation to know Him more. When we are gripped by this kind of hunger, this atmosphere creates an abandonment to God in our lives. It releases the hand of God to do in and through us whatever He desires.

This is spoken of often in the Scriptures. God speaks through the Proverbs saying, **"And those who seek Me diligently will find Me,"** (Proverbs 8:17). He declares through the prophecies of Isaiah, **"I did not say to the seed of Jacob, 'Seek Me in vain'; I, the Lord, speak righteousness, I declare things that are right,"** (Isaiah 45:19). And through the voice of Jeremiah the Prophet God said, **"And you will seek Me and find Me, when you search for Me with all your heart,"** (Jeremiah 29:13). Hear the cry of Amos, **"For thus says the Lord to the house of Israel: 'Seek Me and live;'"** (Amos 5:4).

The Society

The society is the second natural element found in this verse. Luke uses an unusual combination of words here. He links them together to give us a phrase which seems to have been used with a clear distinction. In the Greek language, as Luke wrote it, the order of the words is "number, names, together." This unusual turn of phrase is used in the Old Testament translation from the Hebrew into the Greek, which is called the Septuagint. It refers to a gathering of persons or a crowd of names. It is used to describe the census that opened the nation of Israel's register (Numbers 1:2, 8, 20; 3:40, 43; 26:53). Could Luke be using this unusual phrase for the opening register of the Church?

Perhaps he was saying this is the church roll or the church

Part Six: A God Ordained Board Meeting: The Proposition

membership book. This is the society of believers. But we have no right to limit the believers in Christ to this group of one hundred and twenty. No doubt there were many others who were not gathered in this upper room at this business meeting. But why are these here and the others are not? What is it that makes these one hundred and twenty a society, a group of names gathered together?

This is the very thing we have been discussing. It is this openness, hunger and desperation for the new level of intimacy which the Father promised. The disciples had believed in a military emphasis. They wanted Jesus to replace the political structure in the city of Jerusalem by force, and thus end the Roman occupation. This now no longer mattered to them. They now have a new focus on Christ, and what they once wanted has been replaced by a burning desire for His presence. Jesus' resurrection presence has captured them to the degree of an obsession. Their focus on Him drives and motivates them as if nothing else matters. Their only concern seems to be Jesus and the fulfillment of what He desires for them.

If this group has any other focus than Jesus, they are not a society, but a divided and warring number of cliques. If they focus on leadership, they have heated arguments about, **"Who then is greatest in the kingdom of heaven?"** (Matthew 18:1). If they focus on nationalities, you will hear the cry, "Let's **command fire to come down from heaven and consume them, just as Elijah did,"** (Luke 9:54). If ministry is the focus, there will be those who report, **"Master, we saw someone casting out demons in Your name, and we forbade him because he does not follow with us,"** (Luke 9:49). When age is the focus, then these words of Jesus need to be repeated, **"Let the little children come to Me, and do not forbid them; for of such is the kingdom of heaven,"** (Matthew 19:14).

We can only have one focus. It is Jesus! It comes in the form of openness, hunger and desperation to know Him. This is what made this group the society who could receive the Promise of the Father. Is there a lesson here for us to learn? Can we come to one motivating desire? Can we clear the slate, set the committee meetings aside, and let our hearts beat for one thing alone?

The Speaker

Luke clearly states who is conducting this meeting. *And in those days Peter stood up in the midst of the disciples,* (Acts 1:15). Is this a good thing? We have three years of examples of what Peter is like. He has always responded in one way, protecting his position and commanding authority. He has generally been responsible for the arguments among the disciples, and he has continually created friction. He has never been seen as a peace maker. He consistently defends himself and is quick to criticize others. When Jesus told the disciples, *"All of you will be made to stumble because of Me this night,"* (Matthew 26:31), Peter quickly responded that the others might stumble, but certainly not him. His actual words were, *"I will never be made to stumble,"* (Matthew 26:33).

But something has happened to the disciple group. They no longer respond as in previous days. Peter is no longer the same, and neither are the others. This verse reveals that all of the disciples have been greatly affected by something or someone. The Scripture says that *Peter stood up.* The customary position of one who leads, gives laws, or has supremacy over the rest of the body is sitting. Peter stood to his feet as one who had a motion or suggestion to make to the group. Does this resemble the Peter we have read about over the three-year Gospel account? What has happened to him?

Peter stood *in the midst of the disciples (altogether the number of the names was about a hundred and twenty),* (Acts 1:15). If Luke had written that Peter stood *in the midst of*

Part Six: A God Ordained Board Meeting: The Proposition

the disciples, we would assume the eleven had formed a select group against those who were now pressing their way into authority. But he clearly says that Peter made this suggestion or motion before the entire group. This restates the message. ***These all continued with one accord in prayer,*** (Acts 1:14). This does not sound like the Peter we know from the Gospel accounts. What has happened to Him?

There can only be one explanation. Peter, along with the others, has been captured by the resurrected Christ. They have spent forty days with Jesus. They are compelled by the message of the Kingdom of God being within them. They see the possibility of God indwelling them, ruling over them, and enhancing their lives. They are thrilled by the prospects of the Promise of the Father. They are focused on the expansion of the person of Christ in their lives. They realize that Christ is going to move from being with them to being within them, and this compulsion has overridden them.

Pentecost has not happened. They are waiting in Jerusalem as Jesus instructed them. The fullness of the Holy Spirit has not yet come, so the change in the lives of the disciples at this point is not due to the Holy Spirit. Their anticipation for the fulfillment of the Promise of the Father has changed them. There seems to be only one thrust in their lives. They are overwhelmed with one passion; it is the fullness of Jesus within them.

What will this do to your life? Far too often we have plateaued in our spiritual experience. Our attitude is one of arrival. We cease to seek, which means we are not open to the new level to which Jesus wants to take us. What the disciples experienced in the setting of Pentecost is missing from our lives. Does this means we will miss Pentecost as well?

Acts 1:16

THE SPEAKING OF GOD

In Acts 1:15-26, Luke records the early church's first business meeting. We have previously outlined this passage for you to provide for your understanding of Luke's proposition.

I. SETTING - Acts 1:15
The Context

II. STORY - Acts 1:16-17
The Concept

III. SADNESS - Acts 1: 18-19
The Conclusion

IV. SCRIPTURE - Acts 1:20
The Certainty

V. STANDARD - Acts 1:21-22
The Conditions

VI. STRATEGY - Acts 1:23-25
The Consultation

VII. SOLUTION - Acts 1:26
The Chosen

Part Six: A God Ordained Board Meeting: The Proposition

We have a slight dilemma with the interaction of verses fifteen and sixteen. The verse divisions were imposed by man. Based on the content, the beginning of verse sixteen should go with verse fifteen, and the end of verse sixteen should be included with verse seventeen. Before Luke gets into the actual recounting of the story of Judas, he gives additional insight into the context of what happens in the business meeting.

The context of this scene comes from the phrase, ***And in those days.*** It takes place during the last seven to ten days prior to the outpouring of Pentecost. There are one hundred and twenty (Acts 1:15) people, in a state of continual prayer and worship (Acts 1:14), seeking all God wants for them. They are united together as a society of believers. They are focused on the resurrected Christ, knowing He will fulfill the Promise of the Father. Peter, from a position of humility, leads the society of believers, offering truth for their response.

Verse sixteen gives additional information as to the setting of this business meeting. The difficulty with this verse comes in the English translation. It relates to Luke's order of associated items. As written in the Greek language, there is no difficulty. How does one translate this into another language? The main focus of concern is the phrase, ***this Scripture had to be fulfilled.*** Peter continues the story of Judas. Every detail of Peter's account comes under the scrutiny of absolute certainty of Scripture.

Peter presents the truth that ***this Scripture had to be fulfilled.*** Then comes the deep awareness that ***the Holy Spirit spoke before.*** He spoke ***by the mouth of David,*** and the message he gave was ***concerning Judas.*** The main focus of this presentation is that the Scriptures had (must) come to pass as stated. What would happen in your life if I could convince you I have a written document which is so supreme that every single statement has to come true? There are no exceptions. If you can find the reality in this document's statements, you will find the infallible revelation of truth.

We have spoken before of the importance of the verb Peter uses in his statement. It is translated *had* or *must.* It has the idea of absolute necessity. It is the necessity of logic and Divine decree. This idea is not an isolated approach in Scriptures. In His resurrection form, Jesus appeared to the two men on the Emmaus Road. Thinking He was a stranger, they attempted to explain to Him the events leading to their discouragement. He simply opened the Scriptures to them of **the things concerning Himself,** (Luke 24:27). In the process of this He said, **"Ought not the Christ to have suffered these things and to enter into His glory?"** (Luke 24:26). The Greek word translated, *ought,* is the same word Peter uses.

When the resurrected Jesus appeared later to His disciples, He said, **"These are the words which I spoke to you while I was still with you, that all things MUST BE fulfilled which were written in the Law of Moses and the Prophets and the Psalms concerning Me,"** (Luke 24:44). The Greek word translated, *must be,* is the same one Peter uses here. This would lead us to conclude that in this business meeting Peter is expressing the very truth Jesus proposed.

Jesus had been in the heat of battle with the leaders of Israel. They were arguing as Jesus tried to reason with them concerning their view of Him. They became so inflamed they **took up stones again to stone Him,** (John 10:31). A discussion followed as to why they did this. In the course of the debate, Jesus quoted an obscure phrase from a Psalm. **Jesus answered them, "Is it not written in your law, 'I said, "You are gods'?" If He called them gods, to whom the word of God came (and the Scripture cannot be broken),"** (John 10:34-35). Jesus' view of the Scripture is that it cannot be undone, dispersed, or brought to an end. **This Scripture has to be fulfilled.**

Peter relates this same certainty to the fulfillment of the story of Judas. This does not eliminate any responsibility on the part of Judas. He was as free in his betrayal of Jesus, even though it was prophesied in the Scriptures. What would happen in your life if I could convince you of a document that lays out the future, and every single statement in that document will come true? There are no exceptions. If you can find the reality of the statements in this document, you will have found the infallible revelation of truth.

How can we put that much weight of importance upon one book over against all other books? Peter makes that perfectly clear as he continues in the order or focus of this verse. In his second statement he declares, **which the Holy Spirit spoke before,** (Acts 1:16). There seems to be no question in Peter's mind that the Psalm which he quotes in verse twenty is a direct quotation of the Holy Spirit. God Himself is responsible for these words. The author, the one who gets the credit for these words, is the Holy Spirit.

Do you know how many times this kind of statement is made in the Book of Acts? *So when they heard that, they raised their voice to God with one accord and said: "Lord, You are God, who made heaven and earth and the sea, and all that is in them, who by the mouth of Your servant David have said"*: (Acts 4:24-25). The verse continues with a quotation of another great Psalm. *So when they did not agree among themselves, they departed after Paul had said one word: "The Holy Spirit spoke rightly through Isaiah the prophet to our fathers, saying...* (Acts 28:25-26). This is then followed by a quotation from Isaiah. Paul, as a Jew, and later as a Christian, held the high view that every word in the Old Testament was "the authentic voice of God." This cannot be overstated.

How would you react to my assurance that I have a document which was actually spoken by God? The contents of this document are certain and sure, and what it says always comes true. It holds the certainty of life or death for you. If you want to discover the truth from any book, this is the one you must come to. Saturate in it. Give your mind to it. Let it be the guide for your life. Why would I do this? It is simple. This book is spoken by God!

Peter speaks this same truth in his epistles. ***For prophecy never came by the will of man, but holy men of God spoke as they were moved by the Holy Spirit,*** (2 Peter 1:21). Again, this passage's emphasis is one of Divine origin. The context of this passage holds a startling revelation. Peter declares the ***prophetic word*** to be more ***sure*** than even the eyewitnesses of Christ's glory as seen on the Mount of Transfiguration, (2 Peter 1:17-19).

Peter highlights the supernatural quality of the Scripture in this section. Scripture owes its origin to the Divine initiative, not the human initiative. We can see this in the series of statements where Peter strongly emphasizes the reliability of the Scriptures. He says, ***knowing this first, that no prophecy of Scripture is of any private interpretation,*** (2 Peter 1:20). There is some controversy among Bible scholars concerning the words in this verse. Some think the Greek word translated ***interpretation*** has to do with origin, and the verb translated ***is*** has the meaning of "emerging." However, this argument is settled when we understand there is no possibility of understanding the Scriptures unless the Divine Author, who spoke the original, gives illumination to it now.

Next Peter says, ***for prophecy never came by the will of man,*** (2 Peter 1:21). If the first statement tells us we cannot understand the Scripture without the illumination of the Holy Spirit, this statement definitely tells us that the Divine is solely responsible for the origination of the Scriptures. Man is not the source of the Scriptures.

Then Peter writes, ***but holy men of God spoke as they were moved by the Holy Spirit,*** (2 Peter 1:21). Another translation strengthens the Divine quality of the words by saying it this way, ***men moved by the Holy Spirit spoke from God.*** The Greek word translated, ***moved,*** means "to bear along." It implies an activity more specific than mere guidance or direction. These words

Part Six: A God Ordained Board Meeting: The Proposition

have Divine origin behind them.

How would you react to my convincing you that I have a document which is actually spoken by God? It is sure and true. Everything it says crosses the time barrier and cultural involvement. When you go to the depths of its truth, it becomes a private conversation between you and God. There is no where else to seek truth!

The focus of this verse is ***this Scripture had to be fulfilled,*** (Acts 1:16). The reason presented by Peter is ***which the Holy Spirit spoke before.*** Now comes the secondary agent of the Scripture. Peter says, ***by the mouth of David.*** To best translate this idea, the use of a causative statement reproduces it to read, "caused David to speak."

We must carefully think this aspect through. The Scriptures, as an end product, are certainly of God. There is no attempt to indicate they were partly man and partly God. Peter states this forcefully when he says, *"which the Holy Spirit spoke before."* He boldly declares the Scriptures to be inspired, not simply the men who wrote them. Thus, the Biblical concept of inspiration is that the writings are inspired, and not writers.

The Scriptures were not verbally spoken by the Holy Spirit and then written by David. The Holy Spirit inspired them within David, and the words flowed from his voice and his pen. His personality was used by the Holy Spirit, and the Holy Spirit is present in the writings. The words were forcibly guarded, protected and designed by the Holy Spirit, being spoken by Him through David.

What if I could convince you that there is a document which was clearly spoken by God? It is absolute truth in every aspect. Every statement has validity. What is spoken in this document will come true! It will happen as it has been written! This document is focused on God's concern and involvement with mankind. God did not involve angels in this speaking. He did not speak it through animals. God spoke this as man to man.

You cannot say, "Well, this is not practical." God is simply giving us His view from some lofty place in the sky. He thunders His ideas from the high clouds of the universe, but He does not speak from my streets. Absolutely - NO! God speaks His truth from one place of abode. He spoke **by the mouth of David.** He spoke His Word through the dirt and grime of our dwelling. He speaks clearly to our situations. David, who knew the depth of adultery and murder, became the mouthpiece of God. He is definitely from our world.

Why would you not cling to this Book? Why would you not search it diligently and base all of your being on it? Why would you not become intimate with the Author and allow Him to reveal direction and purpose for your life? Why would you complain over your circumstances as if He is to blame, when He has been trying to explain them to you through the Word? Why would this Living Word and Written Word not become your very life?

I have a document which is the spoken word of God. It is absolutely true and is being fulfilled in every life. God spoke this through the lips of men on our level. He is focused on our lives and on our needs, and He continues to speak through His Word to our present living.

Acts 1:16
BEING A GUIDE

We have been studying the first recorded business meeting of the early church. This passage gives us great insight into what the disciples were feeling and thinking during their "waiting period" in Jerusalem. This time period falls after the ascension of Christ and before Pentecost. We have called this period the SETTING (Acts 1:15). Peter is making a proposal based on the authority of the Scriptures. After proclaiming the Scriptures as the highest authority, Peter moves into the STORY (Acts 1:16-17) of Judas.

Peter presents the betrayal of Judas to those present (one hundred and twenty in number). They were all familiar with the details, and they would not have disagreed with Peter's proposition. Judas ended his life in death and destruction, but Peter presents an important concept about his life. He says, "*... concerning Judas, who became a guide to those who arrested Jesus;*" (Acts 1:16). He says that Judas, in his betrayal of Jesus, is *a guide.*

Proposition of the Concept

I would like to expose you to some other passages where the concept of *a guide* is a positive thing. One of the most beautiful passages is in the Gospel of John. Jesus is giving His final instructions to the disciples. He wants to encourage them, and He assures them of His continued presence. He says, *"However, when He, the Spirit of truth, has come, He will guide you into all truth; for He will not speak on His own authority, but whatever He hears He will speak; and He will tell you things to come,* (John 16:13).

The word Jesus used concerning the Holy Spirit is the exact same word used by Peter in his description of Judas. He is to be a **guide.** This Greek word is used ten times in the New Testament. It is used five times as a noun (Matthew 15:14; 23:16; 23:24; Acts 1:16; Romans 2:19), and five times as a verb (Matthew 15:14; Luke 6:39; John 16:13; Acts 8:31; Revelations 7:17). I investigated many translations, and it is most often translated "guide." There were a few places it is translated "lead."

This word has a much deeper meaning than to transport something from one place to another. You can do this to cargo, but not to human beings. People must be guided. This word comes from two Greek words. One has to do with a road, and the other has to do with a strengthened form of the word, lead. You must think of the Holy Spirit in this activity. He comes to indwell. Within His capacity is **all truth.** He will gently take your hand, lead, instruct, teach, reveal, and guide you into all truth. This goes beyond the memorization of facts or the learning of techniques. This has to do with grasping the information with wisdom and understanding. The phrase, **He will guide you into all truth,** may be expressed as a causative. It could be translated, **He will cause you to know all the truth.** There are vast elements contained within this meaning. The Holy Spirit is responsible for causing you to comprehend the truth about Jesus. There is no way you can know it otherwise! This will not happen by some magical feat where the truth is dumped into your mind. It only takes place through your seeking, openness, and response, and it comes through the circumstances of your life. Your trials are a vital part of His guidance into all truth. As we seek, He carefully

Part Six: A God Ordained Board Meeting: The Proposition

moves us through the classes of truth learning.

We want to investigate another passage where the same Greek word is used. This passage describes the ministry of Jesus, the Lamb of God. Many people have come out of the great tribulation. He visualizes them as, ***Therefore they are before the throne of God, and serve Him day and night in His temple. And He who sits on the throne will dwell among them. They shall neither hunger anymore nor thirst anymore; the sun shall not strike them, nor any heat; for the Lamb who is in the midst of the throne will shepherd them and lead them to living fountains of waters. And God will wipe away every tear from their eyes,*** (Revelation 7:15-17). Did you notice ***the Lamb will lead*** (guide) ***them to living fountains of waters?***

Jesus has always been characterized as the good shepherd, working in our behalf. The shepherd is a picture of loving care for his flock. From the Scriptures, we can piece together the duties and normal daily pattern of the shepherd. In the morning he leads his flock from the fold. He would go before them and call them. Each shepherd had his own guttural sound to which his sheep would respond. Even though several flocks of sheep might be intermingled together, the sheep knew their shepherd's sound and would easily follow him. Upon arriving at the pasture for that day, the shepherd would watch his flock with the assistance of dogs. If any sheep strayed, the shepherd would search for it until he found it. The shepherd supplied his sheep with water from either a running stream or at troughs attached to wells. At evening he would bring them back to the fold and check to see that none were missing. The shepherd counted each sheep as it passed "under the rod," entering the door to the fold. The shepherd watched the entrance of the fold throughout the night, acting as the "door" (John 10:3). Nothing could get to the sheep without going through the shepherd.

Everything concerned with care and watchfulness of the good shepherd comes under the concept of ***to guide.*** This is an opportunity for us. We can be the sheep of His pasture. The Spirit of Jesus wants to carefully guide us to the pasture of His truth. He will guard us from every intruder who would distract us from His revelation. His strong staff covers everything in our daily activities. As His sheep, we have his constant presence and companionship. He is our provision. He has already supplied all of our needs. We can rely on Him totally *to guide* us through life.

This is a beautiful picture of what the Spirit of Jesus does in my life! But we must now return to the passage at hand (Acts 1:16). It is the negative view of a guide, *"... concerning Judas, who became a guide to those who arrested Jesus."* As discouraging as it might be, we must take what we have learned from the usage of the word in the positive and apply it to the negative. Judas did not simply give directions to those who were desperate to crucify Jesus. If that were the case, he could have drawn them a map. Judas acted in the capacity of a shepherd over the people involved in the betrayal.

Matthew writes of Judas' involvement in the betrayal. *Then one of the twelve, called Judas Iscariot, went to the chief priests and said, "What are you willing to give me if I deliver Him to you?" And they counted out to him thirty pieces of silver. So from that time he sought opportunity to betray Him,* (Matthew 26:14-17). Judas actually initiated the contact with the leaders of Israel. He bargained with them over what he would be given. He was the one who oversaw the time and the place of the betrayal. He was the mastermind of the plot, and he carried it out in the Garden of Gethsemane. The leaders of Israel could not have accomplished their task without the guidance of Judas. This involved much more than locating Christ. They could have seized Him on any given day without the help of Judas. When they came to the garden, Jesus said,

"When I was with you daily in the temple, you did not try to seize Me," (Luke 22:53). Judas was the shepherd guide for the betrayal of Christ.

Part Six: A God Ordained Board Meeting: The Proposition

Progression of the Concept

Here again is the statement of Peter. *"... concerning Judas, who became a guide to those who arrested Jesus;"* (Acts 1:16). The word, *became,* comes from the idea "to come to acquire or experience a state." It is the idea of "to possess certain characteristics, with the implication of their having been acquired." You can see this in the progression within this word. Judas did not become a *guide* without choice or seeing it progressively take place in his life. He made deliberate choices in his life that brought him to this moment. This is evident in the story of the betrayal. We were told nothing about how Judas became a disciple. As you read the Gospel account, suddenly Judas appears in the list of chosen disciples. We have no reason to expect that his selection and response were any less significant than the other disciples. As the disciples became an organized group, traveling, receiving money and other offerings, distributing to the poor, it became necessary that someone would act as the treasurer. This responsibility was given to Judas. As things moved forward, he is accredited with being a thief. John highlights this in the account of Mary anointing the feet of Jesus with the costly oil. The record shows how Judas felt about her actions. *"Why was this fragrant oil not sold for three hundred denarii and given to the poor?"* (John 12:5). Then John adds this commentary. *This he said, not that he cared for the poor, but because he was a thief, and had the money box; and he used to take what was put in it,* (John 12:6).

Judas could have changed directions at any time, but we read of his progression when he goes to the chief priests and says, *"What are you willing to give me if I deliver Him to you?"* (Matthew 26:15). He uses the betrayal of Jesus for financial gain. It is amazing! Even in the midst of the strong influence of the person of Christ in day to day ministry, Judas progressively moves to be the shepherd of the betrayal. He has experienced the power of God moving through him in successful ministry, yet he continues to be a guide for evil.

Production of the Concept

We need to inject one other element into the story. It has to do with source. We need to understand that none of this had to happen. There was someone beyond Judas who was acting as a guide to all that happened. Judas had a choice. He was acting from his own free will. However, there was a guide to the one who became a guide. We cannot ignore this factor.

The leaders of Israel are deeply concerned about Jesus' influence upon the people. The Gospel accounts are full of the repeated phrase, *for they feared the people* (Luke 22:2). These leaders are convinced they must get rid of Jesus. Luke writes, *And the chief priests and the scribes sought how they might kill Him,* (Luke 22:2). The time for the Feast of the Passover was drawing near. Hundreds of people would flood the streets of Jerusalem for this one week celebration. How could the chief priests and the scribes possibly arrest Jesus and bring Him to death with such a crowd present? They had no plan.

Then Satan entered Judas, surnamed Iscariot, who was numbered among the twelve. So he went his way and conferred with the chief priests and captains, how he might betray Him to them, (Luke 22:3-4). This is a great statement of insight. Judas was not acting on his own. He had become an instrument of demonic activity. As the Spirit of Truth indwelt believers and guided them into truth, so Satan entered into Judas and became a guide for the betrayal and destruction of Jesus.

John also verifies this after the fact. The disciples are in the upper room, just having finished the Last Supper. *And supper being ended, the devil having already put it into the heart of*

Part Six: A God Ordained Board Meeting: The Proposition

Judas Iscariot, Simon's son, to betray Him, (John 13:2). John does not seem content to forget this issue. Later in the same chapter he records how each disciple is concerned about being the betrayer. John leans back on Jesus' breast and asks Him, *"Lord, who is it?"* (John 13:25). ***Jesus answered, "It is he to whom I shall give a piece of bread when I have dipped it." And having dipped the bread, He gave it to Judas Iscariot, the son of Simon. Now after the piece of bread, Satan entered him. Then Jesus said to him, "What you do, do quickly."*** (John 13:26-27). Judas was certainly being sourced by something evil. It was far bigger than Judas could personally imagine. He yielded himself to a pattern, and therefore a person who was overshadowing and manipulating his every activity. Judas played a key role in the unfolding of demonic strategy. Satan used Judas as ***a guide to those who arrested Jesus.***

We have looked at both the positive and the negative of the concept ***to guide.*** Now we must dare to bring this into our lives. Could we conclude that God has ordained that everyone be ***a guide?*** Every person has a strong influence. We do not have influence over everyone, but we each have influence over someone. It is the construction of which relationships are made. Each of us has influence over our children, our extended family, our church body, job relationships, and our neighborhoods. Each of us is ***a guide!***

God wants to indwell you and be ***a guide*** to you. He wants to shepherd you from within. This is the message of the cross style. From the breaking of morning until the dawning of evening and through the night, Jesus wants to be the Shepherd from which all your provisions come. His focus is not on what you can do for Him, but on what He can provide and do through you. He is not interested in you using your talents for Him; He wants to use His talents through you. Will you give up the right to live your life, so He can live His life through you?

But what if I refuse to allow Him to be my ***guide?*** The

Scripture says we only have one other choice. Judas stood in the middle of that choice. He had an incredible opportunity as a called disciple. Everything God planned for the disciples was available to him. He could have experienced Pentecost and could have become *a guide* to the world. The **Guide** wanted to indwell him. All of this was within his grasp, and he made the choice to miss it. In his refusal, he became *a guide to those who arrested Jesus.* He found himself under the influence of Satanic guidance and was used for destruction and death. Now you are faced with this question. What kind of *a guide* will you be?

Acts 1:17

ASPIRING TO BE JUDAS

In order to arrive at the conclusions presented in this study, I had to make some major adjustments in my thought process. This is not an easy thing to do. The adjustments seemed to center more in my attitude than in my logic. I had judgment and condemnation focused on Judas for his betrayal of Christ. I could not see him blending into a crowd. Certainly he must have had horns on his head, or at least a brand on his forehead. But the Lord has helped me set aside those attitudes and see the truths of verse seventeen.

We have established the SETTING (Acts 1:15). Jesus has ascended, but the Promise of the Father has not yet been given. It is a period of seven to ten days during which time the disciples gathered as a society of believers in Jerusalem. There are one hundred and twenty in the group. Peter is making a proposal to them. He is not doing it as a dictator or boss, but as one who is making a suggestion. The vacancy left by Judas in the apostle group must be filled. This Scripture is the basis for Peter's proposal.

Peter reminds them of the STORY (Acts 1:16-17). They were all familiar with the painful details of Judas' actions. Peter does not need to review the details, but he does give a concept of the person Judas was, and the position of his actions. Peter says Judas is one **who became a guide to those who arrested Jesus.** He became the shepherd guide of the betrayal. He was the overseer of the evil event. He misused his office of apostle, the position to which Jesus had called him. He was called to be a shepherd guide.

Peter expands the position of Judas when he says, *for he was numbered with us and obtained a part in this ministry,* (Acts 1:17). The concept is the same, but Peter gives additional information. This information establishes the strategy for the selection of another apostle (Acts 1:23-26). Peter uses the same language he will use in proposing they select two individuals and cast lots for one of them. While we know Jesus did not choose His disciples by casting lots, Peter uses that kind of language in describing the selection of Judas as an apostle.

He was CHOSEN

Peter says, *"For he was numbered with us,"* (Acts 1:17). The Greek word translated, *numbered,* is only used here in the New Testament. It is an interesting choice of words. It proposes the idea of "to be counted as a member of a group or to belong to." Peter could have said that Judas was a disciple or one of the twelve as the Gospel accounts often relate it (Matthew 26:14, 47; Mark 14:10, 43; Luke 22:3, 47; John 6:71). Peter emphasizes that Judas really belonged to the group because he was chosen.

Jesus certainly counted Judas among the apostles. His name is in every list of the disciples given by the Gospel writers (Matthew 10:4; Luke 6:16). Judas is included in every incident. No doubt he was selected in the same manner as the rest of the disciples, but we have little information about how the majority of them were chosen. Judas participated in all of the activities with the other disciples. He was present at the Sermon on the Mount, and he heard the parables just as the others did. He was exposed to the same training as the rest of the group.

The ministry opportunities Jesus offered to the "other

Part Six: A God Ordained Board Meeting: The Proposition

seventy" included Judas. Jesus took something of the power which was His and transferred it to His disciples (Matthew 10:1). In this passage the disciples became apostles. He sent them out to minister. They returned with glowing reports of the success of His ministry through them. Judas was included in all of these experiences.

Judas was a part of the intensive training by Jesus. During the last six months he would have heard much about the coming crucifixion. Judas was involved from the beginning in Caesarea Philippi (Matthew 16:13) to the ending in the passion week, including the Garden of Gethsemane (Matthew 26:36). One would think that seeing the Rich Young Ruler (Matthew 19:16) would have awakened Judas to the gripping control of money. Would he not have identified with the Rich Young Ruler? Jesus preached his final message on Tuesday after Palm Sunday. Surely that must have stirred Judas. The exposure of legalism and empty religion was so strong in his life that he must have felt Jesus was preaching to him alone. Judas was present when the disciples gathered around Jesus on the Mount of Olives (Matthew 24:3). They pressed Him with the question, *"Tell us, when will these things be? And what will be the sign of Your coming, and of the end of the age?"* Judas heard both the theological answer (Matthew 24:4-31) and the Parables of Judgment (Matthew 24:32-51; Matthew 25).

The disciples had financial obligations, and Judas was included in these. It was the financial responsibility of every Jewish male to contribute to the temple ministry every year. Money was gathered often for the feeding of the poor. Jesus was always giving. As the treasurer of the disciples, Judas would have been intimately involved in this aspect.

Judas was present for all of Jesus' teachings on the "Promise of the Father." Jesus shared His heart with the disciples in the upper room. He said, **Helper, the Holy Spirit, whom the Father will send in My name, He will teach you all things, and bring** *to your remembrance all things that I said to you,* (John 14:26). Judas was not left out of anything heard by all of the disciples. Indeed, *he was numbered with us.*

Was there anything different about Judas? The only difference was within Judas himself, and it was self imposed. He had the same opportunities as the other disciples. It was not a matter of understanding or intellectual comprehension. Every disciple betrayed Jesus to some degree in His final days. But there was something beyond their betrayal in the heart and soul of Judas. *He was numbered with us*, but he refused the invitation.

We are forced by Scripture to see this statement written about our lives. Your name and my name are included in *he was numbered with us.* God has manipulated the plan to include us. Some disciples were present at the Mount of Transfiguration, and others were not (Matthew 17:1). Not all of us experience the same events, but God has numbered us among His chosen ones. He did not choose the masses, but He chose each disciple individually. It is still true for today. God is focused on you.

You probably can come up with many reasons why you should not be numbered with us. None of us are ever satisfied with our accomplishments, and we are more often discouraged with our actions. But if Jesus numbered Judas with us, certainly He has included you. None of us have gone lower than Judas. He rejected Christ in an unusual way, yet he was still numbered with us. Jesus has called you!

He had CUSTODY

Jesus had chosen Judas to be a disciple. Knowing Jesus chose Judas, who became His betrayer, is startling but true. Peter boldly states this in the verse we are studying. He said, *"for he was numbered with us and obtained a part in this ministry,"* (Acts 1:17). The word, *obtained*, is extremely important. Jesus chose Judas and included him in His ministry. The definition of the Greek word translated, *obtained,* has the idea of being selected by a decision based on the casting of lots, with the possible implication of reflecting Divine choice. This same word is used for the choosing of Zechariah, a priest and the father of John the Baptist. The Scripture states, *according to the custom of the priesthood, his lot fell to burn incense when he went into the temple of the Lord,* (Luke 1:9). The word translated, *lot,* is the same as the word translated, *obtained.* Now it is certain that Jesus did not choose Judas as His disciple through the method of casting lots, but Peter is expressing a concept. Judas was not a candidate for the position. It was actually his! His name plate had been made and fastened to the door. The fact he rejected it by his betrayal of Christ does not lessen the reality that he had been chosen and had received the position of apostleship.

This concept applies to our lives. There is no way to overstate this fact. The Scripture plainly states that you and I have been chosen and have received all that is involved in this choosing. We are not on probation to see if we can fulfill the role. We are not being tested to see if we can accomplish the standard of His requirements. He has not provided some of the benefits of the position, but held back the majority of the perks until we prove ourselves true. He is not withholding the bonus until we pass the test. He has placed in our hands everything He desires for us that we might experience Him.

God speaks this with great power in the Book of Ephesians. We have covered this material at other times, but it is worth my reminding you of these words. God, the Father, has been required by His own nature to act in your behalf. His actions have taken on the form of His creative speech. He has spoken into existence everything He wants you to have. He wants you to have the person of Christ (See Ephesians 1:3). He *chose us in Him* (Ephesians 1:4). He has numbered you and counted you as included. He did this for you *before the foundation of the world*

(Ephesians 1:4). His choice has been long standing. *He made us accepted in the Beloved* (Ephesians 1:6). He not only chose you, and hoped this for you, but He made it so. It is actually yours. He does not have to forgive you; He has already forgiven you. He does not have to deliver you; He has delivered you. He does not have to give you victory; He has already handed it to you.

Are you getting the sense by now that God means all of this for you? He is not playing a game or experimenting with you. He is extremely serious about you. Peter is telling you the same thing about Judas. If God did this for Judas, the betrayer, He has certainly done it for you. Could it be that all you need to do is accept it? Can you, by faith, accept His choice for you?

The Scriptures are full of this idea. Paul shouts it out based on the crucifixion and resurrection of Christ. *Likewise you also, reckon yourselves to be dead indeed to sin, but alive to God in Christ Jesus our Lord,* (Romans 6:11). The idea of *reckon* is to compute, to realize, or to understand. You need to see the reality of what God has already put into place for you in Christ. Visualize it as yours. He has already given you victory over sin, holiness in abundance, joy and peace in every circumstance, wisdom for all situations, and power for every temptation. He has made every provision for you in Christ, and you have custody of it all now.

He was COUNTED a place

Each of these ideas links together and overlaps. Judas was chosen. He had custody. He was counted a place. Peter said, *"For he was numbered with us and obtained a part in this ministry,"* (Acts 1:17). Judas was chosen by Jesus as a disciple *(he was numbered with us).* All the privileges of apostleship were his because he was chosen. He had custody of this position and all that went with it *(... obtained ...).* Jesus withheld nothing from

Part Six: A God Ordained Board Meeting: The Proposition

him. He was counted a place *(a part in this ministry)*. The spot, the office, the position, and the space he was to fill were his.

Now let me remind you that Peter is using the language connected with the strategy he is proposing for choosing the one to replace Judas. It is the language used with the idea of casting lots. The actual Greek word translated, *part*, refers to a specially marked pebble, piece of pottery, or stick which is used in making decisions based upon chance. It is the same Greek word used in connection with the activity of the soldiers at the foot of the cross. Matthew writes, **Then they crucified Him, and divided His garments, casting lots,** (Matthew 27:35). This word refers to the instrument used in the act of the selection. It is frequently a term which refers to "dice."

Peter said that Judas received the "lot." Then he goes on to propose they cast lots for the person who will take the place of Judas. According to verse twenty-six, this pebble, dice, or lot actually fell to Matthias so the position of apostleship was his. In the same manner this lot, pebble or dice actually belonged to Judas. This was his place.

Oh, how I need to convince you of this! The Bible speaks of what God has planned and provided for you as if you already have it. It is not forth coming or future tense, but the reality of this moment. Listen again to what Paul had to say, **and raised us up together, and made us sit together in the heavenly places in Christ Jesus,** (Ephesians 2:6). When will this take place? It has already happened! This is true even for the non Christian. The dice have been thrown; the lot has been cast. You have already been selected and the position of all God has dreamed for you is in place.

Why would God do this for me? That is not the right question to ask. Why would He not do this for you? He did this for Judas! If God would act this way in behalf of one who would betray Him in the manner and style of the crucifixion, why would He not include you? None of us has gone lower than Judas. If by a slight chance this may be true, would it not pressure me to simply respond to God and accept what He has put in place for me? Could I resist the embrace of the Father who has jumped off the porch and is running in my direction? I have had fellowship with the pigs, and now I smell like them. I have lived in the far off country. I do not deserve the status of a slave in His household. But He has reserved the position of Son for me. My room is clean and ready. He has killed that fatted calf and planned a celebration for my return. Everything is in place. He has not tossed me out and now has to make another place for me. He has **numbered** me and I have **obtained** all of the provisions in His mind and heart. That *part* is mine. How can I resist such love?

Acts 1:18-19

WHAT DO I DESERVE?

One of the great mind stretching issues of the Christian faith is man's attempt to reconcile the justice of God with His mercy. If we over emphasize the mercy of God, we make him the "Santa Claus of the sky," forgiving everyone and everything. We can easily manipulate Him into extravagant gifts of love, which do not deal with the reality of life. On the other hand, if we over emphasize the justice of God, we make Him a scary, stern God, who has no compassion. He cannot understand my weaknesses, and He certainly cannot forgive me when I break His law. How do the two fit together?

One attempt to reconcile this issue is to keep the justice of God and the mercy of God in tight tension, so they balance each other. We then create two different gods, or at least one God who acts in two different ways in two different time periods. In the present time, which extends back to the cross, we are in the dispensation of grace. God is holding back His wrathful side, and He is extending His mercy and love. At the second coming, this will change. God will push the love and mercy aspect of His character into the background, and He will loose His judgment. This makes our God like Jekyll and Hyde, possessing two personalities. We cannot be sure God can be trusted; He might just turn on us in the end.

Some have proposed that Jesus is the reconciliation of these two sides of God. At the cross we see the mercy and justice of God married in a perfect union of oneness. There is valuable truth in this view, however, it is then easy to view Jesus as compensating or paying off the angry God of the universe. This God has no ability of compassion on His own. If we are not hidden in Christ, the angry, judgmental God of the universe will have His way with us.

I have struggled with these concepts throughout my life. I may have a tendency to be over simplistic, but this does not seem to be a problem in the Scriptures. The justice of God is not violated by the love displayed in Christ. Christ is the display of the Father's heart, so we are really seeing what God is like on the cross. If He had His way, everyone would be forgiven. He has done everything within His power, limited only by the free-will of man, to bring victory to all mankind. He has no desire to punish man. Hell was never His idea for us. Yes, it is a reality! But how can this be?

We are moving into some material about Judas, the betrayer of Christ, which brings us face to face with the wages of sin. These verses vividly describe the terrible death of Judas. *(Now this man purchased a field with the wages of iniquity; and falling headlong, he burst open in the middle and all his entrails gushed out. And it became known to all those dwelling in Jerusalem; so that field is called in their own language, Akel Dama, that is, Field of Blood,)* (Acts 1:18-19).

We are reminded of the words of Paul, *For the wages of sin is death,* (Romans 6:23). In view of the wickedness of Judas, how can we feel sorry for his end? He deserved all of the agony which drove him to such a death. We wipe our hands of him and bless the God who would not allow him to escape judgment. But this is not the picture of the Scriptures. With such actions we are violating the character and nature of God, twisting the truth of the Scriptures.

Part Six: A God Ordained Board Meeting: The Proposition

Contrast

Most Bible scholars believe the verses we are considering were inserted by Luke to give Theophilus (Acts 1:1) the details he may not have known. Those in Jerusalem already knew this information. These two verses (18 and 19) interrupt the speech Peter is giving. Verse seventeen connects perfectly with verse twenty as Peter continues his message and quotes the Scriptures from Psalms.

Luke writes this interlude sentence in a most interesting way. The sentence's first word as given in the Greek language is the subject, which is translated, ***this man.*** The fourth word is translated, ***purchased.*** There are two small Greek words sandwiched between these main words. One is the second word in the sentence, and it is not translated in our English versions. The third word in the sentence is translated, ***Now***, which begins the sentence in our English translation.

I find great interest in the two little words. They have a strong impact on what Luke is saying. The first of these two words is the one not translated into English. It is a primary particle. Its function in the sentence is to provide a shade of meaning, which in this case is emphatic. It has the idea of "in fact." It is usually followed by a contrast, and that is what the next word suggests. This Greek word is translated, ***Now***, in most of the English versions. It is a coordinating, continuative conjunction. The meaning of "coordinating" is the idea of linking ideas. One thing cannot be adequately understood without the other. It is translated in the following ways in the New Testament; and (so, truly), but, now (then), so (likewise then), then, therefore, verily, and wherefore. What Luke will say is based on what he has already said.

The preceding information establishes the lens through which we are to view this section. It presents to us a beautiful picture of the heart of God. To understand what Luke is saying we must be reminded of the previous statements concerning Judas, (Acts 1:16-17). We begin with, *"concerning Judas, who became a guide to those who arrested Jesus;"* (Acts 1:16). Luke is not making a statement of action, but he is presenting a concept. In the previous chapter we discovered the role of the shepherd is linked to being a guide. The shepherd is the one who takes us by the hand and gently leads us down the road. It is the picture of the Holy Spirit who will guide us into all truth (John 16:13). This is the concept of Judas' role in the betrayal. He was a shepherd guide who initiated the betrayal. He is the one who selected the Garden of Gethsemane as the place to identify Jesus. He chose the sign of the kiss of betrayal. He was an instrument of evil for *Satan entered Judas,* (Luke 22:3).

It appears to me the next statement in Acts should be the passage of this study (Acts 1:18-19), but it is not. It describes the end result of demonic justice. Who could dispute the fact that Judas got what he deserved? When you connect the end of verse sixteen with verses eighteen and nineteen, a sense of gladness results. The display of Judas' evil merits the consequence described in these verses. This is exactly the right outcome, and you go away feeling like things have been put right.

BUT if you pay close attention, these two verses are not connected. Something stands in the way of the oncoming judgment. We can see the terrible evil in verse sixteen, but before Judas marches into full justice of judgment in verses eighteen and nineteen, he must pass through verse seventeen. This verse blocks the pending damnation. It is the great dam holding back the torrent of judgmental waters which should sweep over the soul involved in verse sixteen.

It is the GRACE of God. *"For he was numbered with us and obtained a part in this ministry,"* (Acts 1:17). In an earlier study we investigated this marvelous statement of God's love. Judas was chosen by God, which is the meaning of the phrase, *for he*

was numbered with us. The emphasis is on God's choosing, but not on Judas' involvement. He was not chosen because he was qualified. God chose Judas just as he was, and Judas ***obtained.*** He was not on probation; He was included with all of the benefits of apostleship. He had his name plate on the door, and he had received all Christ dreamed for him. These facts stand in the way of verse nineteen.

This information should compel us to see the same is true for our lives. The filth of our sin looms on one side, and the pit of destruction and consequences for those sins presses from the other side. What chance do we have? Why should God not damn us forever? Then suddenly, right in the midst of my sin and the death pressing in upon me, stands God's grace. This is the way out! I have been chosen, and God's mighty hand has placed me in Christ. Forgiveness is mine. Jesus has come to empower and enhance my life by His presence. I am His.

Concern

There is some controversy among Bible scholars concerning what Luke is saying in the remainder of this verse. He writes, ***(Now this man purchased a field with the wages of iniquity)*** (Acts 1:18). Some believe Judas took the thirty pieces of silver and purchased a small farm. It was on this farm that Judas hanged himself. However, the theory cannot be reconciled with Matthew's account of what Judas did. Judas, upon seeing what the leaders of Israel had done to Jesus, was so convicted of his actions, he came to them and attempted to undo their agreement. ***Then he threw down the pieces of silver in the temple and departed, and went and hanged himself,*** (Matthew 27:5). It was later the chief priest ***said, "It is not lawful to put them into the treasury, because they are the price of blood." And they consulted together and bought with them the potter's field, to bury strangers in,***

What Do I Deserve? | Acts 1:18-19

(Matthew 27:6-7). Since the field was bought with the money received from Judas, Luke writes **this man purchased a field with the wages of iniquity.** (Acts 1:18).

We do not find the truth of this statement in the clarity of who purchased this field, but the truth is found in the motive behind the purchase. The Greek word translated, **purchased**, means to gain possession of, to procure, acquire, or to get. But regardless of which of these phrases or words you want to use, you must add "for oneself." The focus of the **wages of iniquity** is for oneself. According to Matthew's account, **Then one of the twelve, called Judas Iscariot, went to the chief priests and said, "What are you willing to give me if I deliver Him to you?"** (Matthew 26:14-15). John's account relates the story of Mary washing the feet of Jesus with a **pound of very costly oil of spikenard,** (John 12:1-8). This annoyed Judas greatly. He said, **"Why was this fragrant oil not sold for three hundred denarii and given to the poor?** John explains that Judas did not say this because he cared for the poor. Rather **he was a thief, and had the money box; and he used to take what was put in it.** Judas' concern was selling the oil so he could steal the funds when they were placed into the treasury.

This shifts the blame from God to Judas. Surely no one could look at this scene and accuse God of being the author of the consequences recorded in verses eighteen and nineteen. This is not God's desire for Judas. God had chosen him and given him a place of authority. Apostleship was placed in his hands. But Judas chose for himself another way. The end result of his choice to get for himself is seen in these two verses.

Paul expresses the results of choosing for oneself in his Romans account. He tells us **the wrath of God is revealed from heaven against all ungodliness and unrighteousness of men,** (Romans 1:18). In the next verse he clarifies that God has revealed Himself and pushed Himself upon mankind to the point **that they are without excuse,** (Romans 1:20). But men continually

Part Six: A God Ordained Board Meeting: The Proposition

choose to purchase "for oneself". Paul explains how the ***wrath of God*** was poured out upon them for this. ***Therefore God also gave them up to uncleanness, in the lusts of their hearts, to dishonor their bodies among themselves, who exchanged the truth of God for the lie, and worshiped and served the creature rather than the Creator, who is blessed forever. Amen,*** (Romans 1:24-25). God allowed what was ***purchased with the wages of iniquity*** to be realized. He takes His protective hands from our lives and allows us to experience the consequences of what we have chosen. This is the expression of His wrath.

God did not have to punish Judas. Judas' choice carried with it its own guilt, destruction and punishment. Jesus expressed the heart of God as He wept over Jerusalem with a cry not of judgment but of brokenness over what would be the consequences of their choosing "for oneself," (Matthew 23:37-39). Certainly God was weeping over Judas as he experienced the full consequences of his selfish choices. Christ, with all of His grace, is standing between the awfulness of my choices and the destruction that should come to my life as a result of them. Verses eighteen and nineteen can be true for my life, but only after I have gone through the Christ who stands in my way!

Compensation

There is one other intriguing truth located in this passage. Luke writes, ***(Now this man purchased a field with the wages of iniquity; ...)*** (Acts 1:18). The Greek word which is translated, ***with***, is a small word having to do with "origin," and it means "out of." The Greek word translated, ***wages***, is also translated "reward." The focus of the statement is on the act of betrayal, and the thirty pieces of silver Judas acquired from it. The destruction Judas experienced was attached to this one single deed of betrayal.

We know there were many sins in the life of Judas. John's

account calls him a thief (John 12:6). John highlights the fact that Judas' attitude was totally wrong and definitely selfish. But none of those sins are mentioned as Judas' life is destroyed. All of the consequences of sin as found in verses eighteen and nineteen have to do with only one act, the rejection of Jesus. One Bible scholar says the Greek phrase translated, **the wages of iniquity,** means Judas paid the fee for the field purchased with the fee paid him for his crime (of a single misdeed).

What if the single issue for which you and I are going to be accountable is what we do with Jesus? What place did you give Him in your life? Was He the focus of your living? Where was He in your priority list? No other deed, thought, action, or motive will be mentioned. It will be as if nothing else matters or all else is a by-product of this one issue.

If you think I am appealing to you to make a decision for Christ and experience what is normally called salvation, you are wrong. Judas made such a decision. He was a disciple! But he did not allow Jesus to become his life. The Christian experience is greater than a decision made years ago or any activity you have accomplished since then. Christianity is about your intimacy and involvement with the person of Christ now! Have you allowed this relationship to expand to its fullest level in the present moment? Judas continued to operate at the beginning level of his relationship with Christ. He was still a disciple, but his relationship had not expanded to its full potential in the present moment.

The single issue of the Christian faith is Christ and your relationship with Him in the present moment. Contained within the grace (Acts 1:17), which stands between what Judas did (Acts 1:16) and the terrible consequences of sin (Acts 1:18-19), is the unlimited potential of the dreams of God. God chose Judas and gave him the full measure of the ministry of His dreams. The fullness of the Spirit of God would be poured out on Judas at Pentecost. God dreamed that Judas would be a part

Part Six: A God Ordained Board Meeting: The Proposition

of establishing the Church. But Judas refused to move in the expanding relationship with Christ, which would have taken him through the cross into the fullness of the Spirit.

How does this apply to you and me?

Acts 1:19

TO KNOW

There is much about Christianity that has nothing to do with good or bad, right or wrong. Christianity is relational, which means it is hard to measure. We do not want to divide Christianity into categories, but for lack of a better term, we might say that there are levels to the relationship we have with Christ. It is important to constantly examine the depth of our relationship with Him.

A person may have been raised in a Christian culture or environment and acquired a moral character which governs his activities. He or she may appear to be Christian, even though they have no relationship with Christ. There are those who have had a personal encounter with Jesus, and have experienced moments of delight in His presence. They maintain habitual involvement with the church and carry out personal Christian disciplines. However, they are not being sourced by His presence in a moment by moment relationship. Then there is the person who is filled with the Spirit of Jesus. He or she experiences an intimate relationship with Christ. This relationship is constantly expanding, and they are **being transformed into the same image from glory to glory, just as by the Spirit of the Lord,** (2 Corinthians 3:18).

There are degrees and stages to all of the above situations. We are on a journey, and God is bringing us to Himself. The essence of relationship means it is fluid. There is no arrival or

Part Six: A God Ordained Board Meeting: The Proposition

time when it is finished. The love within the relationship calls each one to hunger for a new level of intimacy and embrace. What an experience it is to grow in relationship with God. A deeper and greater reality of His presence seems to be constantly unfolding. The intimacy overcomes you, and you find you cannot live without it.

An intimate relationship with God leads to an awareness of others. A new passion evolves and you find the need for relationships with other persons of mankind. It is the wonder of the mind of Christ beginning to form in you. As His heart begins to beat within your being, you feel about others the way He does. The disciples asked the question, *"Teacher, which is the great command in the law?"* (Matthew 22:36). Jesus gave a profound answer which was already a part of their Old Testament training, (Deuteronomy 10:12; 30:6). *Jesus said to him, "You shall love the Lord your God with all your heart, with all your soul, and with all your mind. This is the first and great commandment. And the second is like it: 'You shall love your neighbor as yourself.'"* (Matthew 22:37-39).

Relationship is very important as we approach the story of Judas. What role did the relationship Judas had with the other disciples play in his act of betrayal? There is certainly a question about his relationship with Jesus. The heart of it seems to be expressed in the passage we are considering in this study. *And became known to all those dwelling in Jerusalem;* (Acts 1:19). In this statement, Luke highlights an expression of a level of involvement or relationship.

As we come to the English translation of the New Testament, the words, know, known, knowledge, and unknown, all appear to come from the same basic Greek word. But further investigation reveals this is not so. There are four different Greek words which seem to be expressed in this one English word, known. The beauty of the Greek language is the various pictures it paints by the different words. Greek enables the author to express a depth of meaning which could not otherwise have been written.

One of these Greek words is "ginosko." It signifies "to be taking in knowledge, to come to know, recognize, understand," or "to understand completely. The power of the word is the fact that it frequently indicates a relation between the person knowing and the object known. This presents us with the concept that what is known is of value or importance to the one who knows. This establishes relationship. This is the word used as a verb to convey the thought connection or union, as between a man and a woman. *"And did not know her till she had brought forth her firstborn Son,"* (Matthew 1:25).

One of the greatest Scriptures for investigating this word is in the High Priestly prayer of Jesus, recorded in the Gospel of John (John 17). Jesus uses this word seven times in this prayer. He begins in the early moments of His prayer saying, *"And this is eternal life, that they may know* (ginosko) *You, the only true God, and Jesus Christ whom You have sent,"* (John 17:3). Eternal life is a quality of life which only comes through an intimate relationship with Him. We title this "Life's Relationship." The word, ginosko, expresses a knowledge of God which takes us beyond facts, into God's person, and produces a quality of life which is eternal.

As Jesus continues in His prayer, He says, *"Now they have known* (ginosko) *that all things which You have given Me are from You,"* (John 17:7). This we call "Life's Revelation." As Jesus manifests His life in us, we see, and we "ginosko" that the life coming from Jesus is from the Father. Jesus is a revelation of the Father's nature. He is a product of the Father's generous heart. We now embrace and "ginosko" the same kind of relationship. What Jesus received from the Father can be ours as well.

"For I have given to them the words which You have given to Me; and they have received them, and have known (ginosko) *surely that I came forth from You; and they have believed that You sent Me,"* (John 17:8). The disciples experienced what we

call "Life's Reliance." They came to believe in the Father because they had "ginosko." It is also the foundation of our living. The knowledge of His person multiplies our faith. We need no other argument but the reality of His presence. The very knowing (ginosko) has become the basis of our faith.

As Jesus nears the closing of His prayer, He focuses on oneness. He says, ***"I in them, and You in Me; that they may be made perfect in one, and that the world may know*** (ginosko) ***that You have sent Me, and have loved them as You have loved Me,"*** (John 17:25). This is "Life's Record." Not only will the disciples have to "ginosko," but the world will have to "ginosko" also. The knowledge will flow from Jesus and the Father, to the disciples, to the world. It is a knowledge that goes beyond facts and information. It is a knowledge that flows into relationship. This is evangelism at its best!

Jesus climaxes His prayer with these words, ***"O righteous Father! The world has not known*** (ginosko) ***You, but I have known*** (ginosko) ***You; and these have known*** (ginosko) ***that You sent Me,"*** (John 17:25). This Greek word, ginosko, is used three times in this one verse. Jesus began His prayer with "Life's Relationship," and that is the way He concludes it (John 17:3). He measures everything based on intimacy. Everyone is seen in comparison to our "ginosko." This can only leave us with the sense that this is the heart of what Jesus desires for us. The Kingdom is one of relationship.

A second Greek word which is translated "to know" is the word "oida." It comes from the Greek root word which means "to see." This word, when used in a perfect tense with a present meaning, suggests "to have seen or perceived." It gives us the idea of "to know, to have knowledge of." The differences between "ginosko" and "oida" are exciting to note. "Ginosko" frequently suggests inception or progress in knowledge, while "oida" suggests fulness of knowledge. A second difference is "ginosko" most often implies an active relation between the one who knows and the person or thing known, while "oida" expresses the idea that the object simply comes within the scope of the perception of the one knowing.

"Oida" presents these two basic ideas. There has come within a person's perception a fullness of knowledge. We see this in Jesus' conversation with His disciples in the upper room (John 14). Jesus tells the disciples there is another place being prepared for them. He would not go to all of this trouble for them without being sure they will arrive at this place. He adds, *"And where I go you know* (oida) *, and the way you know* (oida)*,"* (John 14:4). The disciples have already received the "oida" of the directions to this great place. But Thomas reacts strongly to what Jesus has said. He asks the question, *"Lord, we do not know* (oida) *where You are going, and how can we know* (oida) *the way?"* (John 14:5).

We now want to expand this subject to a third Greek word, "epiginosko." You will recognize it as the first Greek word we discussed, with the prefix "epi." The prefix can be translated, upon. This is a strengthened form of the definition of "ginosko." It means the full extent of relationship or participation in the object you are knowing. It is a knowledge which perfectly unites the subject with the object.

An example of the use of the word, "epiginosko," is found in Paul's statement about our future. *For now we see in a mirror, dimly, but then face to face. Now I know* (ginosko) *in part, but then I shall know* (epiginosko) *just as I also am known* (epiginosko), (1 Corinthians 13:12). The first part of the statement, *Now I know in part,* is a translation of the word, "ginosko." It suggests the idea of progression of a relationship which is not completed. Then Paul uses "epiginosko" two different times to describe what the future holds. It is the full extent of relationship and embrace.

These three words give us rich content to the kind of relationship and knowledge we are to have with God and each

Part Six: A God Ordained Board Meeting: The Proposition

other. There is a definite intimacy suggested; in fact, it is a growing intimacy. The fullness of the Kingdom of God, as pictured in our future, is one of intimate knowledge of each other. There will be total openness and interaction on a deep level of fellowship. It suggests not only a fullness of relationship, but a fullness of knowledge as well. It is a startling truth that the knowledge of a person has something to do with the level of relationship with that person.

Now we come to our study in the Book of Acts concerning Judas. ***(Now this man purchased a field with the wages of iniquity; and falling headlong, he burst open in the middle and all his entrails gushed out. And it became known*** (gnostos) ***to all those dwelling in Jerusalem; so that field is called in their own language, Akel Dama, that is, Field of Blood,)*** (Acts 1:18-19). The Greek word which is translated, ***known***, in this statement, is different from all of the above. It is "gnostos." It is used fifteen times in the New Testament, and ten of those are in the Book of Acts. The word is always used the same way in the Book of Acts, with one exception (Acts 4:16), where it means "notable." All other times it means "acquaintance" and has to do with information.

And it became known to all those dwelling in Jerusalem; (Acts 1:19). There is one Greek word which refers to those individuals living in Jerusalem. It is translated, dwellers. It properly signifies "to settle down in a dwelling, to dwell fixedly in a place." Luke is not referring to the visitors who came to Jerusalem for the Feast of Pentecost, but to those who make their home in Jerusalem and have responsibility for the community. These are the people who knew, had information, and were acquainted with what happened to Judas.

The tragedy of the situation is no one in Jerusalem went to the trouble of going beyond the surface level of "knowing" (gnostos). No one was concerned enough to investigate, come along side, or care. Judas was nothing more than an item of information in the local newspaper. He was not a person of value. No one tried to save him. Judas had been treated this way before. He was present outside Caiaphas' palace when they brought Jesus down the stairway in the early morning hours. He saw Christ and knew full well what had happened to Him. They had beaten Jesus severely. Great conviction gripped Judas deep in his heart. The soldiers were leading Jesus down the road to the palace of the governor, Pontius Pilate. Judas ran to the chief priests and the elders. He desperately wanted to undo what he had done. He had conspired with the leaders of Israel to betray Jesus, and he could no longer live with his transaction. The only thing he knew to do was to return the thirty pieces of silver. He cried out to them, *"I have sinned by betraying innocent blood,"* (Matthew 27:4). And how did they answer him? *"What is that to us? You see to it!"* Do you hear the indifference in their response? Judas confessed, and his information simply did not matter to them.

What would have happened to Judas if someone had cared, if someone had known him beyond the level of information? At the moment of his confession, where was the person who would wrap their arms around him and offer support and prayer? Where was the listening ear and the guidance into forgiveness? Oh, Jesus had given him many chances, but there seemed to be no one else to do the same.

Evangelism does not succeed on the level of information and acquaintance. The heart of Christ demands the kind of love which takes us into the level of relationship. If this does not take place, people never get saved. You cannot program relationship, and it is certainly not the result of learned techniques. We become Christ's when we know Him on an intimate level. We are changed because He maintains an increasing level of knowledge with us. This is what naturally calls us to never allow another person like Judas to perish within the realm of our world.

Our communities are filled with people, who because of

Part Six: A God Ordained Board Meeting: The Proposition

their evil life style, demand the punishment of hell. One such person might be a young female who dances at the local bar. She is divorced and the single parent of one child. She is not an asset to our community. We could have an all church meeting, and without a doubt, after presenting her evil life style, openly demand that she should go to hell for her behavior. In a unanimous vote we declare her damned. Then we have to carry out our decision. How can we be sure she will never encounter Christ and be saved? The most obvious way is to simply continue to do exactly what we have been doing! We simply leave her alone! We keep her on the level of information (gnostos) and not knowing about her. She must never enter into the level of "ginosko."

But you say, that is a preposterous idea. No church group would ever do such a thing! Yet, in reality we have done this with hundreds of people all around us. We read about them in the newspapers. We dwell in their community, have knowledge of their situation, but never move to any deeper level of knowing them. It is important to remember our redemption came because God used someone to go beyond the level of acquaintance in our lives. God is calling us to relationship with Himself and then with others.

PART SEVEN
ACTS 1:20-24

A GOD ORDAINED BOARD MEETING:
HIS PREFERENCE

Acts 1:20

MY LIFE IN THE SCRIPTURES

One hundred and twenty people have gathered together in anticipation of the "Promise of the Father." Through a great volume of prayer and the searching of the Scriptures, an issue arises. It is the unresolved issue of Judas. While they do not have to make a decision about Judas as a person, they are required to make a decision about the office he has vacated. Peter stands to his feet and makes a suggestion. He bases his suggestion on the premise that David considered his enemy, whoever he was, unworthy of his office, and desired that it should be given to another. He quotes a statement made by David (Psalms 109:8), **"Let another take his office,"** (Acts 1:20).

As Peter presents this issue to the group of disciples, he applies it to Judas. Judas rendered himself unworthy of his office, and the conclusion that it should be given to another concurs with David's preceding decision. The Greek word translated ***office*** should be considered in a broad view. It means to care, charge, business, or oversight of anything. It is a word used of magistrates who have the office of seeing that the laws are executed. While Judas is gone from the scene and has been found unworthy, the office he vacated is worthy. It remains open and needs to be filled.

Peter speaks of the qualifications required to fulfill this office. The importance of the office is revealed by Peter's concluding statement. **"One of these must become a witness with us**

Part Seven: A God Ordained Board Meeting: His Preference

of His resurrection," (Acts 1:22). Jesus called these disciples to accomplish a task. This statement focuses on that accomplishment. The manifestation of His resurrected life is the secret for spreading the Good News and building the Kingdom of God.

The Scripture Had To Be Fulfilled

The basic ideas from this passage have direct application to our lives. Verse twenty is directly connected to verse sixteen. We have established an outline for this paragraph. "The Setting" is given to us in the opening verse (Acts 1:15). Peter begins to speak in verse sixteen. His opening statement gives us the concept of "The Story" of Judas (Acts 1:16-17). Luke, the author of the Book of Acts, inserts the two following verses. It is an interruption to the speech of Peter. We call it "The Sadness" (Acts 1:18-19). Now we return to Peter's speech, which contains "The Scriptures" he refers to in his opening statement (Acts 1:20).

Peter has a definite purpose in quoting the Scriptures. *"Men and brethren, this Scripture had to be fulfilled, which the Holy Spirit spoke before by the mouth of David concerning Judas, who became a guide to those who arrested Jesus;"* (Acts 1:16). The strongest statement is the powerful and overall declaration that *this Scripture had to be fulfilled.* Immediately under, subordinate and giving content to, is the pronouncement *which the Holy Spirit spoke before.* Coming under this is another explanation *by the mouth of David.*

We must view the actual Scriptures Peter quotes through the lens of verse sixteen. The premise, which sets the stage for these two quotes from the Book of Psalms, is *this Scripture had to be fulfilled.* Peter uses the same verb again. He says, *"One of these must become a witness with us of His resurrection,"* (Acts 1:22). It is in the Greek imperative. It carries with it the absolute necessity which comes from a Divine decree. Mankind has no influence upon the fulfillment of the Scriptures. The choices man makes, or does not make, will not effect the fulfillment of the Scriptures. There is no way to overstate this great truth. The Scriptures are set in concrete and are absolutely sure. They will be fulfilled.

This does not take away from the free will of man. Things are not true because they are in the Scriptures; rather they are in the Scriptures because they are true. Regardless of the prophecy in the Old Testament, Judas would have accomplished the act of betrayal. He was not forced to this evil thing. However, the Scriptures recorded his evil act because it is what he was going to do. The Scriptures had to be fulfilled!

The Scriptures Are Being Fulfilled

You may not immediately see the relation of this truth to your personal life. This is undoubtedly how it was with Judas. He viewed himself as having no major role in the histories of the world, let alone the fulfillment of Scriptures. Yet, he played a key role in the plans of God for the redemption of the world. He read the same Psalms that Peter read, and he would not have recognized them as prophecies concerning him. But think of what would have happened if he had seen the truth! If Judas could have seen the Scriptures acting out upon the stage of his life, he would have responded differently. What a change it would have made in his approach to life! He would have found a completely different pattern for his living.

Well, I have not seen my name in the Scriptures! Have you looked carefully for your name? It is absolutely essential you see your life in light of the Scriptures. Think of the life of John the Baptist. What kept him focused on what he had been called to do? How did he overcome pride to having the most successful ministry in the land of Judea? How could he settle for second place to the ministry of Jesus? What drove him to be faithful to what God had called him? There was a dispute between John's disciples and some of the Jews. It was

Part Seven: A God Ordained Board Meeting: His Preference

over purification. They were a little dismayed over the fact that Jesus and His disciples were baptizing more people than they were. What was the reaction of John the Baptist? He had no problem with it at all! ***John answered and said, "A man can receive nothing unless it has been given to him from heaven,"*** (John 3:27). John recognized his role as one given to him from heaven. God Himself proclaimed it in the Scriptures. John knew his life and ministry was a fulfillment of the Scriptures which had to come to pass. John saw himself as the forerunner to the Messiah. He said, ***"You yourselves bear me witness, that I said, 'I am not the Christ,' but, 'I have been sent before Him,'"*** (John 3:28). John the Baptist knew his role as defined in the Scriptures. The Scriptures were being fulfilled in and through his life. In this he found contentment.

John understood that his baptism was a preparation for the Messianic baptism anticipated by the prophets. For a true cleansing, the nation must wait until God opened a fountain for cleansing in Israel (Zechariah 13:1), sprinkled His people with clean water, and gave them a new heart and spirit (Ezekiel 36:25-26; Jeremiah 33:8). John's baptism was an immediate preparation and a promise of the spiritual cleansing which the Messiah would bestow. ***"I indeed baptize you with water unto repentance, but He who is coming after me ... will baptize with the Holy Spirit and with fire,"*** (Matthew 3:11).

Are there any prophecies which concern you? Here in the Book of Acts, Jesus gathers His disciples together for the last time to emphasize a promise which is theirs. ***And being assembled together with them, He commanded them not to depart from Jerusalem, but to wait for the Promise of the Father,*** (Acts 1:3). What a great prophecy and fulfillment!

Do you not see your name on this page? Is this not spoken directly to you? The Scripture has been and will be fulfilled. You are affected by the outpouring of the Holy Spirit. God has accomplished His dream of intimacy with you. Everything is in place for you to experience the fulfillment of Scripture in your life.

Jesus continues his discussion with His disciples, giving them additional information. He says, *"But you shall receive power when the Holy Spirit has come upon you; and you shall be witnesses to Me in Jerusalem, and in all Judea and Samaria, and to the end of the earth,"* (Acts 1:8). Your name is recorded in this statement. This was spoken directly to you and for you. It is a fulfillment of the promise of being sourced by God. Everything you need to win your world, to walk in victory, and to be adequate for that which He has called you, is yours. The Scripture has been and will be fulfilled. This is a certainty for your life. You do not have to beg or worry yourself or God with the need. It is definite. This prophecy will be fulfilled in your life. Will you allow the Scriptures to be fulfilled in you?

Peter displays this same truth when he makes his request of the society of believers. He does not give the details of the betrayal scene; rather he relates the concept of Judas' action. He refers to him as *"a guide to those who arrested Jesus;"* (Acts 1:16). He relates the position in which Judas was placed by God. As you look at it carefully, and examine it in light of the rest of the Scriptures, you find it describes you. He said, *"For he was numbered with us and obtained a part in this ministry,"* (Acts 1:17). This statement deserves careful and constant consideration. Perhaps you do not see your name here. Maybe you think this relates only to the person of Judas. Judas would not have thought this was about his life either. He would have laughed at the mere suggestion. Yet, the reality of truth is there. There is no question that verse seventeen, which is in reference to Judas, is true about your life as well. You have been *numbered with us.* It is the idea of "chosen." Paul said, *"He chose us in Him before the foundation of the world,* (Ephesians 1:4). We are not hoping to be chosen, or put on probation to see if we qualify. We have *obtained.* Our name

Part Seven: A God Ordained Board Meeting: His Preference

is on the door and the office has been provided. The dream of God is in place for your life. It is in the Scriptures, and the Scriptures are being fulfilled in your life. You can do as Judas did, but you can also experience all God wants for you! It is prophesied in the Scriptures, but you have the choice. The Scriptures are being fulfilled in your life!

The Scriptures Fulfilled Reveal You Are Not Alone

In the passage we are considering (Acts 1:20), Peter quotes two Psalms as the basis for the proposal concerning the office Judas has vacated. The first quotation: ***Let his dwelling place be desolate, And let no one live in it.*** (Psalm 69:25)

This is a Psalm of David. It is one of the many Messianic Psalms. There are several key statements in the Psalms which are distinctly related to the Messiah.

Because zeal for Your house has eaten me up, (Psalm 69:9). The verse is directly applied to the Messiah in John 2:17; 21.

They also gave me gall for my food. And for my thirst they gave me vinegar to drink, (Psalm 69:21). This was done to Christ on the cross as related by Matthew (27:34). The whole Psalm is expressive of deep sorrow for persecution, contempt, weeping, being forsaken, and is applicable throughout to the Messiah.

There is a second quotation. ***Let another take his office,*** (Acts 1:20). This comes from another Psalm of David (Psalms 109:8). It is in the same class as numerous other Psalms (6; 22; 25; 38 and 42). This class of Psalms is believed to have expressed David's feelings during the troubling times of persecution by King Saul, the rebellion of Absalom, and other trials. They are also expressive of the condition of a suffering and persecuted Messiah and many of them are applied to the New Testament.

These Psalms are related to the coming Messiah. This Messiah will reign on the throne of King David, and the enemies of the royal psalmist become the enemies of the Messiah. Therefore, Judas was also included in these Psalms. David could take great comfort in this truth. He is not alone in his battles, for his enemies are the enemies of the coming Christ. Those who attempt to hinder and destroy him are also coming against the redemptive plan of God. David is not alone in the battle.

We are aware that the Scriptures have to be fulfilled. It is a Divine necessity. The Scriptures are being fulfilled in and through our lives this very moment. We are the stage upon which the Scriptures are being acted out. The war that rages upon my life is not my personal war. I am not alone. The enemies which battle my life are coming up against the resurrected Lord. What a reality this is! This is the message of the entire Book of Acts. The Promise of the Father has been fulfilled. The fulfillment of this great prophecy has taken place within us. Everyone who would fight against us comes up against the indwelling Spirit of Christ. This is not our battle.

We must not take responsibility for what is not ours. We must not assume leadership and control over what is not placed in our charge. We must surrender, yield, and live in responsiveness. It is the call of the fullness of the Holy Spirit.

Acts 1:21-22

A RESURRECTION WITNESS

The minutes to the first recorded business meeting of the early church are included in sacred Scripture. They find their position just prior to the event of Pentecost. Peter feels the leading of the Holy Spirit through prayer and reading of the Word. He presents a proposal to the entire group of believers who are waiting on the Promise of the Father. He suggests the selection of two individuals, and they pray for the guidance of God in the casting of lots.

The difficulty with the proposition is the selection of the two individuals. What are the qualifications? Peter has thought this through as well. The STANDARD is established for us. The individual who will replace Judas in the apostleship office must be chosen from among those **"who have accompanied us all the time that the Lord Jesus went in and out among us, beginning from the baptism of John to that day when He was taken up from us,"** (Acts 1:21-22). This eliminates many from the number of individuals who are available. The only ones who will qualify are those called "the other seventy." These have been a part of the ministry of Christ and were sent out to minister as were the apostles.

But Peter makes one more statement in connection with these qualifications. His statement gives us a dominate focus on the reason for this process, as well as the purpose for the office of the twelve apostles. The purpose was not to establish adequate leadership to oversee the various regions where evangelism would take place. Neither was the purpose to establish and promote new programs for the church plants. The purpose was contained in *"one of these must become a witness with us of His resurrection,"* (Acts 1:22). The witnessing of His resurrection was the single reason. This was fulfilled in the preceding ministry of the Holy Spirit as recorded throughout the Book of Acts. *And with great power the apostles gave witness to the resurrection of the Lord Jesus. And great grace was upon them all,* (Acts 4:33). The focus for choosing was on the witnessing of His resurrection.

Remember, as presented by Peter, this purpose contained the word *must*. He states, *"one of these must become a witness with us of His resurrection,"* (Acts 1:22). This is the same Greek word which Peter used earlier concerning the Scriptures. He related that the Scriptures must be fulfilled (Acts 1:16). It has to do with an absolute necessity due to the decree of God. The issue of this whole process is the absolute necessity that there must be an adequate witness of His resurrection.

The Centrality of the Resurrection

It is significant that the focused message of the early church was His resurrection. As we view the Book of Acts, the issue of the resurrection seems to be in every message and conversation. The first message, after the Promise of the Father was poured out upon them, was delivered by Peter. The heart of his message is a quotation from David (Psalms 16:8-11). As Peter interprets this statement, he says, *"He, foreseeing this, spoke concerning the resurrection of the Christ, that His soul was not left in Hades, nor did His flesh see corruption. This Jesus God has raised up, of which we are all witnesses,"* (Acts 2:31-32).

Peter and John are involved in a miracle at the Gate Beautiful. The crowd is greatly moved giving Peter the wonderful opportunity to preach to them. The results were, ***Now as they spoke to the people, the priests, the captain of the temple, and the Sadducees came upon them, being greatly disturbed that they taught the people and preached in Jesus the resurrection from the dead,*** (Acts 4:1-2). There could be no doubt in the minds of the leaders of Israel what the message of the apostles was. They preached Jesus and His resurrection from the dead.

As the Book of Acts unfolds into the evangelism of the Apostle Paul, we see the message of the resurrection being strongly delivered to the Gentiles. ***Then certain Epicurean and Stoic philosophers encountered him. And some said, "What does this babbler want to say?" Others said, "He seems to be a proclaimer of foreign gods," because he preached to them Jesus and the resurrection,"*** (Acts 17:18; see 17:32). Paul's message before the council was the resurrection. ***But when Paul perceived that one part were Sadducees and the other Pharisees, he cried out in the council, "Men and brethren, I am a Pharisee, the son of a Pharisee; concerning the hope and resurrection of the dead I am being judged!"*** (Acts 23:6). Paul came before Felix, the governor. He presented his defense against the accusations of the leaders of Israel, saying, ***"I have hope in God, which they themselves also accept, that there will be a resurrection of the dead, both of the just and the unjust,"*** (Acts 24:15). At the close of his defense, he boldly proclaims, ***"They ought to have been here before you to object if they had anything against me. Or else let those who are here themselves say if they found any wrongdoing in me while I stood before the council, unless it is for this one statement which I cried out, standing among them, 'Concerning the resurrection of the dead I am being judged by you this day,"*** (Acts 24:19-21). Paul then presented his case before King Agrippa. He told the king of his heavenly vision, and ***"that the Christ would suffer, that He would be the first to rise from the dead, and would proclaim light to the Jewish people and to the Gentiles,"*** (Acts 26:23).

A new apostle must be chosen to take the place of Judas. This person was to have been present for all of the resurrection appearances of Christ. He was also to have been present throughout the entire time of Christ's earthly ministry. The individual chosen has to have been there, *"beginning from the baptism of John to that day when He was taken up from us,"* (Acts 1:22). All of the events of Jesus' life gave content to His resurrection. The content of His life did not change after the resurrection, but continued throughout. The resurrection was more than a mere event to be remembered. It was the continuation of the redemptive ministry of Christ, which expanded at His baptism by John. The content of the resurrection is the entire life of Christ. Everything from His baptism through to His ascension was important. Nothing matters but the expression and manifestation of His life.

The Concentration of the Resurrection

The Greek word, which is translated *resurrection,* is used forty-two times in the New Testament. It is a powerful word. It means the resurrection of the body with only one exception. Simeon, the old man at the temple, was waiting for the revelation of the *Consolation of Israel.* Being led by the Holy Spirit, he entered the temple when Joseph and Mary brought in the Christ child *to do for Him according to the custom of the law.* Simeon gave blessing to God for this experience. *Then Simeon blessed them and said to Mary His mother, "Behold, this Child is destined for the fall and rising of many in Israel, and for a sign which will be spoken against,"* (Luke 2:34). Here the Greek word normally translated *resurrection* appears as *rising (again).* Even in this context it has definite connections to the resurrection from the dead.

The content of this Greek word is always focused on

the physical resurrection from the dead. It is about the resurrection of the body. It is never used with the meaning of spiritual regeneration or quickening. The apostles preached and believed Jesus was physically raised from the dead. But what else could they proclaim after experiencing forty days of His resurrection appearances (Acts 1:3)? They had seen Him in his newly resurrected body. They recognized him. They engaged in numerous physical activities with Him, such as eating, communication, and travel. The apostles constantly wrote about, *That which was from the beginning, which we have heard, which we have seen with our eyes, which we have looked upon, and our hands have handled,* (1John 1:1). This was true not only of their involvement with Him in ministry and training, but also of the resurrection.

Jesus Himself verified that He was physically raised from the dead in His appearances to the disciples. They were afraid when He first appeared, and they thought they had seen a ghost. He assured them by saying, ***"Behold My hands and My feet, that is I Myself. Handle Me and see, for a spirit does not have flesh and bones as you see I have,"*** (Luke 24:39).

Why is this so important? Because this is the very basis of the hope we have of our own personal resurrection. Jesus' resurrection is a prototypical event. Jesus' resurrection of the body is declared by the Apostle Paul as ***the first fruits,*** (1 Corinthians 15:23). He declared Jesus to be ***the firstborn from the dead,*** (Colossians 1:18). Paul declared that Jesus established the resurrection of the body for all of us. He was the first one to have the newly resurrected body like that which we shall obtain. What is the guarantee of this? Since Jesus is the first fruit, He gives us the Holy Spirit as the first fruits (Romans 8:23). The first installment for us is the indwelling of the Holy Spirit. This guarantees the redemption of our physical bodies, which is the resurrection (2 Corinthians 1:22; 5:5). What a promise we have been given!

The Cross Style of the Resurrection

However, there is something more here. The resurrection is bigger than mere facts. It is certainly beyond an event. The resurrection of Christ is in a category completely by itself. It is a total focus on the life of Christ, and the continued manifestation of that life. It is not a ceremony or a ritual. It is not a doctrine or concept. It is presence and reality. It is what takes Christianity beyond the realm of religion. Christianity becomes relationship through the resurrection. We must constantly emphasize that the focus of the resurrection is on the life of the person of Christ. No one is focused on doctrine or theology during the resurrection event. No one is arguing over the proper mode of baptism. Everyone proclaims the person of Christ as alive. His life has become the dominant and convincing factor. The hope of the resurrection is not in the establishment of a new religious movement with updated meditations. The person of Christ, who is alive, has become our hope. No one discusses a new philosophy of eternal living. Everyone uplifts the reality of His life. The manifested life of Christ has become the convincing factor. Everything in Christianity revolves around the revealed and demonstrated life of Christ. This is what won the world during the days of the early church! It was their single witness!

Throughout the Book of Acts, a pattern of activity is established. There would be a tremendous demonstration of the power of the resurrected life of Christ. It usually resulted in a miracle or a display of love. An opportunity to proclaim the message of His resurrection immediately followed. Hundreds gave their lives to the Christian faith. Time after time the proclamation of the message was coupled with the demonstration of the resurrected life of Christ. Jesus never just preached a message, but He always included a powerful display of His life.

This is what our world needs. We do not need more stories

Part Seven: A God Ordained Board Meeting: His Preference

or lectures of facts. We need a display of the resurrected life of Christ. It is undisputable. Luke redefines the idea of witnessing to include this factor. Witnessing is not just the sharing of facts, but the demonstration of the reality of His life. The resurrected life of Christ was manifested in and through the lives of the apostles. After a powerful presentation of His life, the leaders of Israel were deeply moved. ***Now when they saw the boldness of Peter and John, and perceived that they were uneducated and untrained men, they marveled. And they realized that they had been with Jesus,*** (Acts 4:13). The leaders of Israel were ignorant about spiritual things; therefore, they did not state it properly. They did not fully realize that what they were seeing was not those who had ***been with Jesus,*** but they were actually seeing the resurrected life of Christ displayed through the disciples.

The resurrection is the only event in Christianity where no other human being other than Jesus is involved. Man participates in all the other great events in some manner. His participation ranges from being a vessel to being a spectator. But the resurrection of Christ is unique. Mankind has absolutely nothing to do with it.

The virgin birth of Christ is an important foundational event of our faith. Christ was born of God. The only explanation for His birth is the movement of God. It is a Divine plan fulfilled. But notice, it took place through the virgin, Mary, and Joseph witnessed the event. The crucifixion is crucial to our redemption. But Peter says in his sermon at Pentecost, that while Christ was ***delivered by the determined purpose and foreknowledge of God,*** He was ***taken by lawless hands, crucified, and put to death;*** (Acts 2:23). Mankind participated in, and watched closely, the death of Christ. This was certainly needed in the historical proof of the matter. The ascension of Christ was also a marvel. The group of disciples stood with their mouths wide open as Jesus disappeared in the arms of the Father.

But the resurrection was distinctly different from all of other events! No man participated in it or was used as an instrument

A Resurrection Witness | Acts 1:21-22

to bring it to pass. No human being was present for the actual event of the resurrection. The power of God for the resurrection from the dead did not flow through any man to Jesus. We are left without any knowledge of the actual event. No details are available to us. We simply witness the tremendous results of this Divine movement.

It is this kind of event which is at the center of the Christian faith. At the heart of Christianity is a total focus on the actions of God alone. Man becomes a vessel for the action of God. My service for Jesus is not impressive. However, when Jesus flows His resurrected life through me, people are impressed. It is not my talents displayed that will win my world. It is the wonder of the demonstrated, resurrected life of Christ now seen through me. It is not my reforms or disciplines which attract my world, but the credible resurrected life of Christ becoming visible in and through me. Jesus' resurrected life must become the source of my living.

Acts 1:21-22

TO BE MADE A WITNESS

In this scene we find Peter standing in the midst of the one hundred and twenty who have gathered in anticipation of the Promise of the Father. Just as the Scripture said it would be, Peter proposes that the office of Judas should be occupied by an individual whom God shall choose. The concern in this passage is not with the state of Judas, but with the position of apostleship *from which Judas by transgression fell.*

There does not seem to be any disagreement concerning God's choosing of such an individual. The difficulty with this matter is the great question, "How?" Peter has done some serious thinking about this issue. The STRATEGY is suggested to us in his proposal (Acts 1:23-25). At the heart of this strategy, Peter prays with sincere faith that God will intervene, selecting the individual He desires. However, who is qualified to even be considered for such a position? Peter gives us the STANDARD which must be maintained in their selection (Acts 1:21-22).

These two verses are contained in one long sentence. There are so many clauses in the sentence, it can be confusing. A sentence diagram becomes difficult. The subject of the sentence is not given until close to the end. It is the Greek word translated *one*. Nearly everything written in the two prior verses gives content to this subject. The prepositional phrase, *of these men*, helps to identify the *one* about whom he is speaking (Acts 1:21). The phrase, *who have accompanied us all the time,* is an adjective clause, which gives content and identifies **these men.** Another clause, **that the Lord Jesus went in and out among us,** gives content to **time.** From there the clauses simply continue. Peter identifies the exact period in which Jesus was among them. The time was **beginning from the baptism of John to that day when He was taken up from us,** (Acts 1:22).

There is one Greek word placed at the beginning of the sentence. It forms a part of the main verb. It is an important word because it brings the activity of the Divine into the heart of the action of the verb. It is the Greek word which is translated **must.** This is added to the verb placed close to the end of the sentence, which is translated **become.** So the main subject is **one,** and the main verb is **must become.** The word translated **witness** is an accusative, which acts as a direct object, meaning it is the primary recipient of the action of **must become.** Peter states this in such a way as to acknowledge the activity of Christ Himself. We see it in the use of the word **must.** The Greek word from which this is translated has the idea of necessity coming from a Divine decree. This same word is used in connection with the Scriptures. **"Men and brethren, the Scripture has to be** (must) **fulfilled, which the Holy Spirit spoke..."** (Acts 1:16). The creative flow of the Holy Spirit is behind this, and the creative speaking of the Holy Spirit is bringing this to pass. As the Scriptures find their necessity for fulfillment in the creativity of the Holy Spirit, so the very existence of the **witness of the resurrection** comes from the Divine activity. Throughout the Book of Acts, Luke highlights the facts that the power of the witness was not in education (Acts 4:13), nor in the power or godliness of the apostles (Acts 3:12), nor in plans or works of men (Acts 5:38). The proposition of this book is that the Holy Spirit is the source of the witness (Acts 1:8).

We see this, not only in the Greek word translated **must,** but also in the Greek word **become** (*ginomai*). This word is the equivalent to the middle passive of *poieo*. This is a word we have

Part Seven: A God Ordained Board Meeting: His Preference

emphasized repeatedly. It is a key expression to the cross style message of the Scriptures. *Poieo* is most often "doing" in the Scriptures, but it has an undercurrent which gives it a different flavor than other words translated the same. It has an artistic value to it! It expresses creative flow from the inner most being. It is the picture of the artist who is painting a masterpiece. The creative juices are flowing through his personality, and with great ease he strokes the canvas with his brush. Colors blend together; objects are remarkably life like. This is contrasted with another Greek word which focuses on duty and obligation. It gives us the picture of a man painting a barn. Both individuals are painting, but the two scenes are vastly different.

In the life of Jesus, His actions were characterized as *poieo*. Everything He did was a direct result of the creative flow of the Holy Spirit within Him. He painted the image of the Father so perfectly that those who saw Jesus saw this invisible Person. It did not flow from His discipline or self-effort. Jesus acknowledged, **"The words that I speak to you I do not speak on My own authority; but the Father who dwells in Me does** (*poieo*) **the works,"** (John 14:10). Now the same creative experience is going to take place within us. **"One of these must become a witness with us of His resurrection,"** (Acts 1:22). This will not be the result of education, talent, or information acquired. The responsibility of making them the **witness of the resurrection** is upon the creativity of the Holy Spirit, who has been promised to them. **Witness** is the direct object of the action of the verb **must become.** It is the primary recipient of the action of the Divine necessity, who is the creative power of the doing.

When Luke wrote the Book of Acts, his intention was to elevate the **witness of the resurrection** high above performance, speeches, seminars, and techniques. The witness, not based in skills or talent, and is much more than the sharing of information. All of these factors may be found in the demonstration which forms the witness, but they are only incidental to the witness itself. The actual creative life of Christ, raised from the dead, is going to dance on the stage of the believer's life and make Himself known. The witness will be the result of the resurrected life itself, contained within the believer. This is not a theological argument or doctrinal presentation, but a living demonstration. Only God can bring this to pass, within and through us.

We can also see this strong concept in the Gospel of John. John presents the eternal Word to us. He contrasts two verbs. One is *een*, which is the imperfect of the Greek word translated "to be" or "am." The second word is *ginomai*, which means to come to existence. This is the same Greek word used in our Acts passage. John begins the presentation with, **In the beginning was** (*een*) **the Word, and the Word was** (*een*) **with God, and the Word was** (*een*) **God. He was** (*een*) **in the beginning with God,** (John 1:1-2). He makes reference to the pre-existence of the Logos, the pre-incarnate Christ. John uses the verb *een* to indicate that Jesus always was, and never ceased to be what He was, even in the incarnation. Before the beginning of creation, the Logos was self-existent and eternal. This is in contrast to a beginning in time and space, which is the verb *ginomai*. A proper translation of these two verses could be: **Before there was any beginning the Word had been, and the Word had been toward God (the Father), and God has been the Word. He Himself was before there was any beginning toward God (The Father).**

In verse three, the perspective is shifted to created beings and things, and the verb *ginomai* is used. **All things were made** (*ginomai*) **through Him, and without Him nothing was made** (*ginomai*) **that was made** (*ginomai*), (John 1:3). Everything in existence has flowed from the creative source of the pre-existent and self-existent One.

In verse four, John shifts back to the Greek word *een*. He again speaks of life that is not acquired, but is inherent. **In Him was** (*een*) **life, and the life was** (*een*) **the light of men,** (John 1:4). This life was not acquired by the Word, but had always been

Part Seven: A God Ordained Board Meeting: His Preference

within Him. This could be translated, ***In Him had been life, and the life had been the light of men.***

In verse six, John again uses the verb *ginomai* as he presents the person of John the Baptist. ***There was*** (*ginomai*) ***a man sent from God, whose name was John,*** (John 1:6). Then in verse eight, he attempts not to confuse John the Baptist with the One who has always been the Light. ***He was*** (een) ***not that Light, but was sent to bear witness of that Light,*** (John 1:8). John the Baptist simply became a witness of the Light which has always been. ***That was*** (een) ***the true Light which gives light to every man coming into the world.*** (John 1:9). All enlightenment comes through Jesus Christ, either in His pre-incarnate state, his incarnate state, or his post-incarnate state.

In verse ten, John contrasts the words *een* and *ginomai*. ***He was*** (*een*) ***in the world, and the world was made*** (*ginomai*) ***through Him, and the world did not know Him,*** (John 1:10). There was never a time when Jesus was not in the world. John clears up the confusion of those who think Jesus made entrance into the world the first time in the incarnation. Certainly He did come in human form, and this was a new manifestation of His presence, but it was not a new coming of His presence. He had been in the world all the time (*een*), and the world through Him came into being (*ginomai*). Christ, as Spirit, had always been in the world that He created. He is still in the world through the dynamic of His Spirit.

In verse fourteen, John returns to the word *ginomai*. The incarnate Word entered into time and space as the God-Man. ***And the Word became*** (*ginomai*) ***flesh and dwelt among us, and we beheld His glory, the glory as of the only begotten of the Father, full of grace and truth,*** (John 1:14). As He speaks to the witness of John the Baptist, John again uses *een*. ***John bore witness of Him and cried out, saying, "This was*** (*een*) ***He of whom I said He who comes after me is preferred before me, for He was*** (*een*) ***before me,"*** (John 1:15).

When Christ made entrance into our world, He made something available that was not in existence. John calls it grace, *or the law was given through Moses, but grace and truth came (ginomai) through Jesus Christ,* (John 1:17). Grace found its source in the person of Christ through His incarnation, crucifixion, resurrection, and ascension. Grace came into being in a new and particular way for us. Men of old heard about its coming, but had no concept of what it would be like.

John thunders out a bold statement concerning the unity between two personalities of the Triune God. He does it by using *een* again. *No one has seen God at any time. The only begotten Son, who is (een) in the bosom of the Father, He has declared Him,* (John 1:18). Jesus always resided in the bosom of the Father, and even when He became incarnate, God the Father as Spirit, and God the Son as Spirit, remained in unity. The Spirit of the Father became the very source of the Son's life.

This gives us an excellent picture of the word *ginomai*, which is used by Peter in relation to becoming a witness of the resurrection. From this I will draw several conclusions.

Silence

Here we can see the idea of something that was not previously in existence now coming into being. Prior to the Book of Acts there was no witness of His resurrection. Many were not even sure there would be a resurrection. The Sadducees did not believe in the resurrection, while the Pharisees proposed it strongly. There was no powerful voice from the prophets of the Old Testament given to such a reality. Everyone was guessing about what might take place until the resurrection of Jesus among us. In this great revelation, clarity came for the first time concerning our hope and future. How would we know now except for the fullness of the Holy Spirit living within us?

Part Seven: A God Ordained Board Meeting: His Preference

The life of the resurrected Christ, living within us, is the *first fruits of the Spirit,* (Romans 8:23). This is the guarantee of our own personal resurrection. This is the first installment which is our hope of that which is to come! Peter was exactly right. It was a Divine necessity that ***one of these must become a witness with us of the resurrection.***

Secret

The coming into existence of this witness was the secret to winning the world for Christianity. It was the central message and demonstration of the early church. In a matter of seventy years Christianity became recognized as the world religion. It was the powerful *witness of the resurrection* which accomplished this. The Book of Acts is definite about this matter. It was not found in their organization, buildings, colleges, materials, or talents. The resurrection was the central message they proclaimed. It is at the heart of all the sermons found in the Book of Acts. Paul attributed all of his persecution to his proclamation of the resurrection of the dead.

If it was the secret to evangelism then, could it be the secret to evangelism now? There are vast cultural differences between now and then. But the inner heart's desire of mankind has not changed. The resurrection of Christ, both as an historical event, and as a spiritual reality, makes us complete in Christ. There is nothing outside of this. Should not our evangelism strategy focus on the demonstration of this reality?

Source

While the resurrection of Christ is the secret to all church growth, it is not the proclamation of fact or event. The witness is contained in demonstrations. The disciples became vessels through which the resurrected life of Christ was manifested. They became *a witness with us of the resurrection.* It was the Promise of the Father fulfilled at Pentecost which empowered the disciples. Their world could not deny the fact that Jesus was still alive. Every deed done by the disciples was attributed to the resurrected Lord. The message of Paul was to join Jesus in His death so we could experience Him in His resurrection. Christ is to be the source of our life.

    This is beyond strategy and good planning. This is a level above discipline or fulfillment of duty. Education and knowledge can never take us to this place. The creative juices of the Spirit of Jesus must flow through us, creating His likeness. As Jesus is the expressed image of the Father, so we must be the revealed image of Christ. His person is the source! I must have intimacy with him.

Acts 1:23-25

WHAT IS THE RIGHT STRATEGY?

Though we have been discussing this material in detail, I believe we need a review to keep the proper focus of the passage. It is important to know how it fits into the flow of the book. It is the "waiting" time between the ascension of Christ and the fulfillment of the Promise of the Father. This does not mean those involved are idle. They are spending much time in ***the temple praising and blessing God,*** (Luke 24:53). The focus of their praise is the resurrection of Jesus. This "waiting" time will last only seven to ten days, and Pentecost will take place.

During this time of prayer and unity (Acts 1:14), Peter expresses a great concern over the emptiness of the apostleship position. The tragedy of Judas is well known to all of them. This is the first recorded business meeting of the early church (Acts 1:15-26). Apparently, it is an important event involved in the preparation for the release of the Holy Spirit. In the progression of our study we have arrived at the section entitled THE STRATEGY (Acts 1:23-25).

In many ways this is the most important part of the entire study. Here is the actual method of action the disciples are going to take to solve the problem at hand. This strategy comes from their tradition. The casting of lots was used extensively in the Old Testament days. On the annual Day of Atonement, lots were

What Is The Right Strategy? | Acts 1:23-25

cast over two goats to determine the selection of the scapegoat (Leviticus 16:8-10). It was the method used to choose the men who would fight in Israel's army (Judges 20:9). Lots were cast to determine which land would be given to the various tribes of Israel (Numbers 26:55; Joshua 18:10). This method was used to divide the spoils and captives among the captors in Jerusalem (Obadiah 11). In a similar way, casting lots determined the appointment of possessions, spoils, or prisoners to foreigners or captors (Joel 3:3; Nahum 3:10; Matthew 27:35). Lots were often cast to settle doubtful questions (Proverbs 16:33). They were also used as a means to detect which individual had committed a crime (Joshua 7:14). We see its function in the appointment of persons to offices or duties, such as the priests (Luke 1:9).

There was no one in the group gathered in the upper room who objected to the strategy suggested by Peter. However, we must note, this was the last time we see this casting of lots in the Christian church. Just as the offering of sacrificial lambs was terminated when the official Lamb of God died upon the cross, so this tradition was ended upon receiving of the Promise of the Father. But up to this time, this method was completely accepted and approved.

I have wondered what would have taken place if we had been there with the current mindset of our generation. I am sure there would have been some long debates. The conservative, traditional group would have felt comfortable with the method suggested, but the contemporary sector would have been extremely upset. "We have always done it this way" would not set well with them. Perhaps if this situation had occurred, the selection of an apostle would never have taken place. We most likely would not have been able to agree on a strategy by which to accomplish this selection.

We live in a world which is focused on strategy. More often than not, the method of accomplishment becomes more important than what we are seeking to accomplish. We see strategy as the solution to every problem. In the business world there is a strong focus on marketing strategy. We have lost sight of quality of product, value of service rendered, and we have become consumed with the method of selling. Even in the church, we have been infiltrated with such approaches. There are training sessions to attend, which teach us advertising techniques, fund raising strategies, and how to make a good first impression. How do we get visitors to attend the first time? How do we get them to return? These seem to be the central focus of church growth.

We consistently see a strong emphasis on leadership strategy. What we wish to accomplish in the church can easily be achieved when we have proper leadership. Equipping leaders becomes the strategy. The book market is flooded with books to give you the information to be such a leader. Seminars are a million dollar business in our day. Management skills are highlighted. A small church can become a large church if its leadership functions as if it were already large. The solution is in the strategy.

Our thought process seems to flow in this direction. Strategy is focused on figuring it out and doing out. It caters to our self-centered carnality. The church grows because the right men came, determined the right strategy, and achieved the goal. Praise be to the man. Our children grow to be respected people, because we parents discovered the right strategy. Praise be to our parenting skills. Our finances are secure and plentiful, because we mastered the proper financial strategy. Praise be to our financial wisdom. Every area of life, with its unique problems, is easily mastered if we find the right strategy. Praise be to our own brilliant abilities!

It is no wonder that the cross of Christ is so counter to our culture. There is nothing about this kind of redemption which resembles a reasonable strategy. It is not about doing; it is about dying. The cross does not focus on "figuring it out" or "mastering the technique." It is certainly not "doing" focused. It is about resting, leaning, and trusting. There is nothing about

What Is The Right Strategy? | Acts 1:23-25

the cross which allows me the warm feeling of accomplishment. No applause will be given for my brilliant wisdom. There is no acclaiming my superior talent. The cross strips me of everything, and I find my all in Him alone.

However, even in the cross style we are prone to strategy. Disciplines and meditation techniques are highly acclaimed. How do we achieve the dying? It is an issue we constantly raise in our conversations. The moment we slip into the "doing" mode, we abandon the cross of Christ! In the cross, strategy is of no concern. Methodology is never highlighted. We see this truth in the Book of Acts. Many have studied the Book of Acts to discover the strategy for winning the world. But the very theme of the book will not allow such a discovery. This book has only one thing to say. It highlights what God does when He fills a life. God calls each of us to abandon ourselves to the activity of Another. We are not told to serve God; we are told to become a vessel through which He serves. We are not a display of talents and gifts; we are the body of Christ. We do not have a brilliant witness of His resurrection; the resurrected Lord actually fills us and displays His resurrection through us.

What a revelation for us to discover that strategy does not matter. Neither failure nor success can be explained because of strategy. Strategy does not matter! We see this clearly in our passage (Acts 1:23-25). The key element in the selection of one to fill the vacant office of apostleship is not strategy. It is as if it did not matter. No matter what strategy the disciples used, it would have been correct. The secret was not in the method of the selection.

What was the secret? It is the same as has been displayed in all of the other situations and occasions. We do not state it in cute phrases or fancy outlines. There are two perspectives. There is the vision of God and the view of man. From the perspective of God, it is simply the movement of the Divine activity. God is going to choose. From the view of man, it is a total openness

Part Seven: A God Ordained Board Meeting: His Preference

to allow God to choose. Man must not tamper with it.

Let us look at this from the perspective of God. The solution to the problem of a vacant office of apostleship is going to be solved because God is going to choose. Did God come to Peter and dictate the strategy for the choosing? We do not find this in the passage. The indication is that Peter simply uses the method comfortable to the group. It is as if God does not care. Can you imagine God's will being blocked because they used the traditional method of casting lots? What if the one hundred and twenty had voted by writing the name on a piece of paper? What if they flipped a coin? The strategy is not the issue. It is all about the wonder of the resurrected Christ being in charge of the situation.

There is no situation in which God cannot move to accomplish His Divine purpose. This is the thrill of the Scriptures. God has no problem handling the wisdom of this world. ***Has not God made foolish the wisdom of this world?*** (1 Corinthians 1:20). On the other hand, neither does He have a problem using the foolishness of this world. ***It pleased God through the foolishness of the message preached to save those who believe,*** (1 Corinthians 1:21). If we offer Him wisdom, He can make it foolish; if we offer Him foolishness, He can make it wisdom. God has no issue with strategy. If we offer Him a cross, He redeems a world. If we give Him a dirty stable and a manger filled with hay, He surrounds it with angels and gives birth to the Messiah. If we offer Him thousands of men to defeat the army of the Midianites, He reduces it to three hundred in order that we might not take glory in our own abilities or strategies (Judges 7:2).

The Apostle Paul expressed it this way, ***But we have this treasure in earthen vessels, that the excellence of the power may be of God and not of us.*** (2 Corinthians 4:7). The immense value of the light of His glory is contained in a common cracked clay pot for the purpose of highlighting the greatness of God. The emphasis is always on Him and how great He is! Strategy is not a problem for God.

What Is The Right Strategy? | **Acts 1:23-25**

When we apply this to our lives we will receive a renewed sense of wonder and thrill. Perhaps we have focused on the wrong thing. Has our emphasis been on strategy? As I view the defeat in my past, Satan consistently highlights my failures. He always turns my attention to strategy. He says, "If you had only done it this way, or if you had simply made this decision." The situation in which I find myself in the present is always a result of the wrong strategy of my past. I turned right when I should have turned left. Did I miss the will of God? I wanted to do His will, but perhaps I missed His voice! Do not believe the Satan's trickery. Remember, *he was a murderer from the beginning, and does not stand in the truth, because there is no truth in him. When he speaks a lie, he speaks from his own resources, for he is a liar and the father of it,* (John 8:44).

Many of us view the lives of our adult children and blame ourselves for their situations based upon our strategy in the past. Things might have been different for them if we had not moved to another town when they were in junior high school. Did they turn out the way they have because I was gone from home too much? Maybe their difficulties are a result of the youth group we had them in. These are all questions which run through our minds in regard to the way we brought up our children. If they are having problems we are quick to blame ourselves. But that is all about strategy. There is no guilt to be found in the strategy of the past. It is not strategy which has brought us to our present position. God has no problem working His Divine will through whatever decisions we may have made. It is simply not the problem.

Then what is the problem? It is not on God's part, but on our part! We must see the need from man's view. We must have a total openness to allow God to display His glory in the midst of the strategy. Let us look at our passage again (Acts 1:23-25). The casting of lots was not the New Testament pattern for finding the will of God. There was a total openness among the one hundred

Part Seven: A God Ordained Board Meeting: His Preference

and twenty which allowed God to act. In the midst of their strategy, *they prayed and said, "You, O Lord, who know the hearts of all, show which of these two You have chosen,"* (Acts 1:24). There was simply no way that God could not accomplish His will. God is sovereign and knows the details of every single heart. God is in charge and has already chosen one of these selected to be the apostle. It is a matter of openness to what God wants to do. The strategy is not significant; our openness and surrender is key to what God wants to do.

This seems to be very difficult for us to learn. In death we find life! The circumstances which surround the occasion do not matter. It is not "through" death, but "in" death. Death is not an experience to accomplish, but it is a state in which we dwell. A radical trust, surrender, and yielding is necessary for God to bring about what He desires. Our world constantly highlights strategy. We must go up against that thought process. It will change the approach of our conversations. Our discussions will be on the depth of our openness rather that the strategy of our accomplishment. We must be very careful about the applause of men and how it affects us. When God successfully brings about His glory through us, the applause of men may come. We may not be able to stop it, and rebuking those who applaud is not always appropriate. But how should this applause affect us? We must let it drive us to Him. Always let it bring us to a deeper surrender and a greater awareness of His presence.

If we fail to accomplish the will of God, it will not be because we did not conceive of the right strategy. It will be for lack of openness for the sovereign God to do through us what He designed. Strategy is no problem! Lack of our total surrender is the only barrier.

Acts 1:24

THE HEART KNOWER

There are certain times in our lives when we are able to look deep into the depths of our souls. At these times, it is impossible to be hypocritical. We express what is really present and what we really think. One of these times is during intense, sincere and earnest prayer. We have all heard the stories of the prayers prayed in the fox holes during war times. All pride is pushed aside. Peer pressure has no control. The real heart and soul of the individual is exposed.

Such is a time in the life of Jesus when He prayed in the Garden of Gethsemane (Matthew 26:36). The cross is heavy in His vision. This is not a time for sermonizing or miracles; it is a time for dying. Everything Jesus preached and taught is now to be played out in His life. This is not a moment to exaggerate or embellish, but to look at things in reality. This is not a seminar on how to handle trials and tribulations. This is the moment of truth. Here is where we see the real heart and soul of Jesus Christ. His commitment to the will of the Father is discovered in its real strength.

Another example of this is found in the "High Priestly Prayer" of Jesus (John 17). He is in intimate communication with His Father. His soul cries out, *"Father, the hour has come. Glorify Your Son, that Your Son also may glorify You,"* (John 17:1). This has the same sense of intensity as in the Garden of Gethsemane. Here Jesus bears His soul to the Father. What He really desires is

Part Seven: A God Ordained Board Meeting: His Preference

displayed. His prayer is completely focused on His relationship with the Father. How He longs for His disciples to experience this same kind of relationship that He has with the Father. It is the entire purpose behind all of the sacrifice involved in His presence on earth. We can hear His heart's cry for unity.

A similar exposure is contained in the prayer of the disciples. The group of one hundred and twenty has been involved in intense prayer (Acts 1:24). It is a "practicing His presence" kind of prayer. It is filled with devotion and fellowship. They are living in God's awareness. They are totally focused through the forty days of the resurrection appearances of Christ (Acts 1:3). Every activity in which they participate comes under the label of prayer. Now in a group meeting they are focused on discovering the mind of God. The impact of the statement, *and they prayed* (Acts 1:24) is that one hundred and twenty of them are involved in one focus. This verse summarizes their hearts' desires before God. Here we see what they really think and believe. Here is the pattern of the hearts that are waiting for the Promise of the Father. Could this be the required condition of the heart that will experience intimacy with the Spirit of Jesus?

There are several key ideas contained in this prayer. *And they prayed and said, "You, O Lord, who know the hearts of all, show which of these two You have chosen to take part in this ministry and apostleship from which Judas by transgression fell, that he might go to his own place,"* (Acts 1:24-25). The idea upon which we want to focus in this study is found in the phrase, *"You, O Lord, who know the hearts of all."* The words *who know the hearts* is a translation of one Greek word. It is the Greek word *kardiognoosta*. The Greek word is actually *ginosko* with *kard* as a prefix. It is a powerful word, and it paints a vivid description of the One to Whom they are praying. The literal translation is "heart-knower."

There are two distinct expressions given to us in these two combined words. They need to be seen in their combination.

One is the idea of "to know." We did a previous study in which the Greek word *ginosko* was highlighted. It is the Greek word translated "to know." You may remember there are four Greek words which can be translated "know, known, and knowledge." Each word paints a slightly different picture. *Ginosko* gives us a distinct picture of affection and embracing. It signifies "to be taking in knowledge, to come to know, recognize, understand," or "to understand completely." The power of this word is the fact it frequently indicates a relation between the person "knowing" and the object known. This presents us with the concept that what is "known" is of value or importance to the one who knows, and therefore the establishment of a relationship. This is the word used as a verb to convey the thought of connection or union, as between man and woman. **"And did not know** (*ginosko*) **her till she had brought forth her firstborn Son,"** (Matthew 1:25).

Now take this concept and place the word *kardia* as a prefix. You immediately recognize it as the word for "heart." What a powerful statement this is! In the Old Testament concept, **the life of the flesh is in the blood** (Leviticus 17:11). The blood is the actual flow of the life of man; since the blood comes from the heart and returns to the heart, the heart is the very source of this life. This is easily translated into the spiritual life of man. The heart is used figuratively for the hidden springs of the personal life. Let us take this concept and place it with the idea of *ginosko*. God is the One Who is the heart-knower. He places great value and importance upon the source of man's life. God is the One who embraces and comprehends the very internal spring of the individual from which the entire life flows.

This word is only used twice in the New Testament. Both times it is used in the Book of Acts. Both times it is used by Peter, if you believe Peter was leading in the prayer which preceded the casting of lots. Both times it is in the context of official business where major decisions were being made. The second time this word appears is in the Jerusalem Conference.

Part Seven: A God Ordained Board Meeting: His Preference

There was a major conflict between **certain men ...** from **Judea,** and Paul and Barnabas, over the Gentiles who were being converted. Those from Judea were preaching, **"Unless you are circumcised according to the custom of Moses, you cannot be saved,"** (Acts 15:1). It was insisted that a meeting be held in Jerusalem to settle this issue. After much dispute, Peter stood up to speak. He relates the experience he had in Cornelius' home with the Gentiles. He says, **"So God, who knows the heart** (kardiognoosta) **acknowledged them by giving them the Holy Spirit, just as He did to us,"** (Acts 15:8). What a powerful thought! One reason this statement is so powerful is because of the background and character of the speaker. He is a Jew who has been raised in the strictness of the Jewish faith. But God had shaken Peter's concepts with the vision of the sheet filled with unclean animals (Acts 10:10-16). Three times in a vision **a voice spoke to him ... , "What God has cleansed you must not call common,"** (Acts 10:15). Peter perceived these animals according to his standard. In his judgment, he only considered what he could see. He did not know that God had actually done something inwardly to the animals. All of this was in preparation for his visit to the home of Cornelius, where the Holy Spirit would be poured out upon the Gentiles just like He was poured out upon the Jews in Jerusalem.

"So God, who knows the heart (kardiognoosta) **acknowledged them by giving them the Holy Spirit, just as He did to us,"** (Acts 15:8). This is the statement of an individual who had been gripped with the knowledge that God goes further than the surface view. He comprehends the hidden depth sources which make us what we are. There is nothing which He does not thoroughly comprehend. God sees through the eyes of an aggressive Lover. He is not a stalker, a prying intruder or a window peeper. He does not simply have information concerning the heart. The individual He knows has great value to Him.

Let us review what we have discovered. It is very significant that the word *kardia* was used as a prefix of the primary word *ginosko*, making this word *kardiognoosta*. Remember the word "know" which is *ginosko* is a relational term. The object which is being known has value to the One who knows. With the word *kardia*, we are given the depth of the knowledge and concern of the relationship. The Lord has knowledge of the individual to the very source of their existence. There is no place deeper than the heart. This is the absolute reality of the person. This is the most intimate level of relationship. When a person is embraced at the heart level, he is affected at the source of his life. There can be no more intimate relationship than is found here.

There is another Greek word which is somewhat of a contrast with this. The author of the Book of Hebrews uses it (Hebrews 4:12). This is the only time it is found in the New Testament. **For the word of God is living and powerful, and sharper than any two-edged sword, piercing even to the division of soul and spirit, and of joints and marrow, and is a discerner of the thoughts and intents of the heart** (Hebrews 4:12). The word **discerner** is a translation of the Greek word *kartikos*. It pertains to the ability to judge legal cases. In this sense it refers to the Word of God being able to judge **the thoughts and intents of the heart.** The picture in the verse is of the skilled surgeon who judges where to cut and divide in order to heal.

Notice there is no relationship in this picture. The surgeon does not know (*ginosko*) the patient. He is simply carrying out the duty of his career. He has detailed knowledge of the individual as he discerns the inner being, but it is from a non-relational position. This is an altogether different picture than the Heart-Knower to Whom the disciples are praying. This Christ of ours is One Who has the deep knowledge of the innermost part of your being. He looks beyond the surface action, or what is being expressed, and goes to the very core of the motive. He sees the source of every detail of your life. He is the One Who knows the heart. But He is seeing all of this through the eyes of a great

Part Seven: A God Ordained Board Meeting: His Preference

Lover. Compassion, concern, and intimacy are all characteristics of His knowing.

Now we must put this in the context of prayer, for they are praying to the Heart-Knower. You could not come making demands of this One. There would be no way to convince One Who knows like this that what you want to do is better than what should be done. The disciples could not persuade the Heart-Knower their choice for the new apostle is better than His choice. The whole issue is that of discovery. They must find out what the Heart-Knower has decided. This changes the element of what we request in our prayers.

However, we must not see this as a simple moment of prayer. The prayer of the disciples during these days was far beyond moments or hours. It was a "practicing His presence" kind of prayer. It was devotion and fellowship. There was no activity taking place which could not be labeled prayer. From the fellowship around the dinner table, to the conversation as they fell asleep at night, to the business meeting they are now conducting, is all about an intimate fellowship with the Heart-Knower.

Can you imagine this kind of intimacy with this kind of Person? I can never con Him! There can never be a dishonest moment, for He will always know the truth. Every true motive is constantly revealed to Him. I am always exposing who I am to Him. Though I take something I have done and see it in the best light, He always sees it in the true light. I must be prepared for continuous instruction and correction. This means change and growth will always take place in my life as I am in this relationship.

On the other hand, there will always be Some One Who will really understand how things are! He will understand them far better than I do, and He can give me great insight into every situation of my life! He is the Heart-Knower. What a relief to be in the arms of the Heart-Knower. There is no safer place to be!

But you can understand the depth of surrender which must be experienced in this kind of relationship. This will require absolute and complete surrender. There can be no token availability. This is the style of relationship, which is characteristic of the cross style. It requires the death of crucifixion on behalf of both parties. There is no question mark about His participation in crucifixion on my behalf. I wonder if I can say the same about me.

Acts 1:24

SURRENDER OF PENTECOST

The passage we are studying (Acts 1) leads us to the event of Pentecost. The call to surrender is strong. You cannot help being struck by the compulsion, obsession, and mastery of each person by Christ. This sets the stage for God to fulfill the Promise of the Father. We see it at every turn throughout the progression of events. A tremendous revolution had to take place in the lives of the disciples as they experienced the Resurrected Lord. This experience caused a major shakeup in their traditions. In the forty days of interaction with the physically risen Lord, these individuals were given a new focus (Acts 1:3). They were called to surrender on a new level. It was a gigantic step for them to take.

As Jesus ascended from their presence, the disciples received a strong call to a new level of obedience. Jerusalem was the symbol of all of their problems, but they returned there anyway. They confronted the leaders of Israel in the temple on a daily basis with their praise and rejoicing over the resurrection (Luke 24:53). As others joined the eleven disciples, a new society of believers was formed. There were other believers, both in Galilee and Judea, but this society of one hundred and twenty came to a new level of surrender. They set aside everything else in their schedule as they waited for the fulfillment of the Promise.

They took a gigantic step as they **continued with one accord in prayer** (Acts 1:14). They had never before entered this level of communication. Prayer has always been in the form of chants, offering of incense, or religious activity. As they come in the name of Jesus, the ascended Lord, they gain a whole new access to heaven. They experience an inward attachment to the heavenly realms.

Peter expresses a new level of commitment in the first recorded business meeting of the early church. ***And in those days Peter stood up...*** (Acts 1:15) suggests a completely new attitude in his leadership. The place of authority was sitting, but Peter is standing. It is the position of suggesting or the making of a proposal. He is not consulting the eleven disciples, but he openly involves the entire society of believers. This is not the normal conniving and manipulating that we have seen from Peter in the past. He has come to a new level of surrender.

Peter and the group are seeking the mind of God concerning the choice of a new apostle. Their prayers are an expression of their new level of surrender. They openly come before the Heart-Knower (Acts 1:24). The expression of this fact can only come from an awareness based in a new surrender. The fulfillment of the Promise of the Father will mean living in the presence of the Spirit of Christ on a moment by moment basis. He is the One who knows the very source of every expression of their being. He has exact knowledge of their motive, so there is no possibility of them coloring the picture for personal benefit. This depth of knowledge comes from an aggressive Lover Who cares about those whom He knows. To live in intimacy with the Heart-Knower requires a new level of surrender. Is this the completion of all surrender? Is it an arrival at the top level? Will there be another place to step? The unfolding of the rest of their prayer reveals a strong call to a new level of surrender.

When you first read verse twenty-four, the opening statement seems to be a bit wordy. The statement ***and said*** (Acts 1:24) appears to be completely unnecessary. As they pray, you would think they were saying something. However, it is not as it appears in the English translation. The Greek word for ***and said*** is an expression used to introduce an alternative form of expression

Part Seven: A God Ordained Board Meeting: His Preference

as an interpretation of what has been said. Luke gives us an explanation and interpretation of the prayer which was made. It is expressed in the phrases "that is," "that is to say," "so to speak" or "in a sense."

Luke wants us to understand exactly what is being emphasized in this prayer. He focuses not on the fact they prayed; rather he highlights the content of the prayer. He does not state a word for word quotation of the prayer, but he summarizes and emphasizes the focus. The content of the prayer gives you insight into their motives. You will be able to understand the depth of their sincerity and the desperation of their hearts. It is in the content of this prayer you will comprehend what they hoped to accomplish.

The emphasis of the prayer is demonstrated in the word **show**. This word is in the imperative mood. This is a command. It is somewhat startling to see the boldness of the disciples as they make demands of God saying, **You, O Lord, who know the heart of all.**

What kind of relationship do they have with the ascended Lord at this time, or in times to come, which gives them the right to demand? What issues or concerns are important enough to come to God with demands?

The writer of the Book of Hebrews encouraged this approach to God. **Let us therefore come boldly to the throne of grace, that we may obtain mercy and find grace to help in the time of need** (Hebrews 4:16). Do you remember the parable Jesus told concerning the widow and the unrighteous judge (Luke 18:1-7)? The widow came to the judge for legal protection against one who was abusing her. He was not going to help her, but then thought *because this widow troubles me I will avenge her, lest by her continual coming she weary me* (Luke 18:5). There is a strong element of boldness involved in the widow's approach to the judge. The disciples exhibit this same kind of aggressive requesting.

As we look at the Greek word which is translated *show*, we will begin to see their boldness is focused. They are not being cocky or demanding their rights. Their boldness in this passage reveals a deep level of surrender. The Greek word translated *show* is *anadeixon*. It is two words put together. The basic word is *deiknumi* which means "to show or to exhibit." However, they added the prefix *ana* to this basic word. This prefix word can be translated "up." What they are demanding and boldly requesting is much more than showing or revealing. This word means to "lift up anything on high and exhibit it for all to behold, to show accurately, clearly, and to disclose what was hidden." They are requesting with great desire that God would lift up on high and openly exhibit the one He has chosen. Their boldness is not in getting what they want, but they are being bold in finding out what God has already done.

We are usually prone to stating our opinion boldly. Boldness comes from the confidence that we have when we think we are right. It flows from the desire to get what we want. But here, in this bold request of the disciples, a new level of surrender is experienced. Their boldness comes from the burning, passionate desire to know His will. They express not only a confidence in Christ's ability to accomplish, but also in the rightness of His choices. It means giving up the right of my own choice in favor of His. This boldness expresses more than the phrase, "He knows best." It goes to the depth of motive and will. There is no grinding under His demands. It is not the spirit of "I have to do this in order to go to heaven. I do not want it this way, but I guess it is best to let Him have His way. I must endure it." The boldness in this passage expresses a level of surrender completely beyond all of this. It is a delight in what He wants. I have so completely become His that His will has become my will. What He wants has become exactly what I want. This gives me the ability to boldly demand!

Boldness always has the characteristic of aggressiveness.

Part Seven: A God Ordained Board Meeting: His Preference

This is not a casual, laid back living, which goes along with the traditional patterns of what is considered God's will. This surrender boldly seeks the choices of God. Those of us raised in the Christian movement have accepted Christian patterns and ideas. In appearance and activity, we have accepted the will of God. However, in reality, we push our opinion and demand our choices. Our desires lean toward what is best for our own personal comfort. It isn't that we are bad; we just think that we know best. After all, we are here in the middle of the situation. We have certain skills and experiences which tell us how things should be. What could be wrong with imposing these upon God, so we can be sure the right thing is done?

Could a new level of surrender be experienced which would bring a new intimacy with Him? As I have aggressively sought after my comfort, could I, in like manner, seek His desires? As I have boldly proclaimed my rights, could I, with the same passion, seek His will? Is it possible to move into a relationship with God where we are not tolerating but passionately desiring? Can something change in the will and mind of an individual so that he is with Christ in intent and motive? Can His mind really be my mind?

In addition to this, you will discover the phrase, **You have chosen,** is in the middle voice. This means that the subject is acting upon Himself. Personal involvement in the action is stressed. In most cases the subject is the only one involved. Also the action is focused on the interest and personal desire of the subject. The subject has allowed, or caused, something to be done in his own behalf. It involves preference and selection among many choices.

The society of believers is recognizing the Heart-Knower has already acted out of His own interests and personal desire. He has selected an individual in whom He is involved. The disciples demand that the Lord lift up on high and reveal in bold fashion His personal preference. It is not a matter of right or wrong in choosing. There were several individuals who would have been adequate. Surely, ***Joseph called Barsabas*** would have been qualified to fulfill this apostleship position. But the society of believers is not satisfied with this. They desperately want the preference of the Lord.

Now this same exact Greek word, translated *show*, has already appeared in this chapter. ***Until the day in which He was taken up, after He through the Holy Spirit had given commandments to the apostles whom He had chosen,*** (Acts 1:2) relates to the time at the beginning of the ministry of Jesus. The occasion when Jesus chose His disciples is recorded by Luke. ***Now it came to pass in those days that He went out to the mountain to pray, and continued all night in prayer to God. And when it was day, He called His disciples to Himself; and from them He chose twelve whom He also named apostles:*** (Luke 6:12-13). Luke is being very consistent in His presentation of the choosing of the apostles by Jesus.

He gives us something of a different impression than the other Gospel writers. Jesus came to John the Baptist for His baptism (Luke 3). It was here Jesus was filled with the Holy Spirit. He then was led by the Spirit into the wilderness temptation (Luke 4:1-13). In the victory, Jesus begins to minister throughout Galilee. In the success of His ministry, He went to Nazareth and found total disbelief (Luke 4:16). However, His ministry began to expand with great power throughout all Galilee. The multitudes are following Him everywhere He goes. There is an abundance of miracles as He meets the needs of the people. This is why Luke makes note that a large group of disciples were consistently with Him. After Jesus had prayed all night, He called His disciples (this large group) to Himself. It was from this larger group that ***He chose twelve whom He also named apostles.***

The Greek word for ***chosen,*** as used in all three of these passages, is two words put together. The first word means "out of." The second refers "to speaking" or "to call by name." There

Part Seven: A God Ordained Board Meeting: His Preference

was a large group of individuals who were available, but Jesus called out of that group these twelve to be apostles. There were several individuals who could have qualified to take the place of Judas. The society of believers has narrowed it down to two individuals, and now they are asking the Heart-Knower to call out of that group the one who satisfies His heart. They want to know what is pleasing to the mind and heart of the Lord. He is to select based upon His own preference and what benefits Him the most.

By the way, this is the exact same Greek word which Paul uses to refer to you and me. ***Just as He chose us in Him before the foundation of the world, that we should be holy and without blame before Him in love,*** (Ephesians 1:4). All the content of this word, as it is used for Mathias, is also applied to us. He has not chosen masses or groups, but you have been chosen as an individual. His passion and love for you has driven Him to a selection which satisfies His heart. You are His preference.

However, there is one additional aspect of this great truth. The phrase, ***You have chosen,*** in the Greek language is in the aorist tense. There is nothing like it in the English language. Normally in translating an aorist verb we place it in the past tense. A definition of the aorist tense is often stated as "of past occurrence: and action or state seen as antecedent to the time of speaking or writing." The emphasis here would be the fact that the Lord has already made up His mind concerning who should take the place of Judas. The disciples do not attempt to talk God into their choice. They desperately want to discover what God has already decided.

This is an entirely new level of surrender! What would it be like to be filled with the Heart-Knower? He not only knows all the activities, but the very center motive of those actions. Nothing escapes His presence and influence. He has already decided a plan. This level of surrender is not an attempt to talk God into something, but to come totally in submission to what

He has already chosen for us. The entire cry of the heart becomes finding what He wants and where He is going.

This is a cross style concept! Death to all we are, and allowing Him to live out His life through us, is the style of the cross. It is not about finding out what He wants me to do and doing it, but finding out what He Himself wants to do and allowing Him to do it through me. It is giving up the right of my own life, in favor of His life. He will become the source of all that is happening in and through me. This will not be for certain moments of ministry, but for my moment by moment living in daily life. Is it possible to be so filled with the Spirit of Jesus, in intimate relationship, that this will be the natural result of my life? Is this true for you?

A GOD ORDAINED BOARD MEETING:
HIS PLACE

Acts 1:24-25

AN AGGRESSIVE USHER

To be an apostle is a great and high calling. What a privilege it would have been to have stood in the great multitude of people who were considered to be the disciples of Christ. Suddenly Jesus appeared before them, having prayed all night. His prayer was focused on discovering what God, the Father, had already chosen. Jesus stood tall and began the selection. He called twelve individuals to be apostles. Each one of them who was chosen undoubtedly was struck with a great sense of awe.

Now one of them is gone *to his own place.* There is a vacancy in the apostleship. Another individual must be chosen. This choosing will be very similar to the first choosing. We are given insight into the very heart of an apostle.

The Compulsion

There are some definite difficulties with the language in this passage. A slight change in a word can indicate a tremendous shift in meaning. Let me give you an example of what I mean. It is offering time in the service, and the pastor stands before the congregation and makes one of the following statements. "We are going to take the offering," or "We are going to receive the offering." How does one differ from the other? In my mind there is a big difference. In receiving, the weight of the action

Part Eight: A God Ordained Board Meeting: His Place

is upon the one who is giving. The usher stands close by and waits patiently for whatever the member of the congregation decides. But in taking the offering, there is a definite, aggressive act on the part of the usher. He places the offering plate in the face of the member. He pokes him on the shoulder, and he may even glare at him. The member must respond because of the pressure exerted on him. When the usher takes the offering, his mannerisms suggest that the member has no choice but to give. When the usher receives, the decision to do so comes from a heart of giving in the member. Now to our verse at hand; what is the right language? The One Who has already chosen stands by quietly awaiting a response from the chosen one. Is the Chooser aggressive and pushy?

The grammar structure of this verse is the only help we have in answering these questions. The Greek word translated *to take* is in the infinitive mood. A word in the infinitive mood may be followed by an accusative, as in the case of this verse. The action of the verb is attached and directed to the accusative. In this case it is the Greek word translated *part.* These words refer to the apostleship as if it is a thing an individual can reach, take or grasp. The idea of taking and the idea of part are attached to the thought of this verse.

This Greek word translated *to take* is in the active voice. This means the subject is responsible for the action of the verb. But it is somewhat misleading in this verse. At first I thought the one who was responsible for the taking of the *part* was **which of these two.** As Luke wrote it in the Greek, the last word of verse twenty-four is "one." In reality, this is the subject of the verb *to take.* Either Matthias or Joseph is responsible for reaching out, grabbing, or receiving the *part in this ministry and apostleship.*

However, the verb *to take* is in the infinitive mood. This means it does not stand alone, but is related to and depends upon the strength of the main verb or another verb. In the case of this verse, it is the phrase *you have chosen.* While response

An Aggressive Usher | Acts 1:24-25

is certainly required from the one who is chosen, the strength of the action comes from the One Who is choosing. The **Lord** is not standing in the shadows quietly waiting. He is aggressive in His choosing. There is a tap on the shoulder; there is an arm around the waist. There is a strong presence that cannot be ignored – He has chosen! This is too important to Him. The entire emphasis of the prayer is that God will reveal and lift up on high the one He has already chosen. He has already made a decision. Matthias will have a choice in the matter, but it is the Lord who has reached out and grabbed Matthias and placed him in this *part.*

Those in "full time ministry" speak often of the call of God upon their lives. They report an experience of such definite magnitude that it captures them. Many report how they ran from the call of God and resisted this pressure. But they always knew if they were to be in proper relationship with Christ, they would have to deal with the issue that they have been called. They have a choice in the matter. The call of God is aggressive in their life. He does not stand back in the shadows waiting patiently; rather He is the aggressive usher. It is the call of God!

Is this the experience of only a few selected individuals who have been called to "full time ministry?" What about the rest of us? This was the genius of the early church. They did not recognize any difference between clergy and laity. Ingrained into the very Christian experience was a call of God to "full time ministry!" There was absolutely no way to have intimacy with Christ and not be called. They knew Christ was very aggressive in this call, and He would do whatever it took to bring about the accomplishment of the call. The individual whom He calls needs to respond. Every call is important to Christ, and He brings all the resource of His being to bear upon its accomplishment. He is not only the aggressive usher Who pushes the offering plate in our faces, but He is also aggressive about the accomplishment of the call itself. The very ministry (to which He has called us)

Part Eight: A God Ordained Board Meeting: His Place

is of extreme importance to Him. He will see to it this call is realized. This is so strong within Him that He has decided to do it Himself. Listen to what Paul tells us; He ***who calls you is faithful, who also will do it,*** (1 Thessalonians 5:24). God has decided to take no chances. He is not only going to be the One Who calls us, but He is also going to be the One Who does it.

Listen to His call! ***For the promise is to you and to your children, and to all who are afar off, as many as the Lord our God will call,*** (Acts 2:39). This statement is a part of the sermon Peter preaches on Pentecost, resulting in the salvation of three thousand souls. The promise to which he refers is the "Promise of the Father." It is the fulfillment of the Spirit of God poured out upon them. God calls you to the fullness of His Spirit. He calls you to live a life which is sourced by Him alone. He wants this so desperately for your life; He has decided to accomplish it for you. This promise is not to be earned, figured out or accomplished by you. It is to be received! Christ ascended to the right hand of the Father. He aggressively reached out and took the promise. He poured it out upon you. He has not only called you, but He has fulfilled the call.

Here is another Scripture that will grip your heart and reveal truth to your mind. ***But God has chosen the foolish things of the world to put to shame the wise, and God has chosen the weak things of the world to put to shame the things which are mighty; and the base things of the world and the things which are despised God has chosen, and the things which are not, to bring to nothing the things that are, that no flesh should glory in His presence,*** (1 Corinthians 1:17-30).

The Greek word translated ***chosen*** in this passage is the identical Greek word we are now considering in our present passage. The one hundred and twenty are praying for God to show ***which of these two You have chosen*** (Acts 1:24). The One Who has called or chosen has reached out ***to take.*** In this Corinthians passage, He has taken the ***foolish things of the world, the weak*** *things of the world, and the base things of the world, the things which are despised, and the things which are not.* These are the things He has called *to put to shame the wise, to put to shame the things which are mighty, to bring to nothing the things that are.* Those who are foolish are going to say, "We can not do this!" Those who are weak will reply, "This is impossible for us!" Why would He place such a strong call upon the *foolish, weak, base* and *despised?* The answer is given *that no flesh should glory in His presence.* Since this is His intent, it is obvious the *foolish, weak, base* and *despised* will not accomplish this. God alone has the power to fulfill this call! God not only calls, but He empowers. This is a demonstration of how aggressive He is in His call.

Do you see the strength of this matter? God does not stand back in the shadows patiently waiting to receive a response. He aggressively takes hold of Matthias. This brings us to the definition of the Greek word being translated *to take.* It actually means "to take hold of something or someone, with or without force." During the great shipwreck, as Paul was on his journey to Rome, he assured those on the ship that all would be saved. They had gone for fourteen days without food. Paul urged them to eat, and immediately *he took bread and gave thanks to God in the presence of them all,* (Acts 27:35). Here the word is used in a non-violent manner. In the parable of the Wicked Vinedressers, the owner's son is sent to collect the rent. The vinedressers plot to kill the son when they see him. *So they took him and cast him out of the vineyard and killed him,* (Matthew 21:39). Here the word is used in a violent manner. In the Upper Room, Jesus gathers His disciples for the last supper. *Then He took the cup, and gave thanks,* (Luke 22:27). Again this usage is non-violent. All of these are examples of the usage of the Greek word translated *to take* (Acts 1:25) in our passage.

How is the word used in our passage? Let me remind you that the idea of God having already chosen is aggressive in nature. The Greek word translated *chosen* is in the middle voice. This

Part Eight: A God Ordained Board Meeting: His Place

means the subject is acting in His own behalf. This has to do with preference and choice which benefits Him. This issue really does matter. God is not casual about this decision. His attitude is not that either one of these men will be fine with Him. No, God has a preference which fits His plan.

Concerning John the Baptist, Jesus said, **"And from the days of John the Baptist until now the kingdom of heaven suffers violence, and the violent take it by force,"** (Matthew 11:12). The verse is somewhat of a puzzle. The verse gives us a strong sense of the Kingdom of God being connected with violence. It is a message about the war against the Kingdom of God. To experience the Kingdom of God, we must seize it with great force and violence.

John Bunyan wrote the great story of "The Pilgrim's Progress." In the second stage of the story, Christian comes to the gate. There is a large sign above it which reads, "Knock, and it will be opened to you!" After knocking several times and crying out, Christian hears an answer coming from behind the gate. It is one named "Goodwill." There is a brief discussion, and suddenly the gate is opened and a hand reaches out. Christian is grabbed and violently pulled through the gate. He immediately inquires about this kind of treatment. The answer is very simple. Close by there is a large tower built by Beelzebub, who is the captain. Arrows are shot at those who come up to the gate with the intent that they may die before entering through the gate.

This is the picture of what is happening in our passage. A sovereign God has chosen. The decision has been made. He reaches out **to take** one He has chosen and places him in the **part in this ministry and apostleship.** In their prayer, the one hundred and twenty recognize this fact. A response must come from this group and from the one who has been chosen, but God is aggressive in His choosing.

The impact of this upon our lives is two fold. You have been chosen. Let no confusion surround this fact. God has called you and has chosen you. It is not a decision He makes now or will make in the future. He decided this *before the foundation of the world,* (Ephesians 1:4). Do not ever question the fact that God has called you to Himself. His desire and passion is for you. The call is not so you can do something for Him, and when it is accomplished the call will be over. It is a call to intimacy. It is a call primarily to be His. He has called angels to service; He has called you to His heart. What a privilege!

God is aggressive in His call. He reaches out and pulls us through to the place of relationship that He has established for us. He is the pushy usher Who stands in the aisle. He will not force you, but He is doing everything possible to bring it to pass. Everything to which He called you, He provides. The resources, removal of every obstacle, inward motivation and ability to decide are all a result of His aggressive pulling. The fact you are aware of the call is evidence of this truth. The hunger you have to be His comes from Him. All that remains is for you to respond as the early disciples did. It is a matter of your surrender and yielding to what He has chosen. He will accomplish it all. He is the aggressive God Who has not only called us, but has done it as well. The question is not "God has called me; how will I do it?" The question is "God has called me; will I allow Him to do it?"

Acts 1:25

WHERE DO I BELONG?

The twelve disciples were the eye witnesses to the earthly ministry of Jesus. Judas, given to his own desires, left a vacancy in the apostleship. This position had to be filled. Matthias met the qualification of eye witness (Acts 1:21-22). The position of an apostle was a unique calling for the twelve disciples. When they had fulfilled their roles, the unique calling came to an end. However, the broader calling of ministry still remained. In the days of the early church, the calling of an apostle became a broader position. Paul referred to himself as an apostle (Romans 1:1). While the function of this first recorded business meeting of the early church was to select a new apostle to take the place of Judas, it also gives insight into the call of ministry and God's design for each of us.

Luke gives us tremendous insight into the ministry to which we have been called. We have been working on an outline for this calling. First, there is the COMPULSION. Jesus is the aggressive Usher Who is persistent in His call upon us. Ingrained into the very fiber of Christian experience is the call to ministry. It is impossible to be Christian without ministry. Christianity and ministry are as tied together as living and breathing. Jesus is very aggressive about the calling. He not only calls us, but He provides the resource for the fulfillment of the call. Ministry is the very essence of Christian living.

Provided

Now we want to view the CATEGORY. As the one hundred and twenty disciples seek the will of God in the selection of the new apostle, they saturate the casting of lots in prayer. Listen to their prayer again. *"You, O Lord, who know the hearts of all, show which of these two You have chosen to take part in this ministry and apostleship from which Judas by transgression fell, that he might go to his own place,"* (Acts 1:24-25). The aggressive action of the Lord is found in the statement, *"you have chosen to take."* The Greek word translated *to take* is in the infinitive mood. It is often followed by an accusative which acts as a direct object. Such is the case in our verse. The action of the verb is focused on the *part.*

This word means "as occupied or filled by any person or thing, a spot, a place, or a room." It is used ninety-four times in the New Testament. It is translated most often "place," but also room, quarters, coasts, etc. It is interesting that the position of an apostle is referred to as a thing, as if it exists by itself. It has an existence apart from the person. The apostleship position is a space, spot, chair, or position in existence apart from Judas. This position did not disappear when Judas betrayed Christ and sought his own place. He left behind the apostleship position *from which Judas by transgression fell, that he might go to his own place.*

This means the ministry was not something to be done as much as it was a place to be. How can we explain this? Visualize the shape of your own being. Think in terms of the fact that your body takes up a certain amount of space. No matter where you are, you always take up the exact amount of space. When you are not present, that space is unoccupied. You were created and you take up a certain amount of space. Consider the opposite. Suppose the exact space you fill was created first. God then

Part Eight: A God Ordained Board Meeting: His Place

made you to fill that space. This is the way it is with ministry. He did not make you and then make the ministry. No! There is a space, room, spot, or office called ministry, and you were designed to fill that office.

What does all of this mean? Ministry is far bigger than me! I am a person of great ability with talent and a charismatic personality. Therefore, I have created a ministry which is dependent upon me. When I am gone there is no ministry. This is far beyond such a concept. It is as if the ministry was established before me, and I was made, called, and commissioned for this ministry. If I do not fulfill the call, the ministry will continue because someone else will fill this place. The ministry exists beyond who I am. I do not shape the calling; the calling shapes me. The ministry exists on its own. It is not produced by me. The ministry from my view is not something I do, but the ministry is something God enables me to accomplish. It is not something to be done as much as a place to be or to occupy. He has called me to fill a place, to be in a position.

But this is contrary to our thought process about ministry. We view ministry as being built, produced or performed by us. The talents with which we are born and the skills which we have developed determine the success of our ministry. We are credited with the ministries' success. All honors are bestowed upon us. We are measured in contrast to others who are not as successful. As we receive the applause of men, we are quick to state it is all for the glory of God. It was only possible through His grace, but we are the ones who are honored.

How can we grasp this spiritual perspective? Ministry is provided by Him. I have been born out of the dreams of God. He has produced me to fill a space or occupy a place. God has called me to ministry. There is only one thing which will destroy the effectiveness of the place to which God has called me. It is self-centered carnality. It is acting as if I produced the place of ministry. Ministry of self performance undermines the very heart of this *part.* I must set quietly in the place to which He has called me. I must respond moment by moment to that which He provides. This brings us to the next part of the concept of ministry.

Parallel

In this passage, Luke records the sample prayer of the early society of believers regarding Judas. Listen to their prayer again. *You, O Lord, who know the hearts of all, show which of these two You have chosen to take part in this ministry and apostleship from which Judas by transgression fell, that he might go to his own place,"* (Acts 1:24-25). The parallel is between these two phrases. *"You have chosen to take part"* and *"he might go to his own place."* The Greek word translated *part* is the same Greek word translated *place.* God has chosen a place, part, office, space or room for Judas. However, Judas preferred his own place, part, office, space or room. The Greek word translated *his own* is much stronger than the simple possessive pronoun. It goes beyond showing possession. It is the place which is peculiarly his. This is the same Greek word used in speaking about the authority which belongs to the Father. *And He said to them, "It is not for you to know times or seasons which the Father has put in His own authority,"* (Acts 1:7). It is extremely personal and private. It belongs exclusively to Him. We discovered this same truth about Judas in Luke's earlier statement concerning the end results of Judas' betrayal. *(Now this man purchased a field with the wages of iniquity;)* (Acts 1:18). The word *purchased* means to acquire or possess, but it requires the addition of the statement "for one's self." Judas' part or place is not forced upon him. It did not come to him even though he did not desire it. This was his personal choice and design. He must take total ownership of this *place.*

On the one hand is the place, spot, office or position to which

God called Judas. He chose Judas for this. It is His preference and design. It is the purpose for which Judas is created. God worked and planned from before the foundation of the world to bring this ministry place into being. He dreamed Judas into existence to fill this place. BUT Judas created his own place. He walked out of the place God designed for him and went his own way. God was not responsible, nor was it His desire for Judas. Was not the redemption of Christ for the purpose of allowing Judas to come back to the place God had for him?

This is a clear message to us about the call of God upon our lives. God created you to fulfill the dream of His heart. Oh, how He is counting on you! Oh, how He needs you! It is no wonder He has called you. The place, spot, office, position or the room is all set. Your name is on the door. Everything has been furnished by God. Will you come and sit in the chair? Yes, you can build your own place. You can allow your life to be shaped by your circumstances. You can allow your past to determine your place. You can be molded by your cultural environment and the customs you have been taught. Your traditions can be so comfortable to you, that even God cannot pull you into the fullness of the place He has designed for you. But why would you miss the dreams of God for your life? It is the reason you exist. God created you for the call of ministry upon your life.

Perpetual

But there is one other important factor for you to consider concerning this call. We have attempted to relate the significance of the apostle position apart from the actual person of Judas. Have you grasped the reality that ministry was present in the dreams of God, and He created you out of that dream? The position of ministry existed before you came into being. He created you to occupy the spot, space, room or office of this ministry. If you do not fill this place, the *part* will continue to exist. This ministry is not dependent upon you for its existence. This is an awesome truth. This truth places ministry on an altogether different level. Ministry is removed from what we do and accomplish. It transforms it from "doing" to "being."

This great truth is emphasized in the disciples' prayer as they seek the will of God for the selection of a replacement for Judas. We cannot see it as clearly in the English translation of this verse. However, in the Greek there is a definite article before the word translated *part* and also before the word translated *ministry*. It is the article "the." Again, in the English translation, it is not included as necessary. But a more literal translation would read, ***And they prayed and said, "You, O Lord, who know the hearts of all, show which of these two You have chosen to take the part in this the ministry and apostleship…"*** (Acts 1:24-25). It is a definite attempt on the part of the author to emphasize the distinctive nature of the apostle position. It is set aside and highlighted by the definite article.

This is a powerful truth. I want to expand it in your thinking to include an eternal perspective. Luke highlights this in the Book of Acts. According to Luke, a terrible tragedy occurred in the very early days of the church. This took place before the first missionary journey of Paul and Barnabas. Much of the ministry was still focused in Jerusalem although there was some movement of the Spirit of God among the Gentiles. According to the record of Luke, Herod the king was beginning to persecute the church (Acts 12:1). This persecution would help to scatter the Christians. God used this to plant churches throughout the world. It was during the early days of this persecution that James was martyred (Acts 12:2). According to Luke's account, James was martyred ***with the sword.*** In all likelihood James was beheaded, which was regarded by the Jews as the extreme humiliation and disgrace.

It is important to establish the fact that James was the

Part Eight: A God Ordained Board Meeting: His Place

brother of John (Acts 12:2), not the brother of Jesus. Matthew records, *Going on from there, He saw two other brothers, James the son of Zebedee, and John his brother, in the boat with Zebedee their father, mending their nets. He called them,* (Matthew 4:21). These two brothers were referred to as "sons of thunder" by Jesus (Mark 3:17). Through their mother they applied for the right and left-hand positions in the coming kingdom (Matthew 20:20). Jesus asked if they were able to drink their Master's cup and be baptized with His baptism. They replied that they were. Jesus then told them they would indeed do that, but that what they sought was under other arrangement. Now James has been martyred for Jesus, indeed drinking of His Master's cup.

The significance of this event is that there was no attempt by the early church to replace the apostle position of James. This is in contrast with the position of Judas. Why would the early disciples replace Judas when he died and not replace James when he died? Upon reflection you can immediately see the difference between the two situations. Judas did not die in the faith as a martyr, but *Judas by transgression fell, that he might go to his own place.* James died in the faith! When Judas left his apostleship he created a vacancy. But when James died as a martyr he carried his apostleship position into the eternal Kingdom of God. The calling to ministry is an eternal calling. It goes beyond thirty or forty years of service and then retirement. The space, room, chair, or spot of ministry for which Jesus designed you is to be occupied forever. God's dreams are not limited to this time period. He has called us with an eternal purpose.

Does this not grip your heart and compel your entire being? How significant are you to the dreams of God? This is a call to total surrender. The call of God must be the consuming factor of your life. When you occupy the place or part of ministry God designed for you, you find the fulfillment of your life. Outside of this spot there is no sense to life.

Acts 1:25

THE MINISTRY

In our last few studies we have attempted to discover the Biblical view of ministry. It is easy to allow our cultural environment to shape and define our role in ministry. It soon becomes cluttered with customs, traditions and personal gain. It seems necessary that we continually come back to the Biblical call.

In our first study we discovered COMPULSION. Jesus, the aggressive usher, is the compulsion for ministry. He is the One Who takes us and positions us in our place. He is very aggressive about this calling; He determines to do the ministry through us. Thus, He is the soul provider of all the resource. His call is to allow Him to place us in the ministry and accomplish His dream.

Our second study focused on the CATEGORY. God created this ministry, and He has created us for this place of ministry. With the ministry in mind, God has shaped us perfectly to fit this spot. It is apart from us. He has an eternal view of this ministry, and there is only one thing that can stop it. It is self-centered carnality when we desire our own place rather than His place.

Now we want to view the COMMISSION. It is hoped we will be able to actually grasp something of the content or substance of this ministry. What are the actual details and activities to which He has called us? The call in our passage is to apostleship. It refers to the *part* which was set aside and

Part Eight: A God Ordained Board Meeting: His Place

provided for Judas who *by transgression fell, that he might go to his own place.* But linked with this is the Greek word translated *ministry. Ministry* and *apostleship* (Acts 1:25) are two concepts which the early disciples combined in explaining the call to ministry. The focus is on apostleship, while ministry gives definite content to the position.

The word "evangelist" is only used three times in the New Testament. Philip, one of the seven deacons, is referred to as *Philip the evangelist* (Acts 21:8). He was led by the Spirit to the chariot of the eunuch, a man of Ethiopia (Acts 8:27). It was from this encounter an entire nation was won to Christ. It says of him, *but Philip was found at Azotus. And passing through, he preached in all the cities till he came to Caesarea* (Acts 8:40). In stating the positions or offices of ministry, Paul said, *"And He Himself gave some to be apostles, some prophets, some evangelists, and some pastors and teachers,* (Ephesians 4:11). Also Paul, in giving instructions to Timothy, encouraged him to *do the work of an evangelist* (2 Timothy 4:5).

The word "apostle" is used seventy-nine times in the New Testament. This does not include the references to "apostleship" and other forms of the word. This is somewhat upsetting to an evangelist like myself. I would like to have thought the role of evangelist was much more important in the early church. It was not until a generation later that the word became more frequently used. The Word which seems to dominate the scene is "apostle." But perhaps it is not as serious as it appears. The apostle was an itinerant preacher who went from place to place being a witness of the resurrection. His role was not one of administration or even supervision in a technical sense. He was in the role to proclaim the Gospel.

This was especially significant because he was an eye witness (Acts 1:21-22). He could speak with the authority of one who had been there. He could boldly say, *"That which was from the beginning, which we have heard, which we have seen with our eyes, which we have looked upon, and our hands have handled, concerning the Word of life -"* (1 John 1:1). You can readily see this in the role of the evangelist.

It is very significant that our passage links two ideas together. One would have thought in their prayer that the disciples would simply have referred to the apostleship. However, they are very careful to link with this apostleship the idea of *ministry*. It is as if the idea of ministry gives content to and helps in defining the idea of apostleship. Perhaps this idea of ministry is the content to all positions and aspects of service within the church. Ministry is the common element making everyone the same. The actual Greek word which is translated *ministry* seems to be used in three different ways in the New Testament.

The Waiter
(at the table)

One of the most vivid pictures of this word is its usage as found in the Gospel of John. It is the first miracle in the ministry of Jesus. The wedding party has used all of the wine. Not to have planned properly is a great embarrassment to those in charge. The mother of Jesus feels it is her responsibility to do something about the situation. She calls upon Jesus to assist her. After speaking to Jesus, she turns her attention to the waiters. **His mother said to the servants, "Whatever He says to you, do it,"** (John 2:5).

The Greek word translated *servants* is the same Greek word which is translated *ministry* in our passage. It comes from the idea of a waiter at the table. It was attached to the idea of providing for physical sustenance. This individual is not in charge of the household. He is not the cook. He simply delivers the goods which have been provided to him.

It is significant that the highest position one could attain

Part Eight: A God Ordained Board Meeting: His Place

in the early church is one which bespeaks the greatest amount of service. This was the very message of Jesus. It was James and John who enlisted their mother in a campaign to occupy the right hand and left-hand positions in the coming Kingdom of God. The other ten disciples were indignant over their attempt. In the midst of the conflict Jesus teaches a great lesson. His first statement was a dogmatic, definite declaration that the Kingdom of God would not tolerate this kind of attitude. Jesus went further in the discussion to reveal the attitude which would dominate the heart of the Kingdom. He said, ***"Yet it shall not be so among you; but whoever desires to become great among you, let him be your servant,*** (Matthew 20:26). Here again is the same Greek word translated ***servant*** as used in our passage for ***ministry.***

The entire function of this ministry as seen in this picture is to make available that which has been provided. You can see how important the aspect of being an eye witness of the ministry of Christ becomes. What did God deposit into the lives of the disciples? What was burning in their bones? What was the focus which had captivated their eye site? This was the content of their ministry. The ministry was not theirs; they were simply offering that which had been provided for them. They were to be waiters at the table. This concept is in distinct contrast to much of our thinking about present day ministry. The basis of ministry becomes talent, personal skills or personality. Our personal reservoir is filled to the brim with education, management and people control. We minister out of this personal reservoir. The problems we face in this kind of ministry involves burnout, moral breakdowns, personality conflicts and ultimately withdrawal from ministry. We were not meant to function in this style of self-sourcing. Oh, God give us a revival of being a waiter at the table.

The Slave
(of a Master)

The Greek word for *ministry* as found in our verse is used often by the apostle Paul. This style of service is strong in his concept of being a minister. However, he uses another Greek word in relationship to this concept. It forms the basis of this kind of servant ministry. It is the Greek word normally translated "servant." This word paints the picture of a slave. Slaves were most often waiters at the table. We are motivated and instructed by the Master to serve at the table.

It is interesting how this relates to Jesus in the passage discussed earlier from the Gospel of Matthew. The mother of Zebedee's sons came to Jesus requesting certain positions in the coming Kingdom for her sons. A dispute arose among the disciples over this aggressive action. In settling the argument Jesus said, **"Yet it shall not be so among you; but whoever desires to become great among you, let him be you servant,"** (Matthew 20:26). As already noted the word *servant* is from the same Greek word translated *ministry* in our passage in Acts. Greatness is equated with the idea of being a waiter at the table. It is found in taking that which has been provided for you and giving it to those at your table. It is a significant picture of ministry.

Jesus continues by saying, **"And whoever desires to be first among you, let him be your slave -"** (Matthew 20:27). This is a translation from an entirely different Greek word. It is a step beyond the idea of being a waiter at the table and forms the foundation for the ability to serve in such a way. Jesus links this statement with the following, **"Just as the Son of Man did not come to be served, but to serve, and to give His life a ransom for many,"** (Matthew 20:28). Now Jesus goes back to the Greek word used in our passage in Acts. He did not come to be waited upon at the table, but He came to be a waiter at the table. The heart of this involvement would be giving ***His life a ransom for many.***

It is understood that the total focus of this kind of ministry is others. Jesus does not serve Himself, but He is possessed with bringing what is needed to those who are seated at the table. His personal needs are not under consideration. His sole function is to be alert to and to meet their every need. It is spoken of in terms of ***to give His life.*** The ministry of an apostle is to be a waiter at the table. It means to meet the needs of others to the point of giving your own life. If Christ is this way, it would not be difficult for one who has the heart of Christ to also be this way. What drives and motivates Christ will be the very motivation of our personal lives. We will share His Divine nature. This cannot be legislated or forced to happen. It springs from the inner heart of one who has truly become the slave/servant/waiter at the table of Christ. True ministry only happens at this level.

The Servant
(of spiritual power)

Perhaps this is the startling conclusion of the entire matter. The ***ministry*** in which the apostle participates is far beyond the accomplishment of duties or activities. It is not a role he fulfills. He actually becomes the waiter at the table and is never anything else. The ministry ceases to be what he does and becomes what he is. He does not possess this ministry; rather this ministry possesses him. It is being produced by spiritual reality far beyond him. The minister has become a servant/slave to this spiritual power.

This is far beyond our normal concept of ministry. A person might conceivably be a mechanic in his day job, and then have a week end or evening job at a restaurant where he is a waiter at the tables. A waiter at the tables does not describe who he is; it only describes what he does on a part time basis. If he is asked what he does, he would probably say that he is a mechanic. A waiter at the table is only a side, incidental or minor issue. We seem to view ministry in this perspective. Our ministry is teaching a Sunday school class. It only occupies a brief time of preparation and actual teaching. It is a side issue and certainly does not describe who we are.

However, this is not the concept of these early church leaders. They consider ***ministry and apostleship*** as an actual place, spot, or office created by God. You have then been created in the shape of this place. God Himself has not only created you, but has selected and placed you in this place. You are not there to do anything but be a waiter at the table. He is going to provide the resource for the accomplishment of any duties or activities involved. You are a servant to the spiritual power He provides. Any service rendered is never a result of your talent, personality or skills. It is a direct result of your total availability to the resource of His person.

This is stated forcibly throughout the New Testament. We see it both from the aspect of good and of evil. Paul exposes some ***false prophets, deceitful workers, transforming themselves into apostles of Christ.*** He explains why we should not be surprised at this. ***For Satan himself transforms himself into an angel of light. Therefore it is no great thing if his ministers also transform themselves into ministers of righteousness, whose end will be according to their works,*** (2 Corinthians 11:14-15). The Greek word for ***ministers*** is the same as ***ministry*** in our Acts passage. Obviously these ministers of evil are operating under the control of the power and nature of Satan. They are waiters at the tables. What they bring to the table is what they have provided to them by the evil one. It is the spiritual power of wickedness. It flows through them.

Paul describes himself in this same way. He tells of the special revelation which came to him. In other ages this

Part Eight: A God Ordained Board Meeting: His Place

revelation was a great secret, but it has now been revealed to the apostles and the prophets. The purpose of the revelation is *that the Gentiles should be fellow heirs, of the same body, and partakers of His promise in Christ through the gospel, of which I became a minister according to the gift of the grace of God given to me by the effective working of His power,* (Ephesians 3:6-7). Paul refers to himself as a "waiter at the table" in regard to the Gentiles. This position was *according to the gift of the grace of God given to me by the effective working of His power.*

Paul, in speaking to the people of Corinth, focuses on what has happened to us. *Not that we are sufficient of ourselves to think of anything as being from ourselves, but our sufficiency is from God, who also made us sufficient as ministers of the new covenant, not of the letter but of the Spirit; for the letter kills, but the Spirit gives life,* (2 Corinthians 3:5-6). We are waiters at the table. Our sole function is to provide that which has mastered us. Our sufficiency is contained in the very Christ who has filled us. We can only offer what we have! We have become slaves to the spiritual power which is either good or evil. Perhaps it is time for self examination.

Acts 1:25

THE APOSTLESHIP

Every individual has an important ministry. This has been the focus of our last few studies. This is the general thrust of the New Testament, not simply an isolated case. It was a significant part of the evangelism which won the world in a period of seventy years. It is not a token concept to make everyone feel a part, but it is an expression of the heart of God's plan.

We see this clearly in the picture of the aggressive usher. Christ is the One Who takes the individual and places him in the position of ministry. Luke highlights this in the prayer of the disciples when they cry out, *"show which of these two You have chosen to take part in this ministry and apostleship,"* (Acts 1:24-25). You might think that one of the two individuals they have chosen is reaching out to take the part in this ministry. However, the grammar emphasizes that Christ, the One Who has chosen, is being asked to take the selected individual and place him in the position of ministry. The focus is on the selection of the one who will take the office of Judas. The New Testament reveals this as the picture of all believers. God is the aggressive usher Who has selected you for the fulfillment of His dream.

The word *part* has become very important in this study. It highlights a place, spot, office or chair. This ministry exists apart from us. We do not source it, and it will not end when our talents are no longer involved. God has built this place of ministry and then made the individual to fit the spot. Each of us has a destiny.

Part Eight: A God Ordained Board Meeting: His Place

We discover in this passage (Acts 1:25) that Judas decided to produce and occupy his own place. He was not satisfied with the place God had provided for him. In our passage, the disciples are focused on the necessity of replacing the Judas position. The New Testament reveals that God has done this for each one of us. God created you to fulfill His dreams. God has a particular place for you. He takes careful measures to fill each individual spot, and He created and especially designed you for a spot like no other. You were built by God for this ministry.

We discover this same truth in the Greek word translated *ministry.* There is a definite article (the) before the word *part* and before the phrase *ministry and apostleship* in our passage. Ministry and apostleship are linked together. It suggests that ministry gives proper content to the apostleship. It is the concept of servanthood. The actual Greek word means "the waiter at the table." He does not prepare, cook or determine the end result. The waiter simply delivers! Would you allow Jesus to put you in your place and just be a waiter at the table? The base of this is not talent, knowledge, a special personality type or activity. This is God's doing alone. What a privilege to be a full time, called of God person, created for the fulfillment of His ministry dream.

Let us now gain insight into our personal ministry and calling through the passage of our study. The Greek word translated *apostleship* has something definite to say to us. The surrounding context verifies this.

Singularly Selected

The concept of being singularly selected is common to all the writers of the Gospel accounts. They had a firm belief that membership in the apostleship is a matter of choice on the part of Christ; there are no volunteers. The one hundred and twenty disciples gave strong expression to this in the first recorded business meeting. They searched through their group to see who would qualify for the position vacated by Judas. It had to be someone who had been with Jesus from the time of His baptism by John through to His ascension (Acts 1:21-22). Their investigation evidently only revealed two individuals, Joseph and Matthias. Having narrowed the choice down to these two individuals, it was a simple matter of discovering whom Christ had already chosen. These two men did not volunteer. There is no indication that either of these two even desired the position. The selection is in the realm far beyond their decision.

The Gospel accounts agree with this concept. Luke is very specific on this issue. ***And when it was day, He called His disciples to Himself; and from them He chose twelve whom He also named apostles:*** (Luke 6:13). This choosing by Jesus transpired after He had prayed all night. There were a huge number of disciples who were following Jesus during those days. Certainly there were many within this group who would have desired to become special ministers of the Messiah. But the choice of the twelve was not decided by their desire; Jesus selected.

For several years now our society has become enamored with their personal rights. We cannot imagine anything connected to our lives in which we do not have the determining vote. This has become a dominate trait we have naturally attributed to our personal wills. If it does not originate from our thoughts, how can there be any value to it? However, this is where we are destined by God. He has created a place from His sovereign will. He has shaped you to fit exactly in that place. You did not choose to be born. Your parents were not selected as a result of your desire. Even your culture and upbringing were not your decision. All of this resulted from the place of God. He molded you in the shape of His place for you.

You have a choice as to whether or not you will fill His place for you. Our passage shows us the choice of Judas. He was not satisfied with God's place for him; he created and sourced his own place (Acts 1:25). You have this same freedom of choice. But the place you initiate and the place sourced by God are as different as night and day. God is not seeking volunteers. He is longing for availability. Will you allow yourself to be put into the place God has dreamed into existence for you?

Significantly Sent

The Greek word translated *apostle* reveals much to us. In the Septuagint (the Greek translation of the Old Testament) the Greek word for apostle in its verb form is used around seven hundred times to translate the Hebrew word *shaalach*. This Hebrew word means "to stretch out" or "to send." But more than the act of sending, this word includes the idea of authorization of a messenger. The noun form of apostle is only used one time in the Old Testament (1 Kings 14:6). The idea of the commissioning and empowering of a prophet is clearly presented. So in the Septuagint, the apostle word-group conveys the authorization of an individual to fulfill a particular function, with emphasis on the One Who sends, not on the one who is sent. "The one who is sent is the same as the One Who sent him" was a common understanding of the use of the apostle word-group. This forms the basis for the use of the concept in the New Testament.

The Biblical use of "apostle" in the noun form is almost always confined to the New Testament. It occurs seventy-nine times. It appears ten times in the Gospels, twenty-eight times in Acts, thirty-eight times in the epistles, and three times in the Revelation. Our English word "apostle" is a transliteration of the Greek word *apostolos*. This Greek word is derived from the verb form *apostellein* which means "to send." There are several different Greek words in the New Testament which are translated "send." The word picture given by the apostle word-group is unique. It describes a far greater picture than merely being sent to a certain location. As described by its usage in the Old Testament, the concept of being commissioned is highlighted. The emphasis is on the authority of and responsibility to the Sender. Apostles are sent on a definite mission. They act with full authority on behalf of the Sender and are accountable to the Sender. Delegation for a particular purpose is involved and the cause for sending is stressed.

This is the picture of the minister (the waiter at the table). The apostle has no personal authority or message. He is only a deliverer of the message. What he says, the manner of his speaking, the certainty of his message are all derived from the One Who sent him. He makes no demands for his personal rights; only the rights of the One Who sent him. He does not complain about his personal needs; he only desires to fulfill the dreams of the One Who sent him. He has no expectations of personal gain; his only desire is to accomplish the mission of his sending.

Let it be known that the more the apostle knows the Sender, the more authentic his apostleship becomes. When the apostle knows the very heart and thoughts of the Sender, he is able to convey His wishes and desires. The ideal is for the apostle to be intimate with the Sender. If the thoughts of the Sender are understood by the apostle, what a representative he can be. The apostle must comprehend the plans and dreams of the Sender. He must experience the Sender so deeply that he knows his spontaneous reactions. The apostle is to be the true reflection of the One Who sends him.

This is the intent of God for the believer. It is not based upon talent or personality, and it is certainly not based upon education. Peter and John went to the temple for the hour of prayer (Acts 3:1). This led to the miracle for the one who lay ***daily at the gate of the temple which is called Beautiful.*** From this great witness, five thousand men came to believe in Christ (Acts 4:5). The Jewish council took exception to this demonstration and witness. Upon interviewing the apostles, these leaders **perceived that they were uneducated and untrained men** (Acts 4:13). Luke then gives us a statement which highlights the essence of apostleship. **And they realized that they had been with Jesus** (Acts 4:13). The verb in this statement is in the imperfect tense. This refers to an event which took place in the past and still exhibits its influence in the present.

This is the reason the criteria for the selection of an apostle is so strongly stated (Acts 1:21-22). For the individual to qualify he had to have been with Jesus the entire time of His earthly ministry, from His baptism by John the Baptist to His ascension from this earth. All of this had to do with being a witness of His resurrection. It was a witness far beyond the testimony of an event. They had to be eyewitnesses of His actions. They had to be with Him in the hours of fame and glory as well the pressure, grief, criticism and crisis. How could they possibly take all He is and deliver this to the table if they did not know Him intimately? On the other hand, if they knew Him intimately, how could they not represent Him adequately?

You can see the call of apostleship is a loss of who one is! It is giving up the right to live your own life! The constant attention of the apostle must be focused on expressing the One Who sent him. This concept is consistently attached to the idea of evangelism or witnessing. This is the kind of witness with which the early church won their world to Christ in some seventy years.

Sovereignly Sourced

This great truth is an absolute necessity in light of Pentecost and it is another strong element in apostleship. It is the foundation of all Jesus was and all He called His disciples to be. We can see this in the Gospel of John. In this Gospel, the verb form of apostle is used by Jesus when His concern is to establish

God as His authority. God is the One Who is responsible for His words and works, and He guarantees these right and truth. The woman at the well returned to her city and told all that had happened to her. The disciples returned at that time with food for Jesus to eat. He told them, *"I have food to eat of which you do not know,"* (John 4:32). The disciples thought someone else had given Him food, but He explained, *"My food is to do the will of Him who sent Me, and to finish His work,"* (John 4:34). Jesus is commissioned of the Father; He is an apostle in the true sense.

In chapter five of the Gospel according to John, Jesus gives a great discourse. He was correcting the misunderstanding the Jews had about Him. Numerous times He refers to the fact He has been sent. It is the verb form of apostle. Jesus said, *"All should honor the Son just as they honor the Father. He who does not honor the Son does not honor the Father who sent Him,"* (John 5:23). This is a clear statement of apostleship. Jesus is the messenger Who has been sent. He is the same as the One Who sent Him. He goes on to say, *"Most assuredly, I say to you, he who hears My word and believes in Him who sent Me has everlasting life,"* (John 5:24). Do you see the emphasis on the message and the One Who sent Him to deliver such an offer to us? In this same discourse Jesus boldly proclaims, *"I can of Myself do nothing. As I hear; I judge; and My judgment is righteous, because I do not seek My own will but the will of the Father who sent Me,"* (John 5:30). He is the apostle Who set aside His own life and will for the sake of the One Who has sent Him.

The emphasis of the above verses is on the authority received from the Father. God, the Father, is responsible for the words and works which Jesus is speaking and doing. This verb form of apostle is used thirty-one times in the Gospel according to John. It is a strong and significant statement of this Gospel. However, equally strong and important is another Greek word which is not normally a part of the apostle word-group. It is the Greek word *pempo*. In the Gospel of John, this word is used

Part Eight: A God Ordained Board Meeting: His Place

synonymously with the apostle word-group. This word is used by Jesus when He wants not only to affirm that God is responsible for the words and works which are taking place through Him, but God is actually participating in the speaking and actions. Therefore, John presents a two fold thrust in the relationship between Jesus and the Father. The words and works which Jesus does originate in God's work, and it is through Jesus that God speaks and works.

This is dramatically displayed in His resurrection appearance to the disciples. He shows them His hands and His side. ***So Jesus said to them again, "Peace to you! As the Father has sent Me, I also send you,"*** (John 20:21). Jesus uses the verb form of apostle to refer to Himself. His emphasis is on the authority He has received from the Father. Based upon this, he sends (*pempo*) them. He is not only giving them a commission but is actually going to accomplish this commission through them. He is going to come alongside them to accomplish the task. He is passing His own apostleship and all it contains on to His disciples.

This brings us back to the fundamental truth of the cross style. Apostleship ministry is focused exclusively on the One Who has sent us and is reliant only on Him as He accompanies us in the task. The moment we act out of ourselves, either in the realm of talent, wisdom or resources, we destroy our apostleship. We see this clearly in Judas. Christ gave him a place with all of the resources to accomplish the purpose of the place. However, Judas refused to get in his place. He ***by transgression fell, that he might go to his own place,*** (Acts 1:25). May it not be written of us!

Acts 1:25

TRADITIONS BEYOND JESUS

Matthew begins his Gospel account with a remarkable revelation. The details of the entrance of Jesus into the world are displayed even before He is born. Joseph is in a moral dilemma (Matthew 1:19). He is struggling with the devastating news that Mary is with child. Joseph is a just man. He must separate himself from this situation as far and as quickly a possible. He retires for the night with the plan of divorcement in place. But an Angel of the Lord appears in the night hour boldly proclaiming the purpose of Christ's coming. He makes this amazing announcement. *"And she will bring forth a Son, and you shall call His name Jesus, for He will save His people from their sins,"* (Matthew 1:21). Before the rest of the Gospel story is made known, we know everything Jesus will accomplish. He will deliver His people from their sins. It is boldly declared before He is born.

A mere surface study of Christ's crucifixion brings to light the issue of sin. The Old Testament preparation for the Messianic atonement was focused on sin. *And according to the law almost all things are purified with blood, and without shedding of blood there is no remission* (Hebrews 9:22). Such statements as this summarize the concept. Through the blood of Christ we experience forgiveness and pardon for our sins. It is a major issue in the atonement.

When we proclaim Christ we should also portray this emphasis. We are called to a clear understanding of the nature of sin. How

Part Eight: A God Ordained Board Meeting: His Place

important is a person's motive in defining sin? How important is the content of the deed of sin? Did Jesus really accomplish His task for this life or is it for the life to come? All of these questions seem to be major issues which need to be addressed!

Let us now thrust ourselves into the middle of these issues in the study at hand. The New Testament writers definitely consider the activity of Judas' betrayal in the category of sin. The leaders of the early church express it in the first recorded business meeting. Peter boldly describes Judas when he says, **who became a guide to those who arrested Jesus,** (Acts 1:16). Luke inserts two verses which contain statements of the guilt and consequences of this sin (Acts 1:18-19). Even in their prayer for the guidance of God in replacing Judas, they cried out, **"Judas by transgression fell, that he might go to his own place,"** (Acts 1:25). Sin and its consequences are vividly made known to all those dwelling in Jerusalem through the life and death of Judas (Acts 1:19).

Sin is the issue! It is the essence of leaving God's place for our lives and going to our own place. It is never isolated to us personally, but always influences others as we become a **guide** (Acts 1:16). Sin is always seen in contrast to the powerful grace of God. We can never compare ourselves to ourselves and have a reality view. We must compare ourselves with Jesus to see who we really are. Our hate contrasted with Jesus' love always shocks us into reality. Our betrayal compared to His faithfulness gives us a true picture of our sin.

The true concept of sin believed by the society of believers is expressed in one basic Greek word as stated in their prayer. It is amazing how they describe **this ministry and apostleship.** They refer to it as **this ministry and apostleship from which Judas by transgression fell, that he might go to his own place** (Acts 1:25). The Greek word which best describes their concept of sin is translated **by transgression fell.** The basic meaning of the Greek word is "to go." However, it more distinctly indicates procedure or course than other Greek verbs which can also mean "to go." When used in the sense of transgressions it has the idea of "to overstep," "to pass over" or "to go beyond."

This Greek word as used in the New Testament sense gives us a vivid picture of sin as seen in the new covenant. The basic concept of sin in the Old Testament was the breaking of the law of God. God gave commandments. They were to be obeyed. When this was not the case, man sinned. Sin was thus defined as the breaking of the law (commandment) of God. We know that disobedience of the known law of God does not "break" the law of God. Sin does not damage or injure the law of God. The law is still whole and in place. It is man who finds himself inwardly changed and damaged. This quickly moves us into the New Testament view of sin. It has to do with the motive, intent, and procedure operating within the heart of man. It pictures one who is going beyond the moral and relational limits established by God.

The concept of this Greek word in our passage focuses on the self-will of Judas. It is in the active voice which means the subject is responsible for the action of the verb. The total responsibility of the final dwelling place of Judas and his going there rests upon the shoulders of Judas himself. Luke distinctly highlights the choice of Judas in this matter. He wanted his own place instead of the place provided by God. He went beyond the place God had selected for him.

This Greek word (going beyond) is very rare in the New Testament. It appears four times in only three different situations. We need to examine these three occasions in order to understand the passage.

Tradition Not Christ

The first situation to consider presents this Greek word (going beyond) twice. It is used once by the scribes and Pharisees

Part Eight: A God Ordained Board Meeting: His Place

concerning Jesus and the second time by Jesus concerning the scribes and the Pharisees. The opening verse of this passage gives us a clear indication of how important and pressing the need to trap Jesus was to the leaders of Israel. ***Then the scribes and Pharisees who were from Jerusalem came to Jesus, saying,*** (Matthew 15:1). It appears these scribes and Pharisees have come from Jerusalem to spy on Jesus for the purpose of accusing Him. This occasion takes place in the **land of Gannesaret** (Matthew 14:34). This would be on the western shore of the Sea of Galilee approximately one hundred miles from Jerusalem. This reveals their dedication to their traditions. They go to great personal sacrifice in order to correct any violations. They especially target Jesus Who seemed to be leading the people to a superficial consideration of their sacred traditions.

The scribes and the Pharisees quickly state their accusation. ***"Why do Your disciples transgress*** (go beyond) ***the tradition of the elders? For they do not wash their hands when they eat bread,"*** (Matthew 15:2). The leaders of Israel accuse Jesus' disciples of "going beyond" the tradition of the elders. In regard to the issue of ceremonial cleansing they are not staying within the bounds of the established traditions. Their concern was not germs from dirty hands, but their prejudice concerning Gentiles. It has been established in their traditions that anything which had been touched by a Gentile had to go through the ceremonial washing to be sure this defilement was not passed on to the food or drink, thus defiling the Jew inwardly. Inward defilement was of great concern to these leaders. The disciples did not seem to have any concern about this issue for they were "going beyond" the tradition of the elders with no expression of guilt or remorse. Jesus was also concerned about inward defilement, but it was not the same as that of the elders. He believed and taught that it was ***"not what goes into the mouth defiles a man; but what comes out of the mouth, this defiles a man,"*** (Matthew 15:11).

Jesus' reply is very strong! ***He answered and said to them,***

"Why do you also transgress (go beyond) *the commandment of God because of your tradition?"* (Matthew 15:3). Jesus used the identical word (going beyond) to accuse the leaders of Israel. His emphasis is that the commandments of God establish the boundaries, not the tradition of the elders. They have allowed their traditions to become higher priority than the commandments of God; thus they have "gone beyond" the commands of God. They focused on their practical applications of the laws of God for their present day world. This caused them to violate and go beyond the commandments of God. They seemed to have no concern about this issue. They were "going beyond" the commands of God with no expression of guilt or remorse.

Jesus immediately gives them a practical example. *"Honor your father and mother;" and "He who curses father or mother, let him be put to death,"* (Matthew 15:4). This command would be applied to the culture and customs of their day. The practical application of the command of God for everyday living established their traditions. This is not wrong, but is very needful. One of the strong applications of this command was that the children should financially support their father and mother in their old age. But the scribes and Pharisees had added a loop hole to this application. Jesus reminded them of it when he said, *"But you say, 'Whoever says to his father or mother, "Whatever profit you might have received from me is a gift to God" — 'then he need not honor his father or mother,'"* (Matthew 15:5-6). If you dedicate all of your finances to God then you do not have to give any of it to your parents. You are not giving all of your money to the church, but you can continue to use it for yourself because it all belongs to God.

Jesus states the conclusion to this action. *"Thus you have made the commandment of God of no effect by your tradition,"* (Matthew 15:6). The leaders of Israel had "gone beyond" the commandments of God through the means of their traditions. The tradition had become of greater value and was more important

Part Eight: A God Ordained Board Meeting: His Place

to them than the commands of God. They had not stayed within the boundaries of the laws of God.

Now let us bring this picture into our world. It is not wrong to make application from the known law of God. There are new situations and customs in our day which were not taking place in the days of the Bible. The great principles of the Word of God must be applied. These applications become our traditions of the elders. They are not wrong! The issue is regarding the priority of these traditions. What is their status in our lives? Are they of greater importance than the words of God? Are we more focused on our traditions than on what God has to say to us?

What are the commands or laws of God? Paul wrote, **For Christ is the end of the law for righteousness to everyone who believes** (Romans 10:4). The Greek word translated **end** has the idea of completion, perfection or the goal toward which something is pointed. The entire law of God is found, fulfilled, completed and accomplished in Christ. So the question is, do our traditions (practical applications) "go beyond" Christ? Is our driving force the achievement of our traditions or intimate relationship with Christ? Is our message and witness reinforcing our traditions or the call to intimacy with Christ?

The Word of God calls us to worship. However, when we are more concerned about the style by which we worship than we are in seeing Him in His fullness, we have "gone beyond" Him. The New Testament labels this activity sin! The call of the Great Commission (Matthew 28:19) is upon all of our lives. But when we focus on methods and programs to accomplish this rather than loving our neighbor (which Jesus said is the same as loving God, Matthew 22:39), we have **made the commandment of God of no effect by your tradition** (Matthew 15:6). This is sin! Anything taking my focus off Jesus quickly becomes sin for it "goes beyond" Jesus.

I want nothing in my life to even threaten the supreme position of Jesus. There must be no law, theology, doctrine or church practice which is more important to me than knowing the heart of Christ. There must be no past training or teaching which hinders me from knowing the new revelation He wants to make known to me. Everything in my life must be a means to bring me to intimacy with His person. Was this not the heart of the Apostle Paul? He loudly proclaimed, *"Yet indeed I also count all things loss for the excellence of the knowledge of Christ Jesus my Lord, for whom I have suffered the loss of all things, and count them as rubbish, that I may gain Christ and be found in Him, not having my own righteousness, which is from the law, but that which is through faith in Christ, the righteousness which is from God by faith; that I may know Him and the power of His resurrection, and the fellowship of His sufferings, being conformed to His death,"* (Philippians 3:8-10).

We must carefully examine our personal lives through the eyes of the Holy Spirit. Have we gone beyond Jesus? We can easily justify our traditions when we focus on the content of the deed. We justify our actions through our patterns of success in the past. Have we gone beyond Him? Any thing beyond the relational boundaries of His Person becomes sin. You cannot set this in order and then forget it. We must constantly be open and adjust our relationship with Him. What may be completely within the boundaries of our relationship one day can quickly shift with the circumstances of life. Will I live in response to His presence?

Acts 1:25

THEOLOGY BEYOND JESUS

You are made in the image of God! This is the standard, conservative truth which has been accepted by the evangelical church throughout the years. You cannot begin a Biblical presentation without being startled by this truth. With His creative energy, God brought about an interesting world. The details of this world are amazing, from the smallest particle of existence to the largest galaxy in the sky. But you are the crowning point of all creation. ***Then God said, "Let Us make man in Our image, according to Our likeness:"*** (Genesis 1:26). ***So God created man in His own image; in the image of God He created him; male and female He created them*** (Genesis 1:27).

The difficulty comes in discovering exactly what this means. Is it physical looks? Is it moral responsibility? There are entire studies on this subject which you can investigate at your leisure. However, for our purposes of study allow me to focus on the idea of "identity." Your personal identity is contained within boundaries of the image of God. Through research I discovered this word is very close to the word "identical." They come from the same root word. In the dictionary one of the definitions of identity is "sameness, as distinguished from similarity and diversity, sameness in every possible circumstance."

"Identity" is seeing myself in "sameness." Who am I to be the same as? I am Stephen Manley; therefore, I am to be the same as Stephen Manley. This supposes that somewhere in existence there is a real Stephen Manley. It is my responsibility to find this real Stephen Manley and be like him in every way. But where is this real Stephen Manley? Since I am unable to find him, I have substituted the method of trial and error. I have tried many things to see if they feel right or are comfortable to me. Is this the way I really am? Some of them I discarded, others I have adopted as mine. I have become a combination of hundreds of qualities I have found in other people for I have not found the real me. Some things I do not like about myself and wish to change, but I do not seem to have the self-discipline needed for that task. As old age sets in, I have accepted myself as I am. What else can I do about it for I have not found the real me?

However, the Bible tells me the real Stephen Manley can be found! His name is Jesus! Jesus is all God has intended me to be! Jesus is the invisible God made visible. I am made in His image. What was vague and without comprehension has become seeable and knowable. Jesus is my identity. I was created by God to be the same as Jesus. Upon discovering this great truth, I began immediately to develop His likeness. I have miserably failed. I simply do not have the self-discipline. It is a worthy goal, but practically, it is impossible. So again I have settled for something less than I was really created to be. But what else can I do?

One exciting element which I have discovered is that Jesus Himself was in sameness as someone else. He had an identity as well. There was a real Jesus Christ which the Jesus of our New Testament was the same as. It was His Father. Jesus gave Himself totally to the Father, Who sourced Him to bring about the proper identity. Jesus did not produce Himself. He was a product of the Father living in and through Him. Jesus was not trying to be like the Father. He was filled with the Father Who was expressing Himself through Jesus. Now in turn, I am to be filled with Jesus (the real Stephen Manley) Who will source me with His life. Thus, I am not trying to be like Him; rather He is demonstrating

Part Eight: A God Ordained Board Meeting: His Place

Himself through me. I have found my identity in Him. It is the end of the search of a life time!

Jesus, being the real Stephen Manley, may be fine for me, but what about you? You do not want to be the real me. Where is the real you to be found? The real you is Jesus! But I thought He was the real Stephen Manley. He is both the real me and the real you. How can this be? Do not ever underestimate who He is! You were built to be in the image of Christ. He is your real identity. The image of God indwelling me is the same image of God indwelling you. As He expresses Himself through my being, so He expresses Himself through your being. It is your destiny. Do not miss it!

This helps to clarify the concept of our passage. Sin must be defined in "going beyond" the boundaries of His image. It is stepping over the limits of my own identity as seen in Him. It is fighting against my own identity. If my identity is found in His life expressed through me, then any expression other than Him is sin. If He is the source of my life in the context of my identity, then anything in my life which is sourced beyond Him is sin. The boundaries of my living are not simply in actions or deeds, but in the very sourcing of my life.

I have often wondered about the issue of stealing. Has God simply made up some rules to put me to the test? Why would He care if I steal? Perhaps I am in a grocery store and I slip a candy bar in my pocket without paying. Why does God get so upset with this action? It isn't like I took it from Him or that He loses anything by my action. Yet, God seems to be very offended by this action. He says, "I will tell you why I am upset with your stealing. I am God and I made you in My image. You were created to tell the truth about God. When you steal, you are saying that God is a thief. I am not a thief! I cannot have you going around telling people I am one!" You were built in the image of God to be filled with God and be the expression of His life. When you steal you are saying, "God is a thief." Your identity is Christ; you are in sameness with Him. In stealing you have misrepresented God.

The same is true for all the deeds of sin. If the very nature of God is love, can you imagine how hate destroys the very image of God displayed through your life? A church split is absolutely unthinkable. It misrepresents the image of God to the whole community. Therefore, sin is "going beyond" the relationship I have with Christ and the very creation of my being. I have been created in the image of God which means His nature is to be the very source of the expression of my being. Anything that goes beyond this source must be considered sin.

The most frequently used Greek word for sin in the New Testament means "missing the mark." It is the picture of the traveler who is lost. He is not evil; he simply made a wrong turn. The warrior has thrown his spear and missed the target. He is not evil; he just missed the mark. The focus is not on the content of the deed, but on the relationship between the deed and the target. I am made in the image of Christ. The target of my life is sameness with Him. Sin is "going beyond" the limits of the target. All aspects of life must be seen in light of the person of Christ in whose image I am to be.

This brings us to the heart of our passage. The early disciples are praying for the Heart Knower to reveal to them the one He has chosen to take the place of Judas. Here is their cry: ***"You, O Lord, who know the hearts of all, show which of these two You have chosen to take part in this ministry and apostleship from which Judas by transgression fell, that he might go to his own place,"*** (Acts 1:24-25). The Greek word which is translated ***by transgression fell*** is used four times in three situations in the New Testament. In the moral sense, it means to overstep, pass over, or to go beyond. The first occasion in which this word is used twice is seen in the previous chapter. It is "Traditions Beyond Christ."

Part Eight: A God Ordained Board Meeting: His Place

Theology Not Christ

There is a second occasion where this Greek word (going beyond) appears in one of the small epistles written by the Apostle John. *Whoever transgresses* (goes beyond) *and does not abide in the doctrine of Christ does not have God. He who abides in the doctrine of Christ has both the Father and the Son* (2 John 9). One of the key elements to his statement is *the doctrine of Christ.* In the context of this verse, John seems to give the simple content of this doctrine. *For many deceivers have gone out into this world who do not confess Jesus Christ as coming in the flesh. This is a deceiver and an antichrist* (2 John 7). The focus is Jesus and Who He really is in the flesh. Many were proposing that Christ came in the flesh, but only in appearance. He was not really incarnate. John refers to the antichrist or deceiver as the individual who goes beyond the person of Jesus as He really is.

We can see the *doctrine of Christ* plainly by the grammar John chose to use. In verse seven he highlights the deceiver as the individual who does not *confess Jesus Christ as coming in the flesh.* The verb *coming* in the Greek language is in the present tense, middle voice and the participle mood. The middle voice communicates the fact that the subject is acting upon its own self. In this case it is Jesus Christ Who is responsible for the act of becoming physical flesh. This was not forced upon Him by the Father Who wanted to accomplish His plan. Jesus was involved in the planning! The redemptive plan for man was the united effort coming from the united heart of the Trinity. Each member of the Trinity is equally involved in the conception of the atonement plan and in its accomplishment. The second member of the Trinity is intimately involved in this plan. It is an expression of His heart.

The participle mood shows us this statement as an adjective

phrase. The phrase, **who do not confess Jesus Christ as coming in the flesh,** gives content to the **deceivers.** The antichrist or the deceiver is defined as one who will not stay within the boundaries or limits of the incarnation of Christ. He is adjusting and compromising who Jesus is as one of us. It does not matter how sincere he is or how many other religious practices he adopts. He is a deceiver when he goes beyond the boundaries of the great sacrifice of God becoming a real man.

The fact this verb is in the present tense tells us the incarnation is a continuing fact which the deceivers flatly deny. John did not write this verb in the past tense. Jesus becoming flesh is not an event of the past. It is a continuing fact now and is still being manifested in the physical ascension, the physical exaltation and His physical second coming. John describes the manhood of Christ as continuing even to the moment of his writing. Jesus did not sacrifice to become a man for a temporary period of time and then abandon His connection with us. He was not man for a period of thirty-three years only. Jesus has made an eternal sacrifice by becoming man for all eternity.

The deceivers and antichrists do not deny that Jesus is the Messiah. What they deny is that Jesus was really a man or that he actually assumed human nature in permanent union with the Divine nature. There was a real incarnation contrasted with their proposal that He came in appearance only to suffer and die or that He merely seemed to be a man. He did not really limit Himself to the realm in which I live. He maintained His omnipotence, omniscience and omnipresence. He did not empty Himself of all that He had as God. He was not a real man. The antichrists "go beyond" Who Jesus really is. The Greek prefix anti means both "instead of" and "against." They are against Jesus as He is in the flesh, and they substitute their own Christ as they want Him.

How important is this issue? It is seen in the severity by which we are to deal with these antichrists. **If anyone comes to** *you and does not bring this doctrine, do not receive him into your house nor greet him; for he who greets him shares in his evil deeds,* (2 John 10-11). There is no toleration at all over this issue. We are not told to work with these individuals and give them a chance to mature in their faith. We are not told to have seminars on the proper doctrine of the incarnation. We are to be very severe in how we treat them. There are other issues which may be adjustable, but this is about Christ, and there is no tolerance of this issue! This is about Christ! The issue is not about the building project of the church, social issues, dress, worship styles or baptism. They have transgressed (gone beyond) Christ. They would not accept the boundaries of Who He is!

Transgression Not Christ

Now we come to grasp the truth of our passage (Acts 1:25). Remember this is an expression of the prayer of the early church. It is not a quote of the entire prayer as they were seeking the will of God for the choosing of a new apostle. This is the concept of their prayer made in a simple statement. Therefore, we see the expression of how they felt about the sin of Judas. Nothing is stated about the fact he was a thief (John 12:6). The act of the kiss of betrayal is not mentioned. Could there have been a lower deed than this?

Evidently in the thinking of the early church, the entire sin of Judas is in the fact of "going beyond." He was not willing to live within the boundaries of the place Christ had for him. Judas had been born out of the dreams of God. God had a great design and plan. Judas was specifically made by God to fit this place of apostleship. It was his destiny. But he would not settle for this. He desired *his own place.*

What was the place Christ had for him? We understand it in the content of this prayer. He was to be an apostle. The early disciples understood this to mean Judas was destined to be *a witness with us of His resurrection* (Acts 1:22). The resurrected life of Christ was going to fill him and be demonstrated through him. The opportunity of being a stage upon which the Spirit of Christ could act was given to him. He had the thrill of being involved in the fresh, empowered life of God. But *Judas by transgression fell.* He would not accept the boundaries of the life of Christ. Evidently he felt that living empowered by God would be far to limiting. He wanted to produce his own life; he "went beyond" Christ. The issue was not good or bad, but Christ alone.

You must prayerfully apply this study to your personal life. Anytime we exert ourselves beyond His sourcing, we have transgressed. We become so accustomed to living out of our talent, wisdom and abilities. We operate the program of the church and call it ministry. We teach our Sunday School class and feel righteous. We sing in the cantata for Easter and proclaim its success. Was it all "beyond" Christ? Have we gone to our *own place?* There must be no other resource or focus but Him. The living person of Christ is our boundary! I will live in Him alone! Will you?

Acts 1:25

OUT OF SHAPE

I have stumbled into an additional thought regarding the ministry to which we have been called. Luke highlights it in the phrase ***that he might go to his own place*** (Acts 1:25). It is the climax of the statement made in prayer by the early disciples as they sought the will of God for the choosing of another apostle. In this statement they are defining the sin of Judas in contrast with the ***ministry and apostleship*** to which he had been called. In our previous studies, we discovered that Judas simply went beyond the limits of the place Jesus had for him. Thus, Judas went to a place he had established for himself.

The Greek words Luke uses to express this truth paint a physical picture. The language is something of a parable describing the spiritual truth of Kingdom ministry. The danger for us is to focus on the physical and miss the spiritual reality to which He draws us. ***Ministry and apostleship*** is never a position within an organization. It is certainly not a job description. It cannot possibly be described apart from your intimate relationship with Christ. It is a by-product of the oneness between you and the Spirit of God which flows through you. It is not something you do, but a result of the creative juice of His Spirit. As you live in response to this flow, ministry is the result. While you may develop certain acceptable social skills, ministry is not based on training, talent or ability. It is a direct result of how well you know Christ. So while the Greek words paint

Out Of Shape | Acts 1:25

a physical picture of this calling, we must never forget it is an attempt to illustrate the wonder of what God is doing through us in the spiritual realm.

Through the years hundreds of young people have come to me with a desire to discuss their futures. "How can I know the will of God for my life?" is their question. They struggle with the three basic "C's" of life - companion, college and career. Who should I marry? Where should I go to college? What is God calling me to do? No one can answer those questions for them. I never want to be critical or judgmental of those discussions, but the questions they ask tell me we have not taught them the proper concepts of *ministry and apostleship*. Their focus should not be on what they are going to do, but upon Jesus. How can I become a part of the mind of Christ? How can I experience the heart of God? How can I embrace the nature of God until His actions are spontaneous through me? How can I live in constant response to God? God's will is accomplished in my life through the intimate relationship I have with Christ.

I have always desired the will of God, for it is best. In the midst of making major decisions I needed guidance to avoid a mistake. I really wanted to be in the place the Lord had for me, but I did not want the shape, character or internal spiritual being to match that place. I wanted God's crystal ball insight to have things work out. I certainly wanted to be happy and have the good life. But my focus was not upon knowing Him regardless of where it took me. I did not abandon all to His person regardless of the consequences. I did not allow Him to bring me inwardly to the shape and size of the spot into which He wanted to place me.

This is exactly what happened to Judas. The consequence of this state was a complete and drastic betrayal of Christ. What Judas became inwardly did not fit the shape of the apostleship into which Jesus wanted to place him. Due to his spiritual condition, he did not belong to the apostleship place, but to another place.

Part Eight: A God Ordained Board Meeting: His Place

He was out of shape. Even if he had wanted involvement in apostleship, now he did not qualify. **Ministry and apostleship** is only experienced when I focus on being intimate with Christ and allow Him to mold my spiritual life into the shape of the chair He has built me to fit.

To see this clearly in our passage, we must examine the strong parallel stated in the prayer of the one hundred and twenty. Let me quote the prayer for you again. ***"You, O Lord, who know the hearts of all, show which of these two You have chosen to take part in this ministry and apostleship from which Judas by transgression fell, that he might go to his own place,"*** (Acts 1:24-25). The parallel is not as clear in the English translation as it is in the Greek language. The first statement is ***to take*** and the parallel statement is he ***might go.*** Each of these phrases is a translation of one Greek word.

Let us review our previous study of the first phrase. The Greek word translated ***to take*** is in the infinitive mood. When it is used, it may be followed by an accusative, as in the case of this verse. The action of the verb is attached and directed to the accusative. In this sentence, it is the Greek word translated ***part.*** This refers to the apostleship as if it were a thing an individual could reach out and take or grasp. This ministry is something which is separate from Judas. Judas is now gone, but his place of ministry remains. Judas did not produce this ministry, thus it did not die with him. God made this place for Judas and molded him into the shape of it.

This Greek word translated ***to take*** is in the active voice. This means the subject is responsible for the action of the verb. This can be somewhat misleading in the verse. At first I thought the one who was responsible for the taking of the ***part*** was ***which of these two.*** As Luke wrote it in the Greek language, the last word of verse twenty-four is "one." In reality, this is the subject of the verb ***to take.*** This means either Matthias or Joseph is responsible for reaching out, grabbing, or receiving the ***part in*** *this ministry and apostleship.*

However, the verb *to take* is in the infinitive mood. This means it does not stand alone, but is dependent upon the strength of the main verb or another verb. In the case of this verse, it is the phrase **You have chosen.** While response is certainly required from the one who is chosen, the strength of the action is coming from the One Who has chosen. He is aggressive in His choosing. There is a tap on the shoulder; there is an arm around the waist. There is a strong presence which will not allow the fact He has chosen to be ignored. This is too important to Him. The entire emphasis of the prayer is that God will reveal, lift up on high, the one He has already chosen. He has already made a decision. Matthias will have a choice in the matter, but it is the Lord Who has reached out and grabbed Matthias and placed him in this place *(part).*

If you understand this first statement, we can now move to our study at hand. The climax of their prayer concerned Judas. They describe the sin of Judas in light of the ***ministry and apostleship.*** It was from this calling **which Judas by transgression fell.** This conveys the idea of "going beyond." Judas was not willing to be within the boundaries of this calling. The end result of this was **that he might go to his own place.** This gives us the parallel statement to what we just reviewed.

The English translation of **he might go** does not properly represent the Greek grammar. As with the phrase *to take,* so this phrase is a translation of one Greek word which is in the infinitive mood. Usually in the English we introduce an infinitive with the word "to." Thus it would read as follows: ***from which Judas by transgression fell, to go to his own place.*** The Greek word translated **he might go** (to go) is a parallel statement of *to take.* Both are in the infinitive mood.

One difference between these parallel verbs is their voice. The Greek word translated *to take* is in the active voice which means the subject is responsible for the action. However, this

Part Eight: A God Ordained Board Meeting: His Place

parallel verb *to go* is in the passive voice. This means the subject is a recipient of the action of the verb. Judas is going to his own place because something is acting upon him. He is not responsible for this action. Remember this verb is in the infinitive mood. This means that this verb does not stand alone but depends upon a stronger verb for support. In this case, the stronger verb is the Greek word translated ***by transgression fell*** (going beyond). This verb is in the active voice and Judas is the subject. Judas was responsible for going beyond the person of Jesus which was responsible for taking him to his own place. Judas is receiving the consequences of going beyond the limits of his relationship with Christ.

Often a verb in the infinitive mood will have an accusative which acts as a direct object. In this case it is the Greek word translated ***place.*** In some Greek text this is the same Greek word which is the accusative or direct object for our parallel verb. It is translated ***part.*** Judas is being acted upon by the action of "going beyond." He is being aggressively taken to a place described as ***his own.***

In the first part of the parallel, the Lord was aggressively acting upon an individual. He took this disciple and placed him in the apostleship place for which he had been built. In the second part of the parallel, Judas is aggressively being acted upon by the results of his choice to go beyond the limits of his relationship with Christ. He is being carried to another place.

The conclusion is that something desperate had taken place in Judas. He had changed. The moment Judas went beyond the limits of His calling, he was no longer in the shape of the chair. He no longer was the size of the spot for which God had created him. His character no longer matched the place God had for him. He was totally incapable of filling the place. He took on a different shape. The end result was he had to go to the place which he now fits.

Let me remind you to think beyond the physical aspects of

the illustration. In the spiritual character and nature of Judas a radical change had taken place. He no longer qualified spiritually as an apostle. What a tragedy! This is completely beyond a deed that he did. This is not about the deed of betrayal, the sign of the kiss, or the plotting against Jesus. This is the character and spiritual relationship of Judas to Jesus. Everything Judas did came from the change in his relationship with Jesus. It is very important to keep this progression in proper perspective. We do not do a deed and then change in our relationship with Christ. We change our relationship with Christ and then become capable of the deed. It is not the deed that has damned us, but the losing of the intimacy in our relationship with Christ. We seem to focus our time and energy on doing the proper and approved activities which are nothing in themselves. Our focus should be on His person and intimacy with Him.

Judas arrived at a place the early disciples described as **his own place** (Acts 1:25). The Greek word translated **his own** means "as belonging to oneself and not to another, one's own, peculiar." It denotes ownership. It means "that of which one is himself the owner, possessor, producer, as my own, your own, his own." Judas went to the place which was proper for him.

The Good News Translation renders this verse as "*who left to go to the place where he belongs.*" The New Century Version says, "*Show us who should be an apostle in place of Judas, who turned away and went where he belongs.*" The translation by Young says, "*to receive the share of this ministry and apostleship, from which Judas, by transgression, did fall, to go on to his proper place.*" Judas has changed size and shape. He no longer fits the spot for which he was first made. He has another place where he belongs.

This leads us to some radical conclusions. Your spiritual condition determines ministry. The basis of ministry is not skill, talent, or education; it is your spiritual relationship and intimacy with God. Remember the sole function of being an apostle was

Part Eight: A God Ordained Board Meeting: His Place

one of these must become a witness with us of His resurrection (Acts 1:22). One can run programs, administrate offices, direct music in the midst of spiritual decay, but he cannot minister as a witness of His resurrection. There is a difference between getting numbers of people into a building and getting numbers of people into the Kingdom of God. It is sad to say, but church growth is not always Kingdom growth. The only ministry which produces Kingdom growth is sourced from intimacy with Christ.

Since this is true, what should be the focus of ministry training either for lay or professional ministry? Obviously, the major focus should be on intimate relationship with Christ. The deeper our intimacy with Christ is, the broader our ministry is to others. However, we are always facing the drawing of self-centered carnality. It is a focus on doing or accomplishment. When "doing" skills are developed, then activities become numerous. This becomes the standard for measuring our success. How big, how many, how much seems to dominate our attention. This quickly drags us away from Him. We become lost in the fury of competition, jealously, even burn out. It is always a sign we have missed His presence in the process.

A second conclusion which needs to be stated is that ministry is inevitable in a right spiritual condition. Ministry is always a by-product of intimacy with Jesus. It is certainly not difficult to discover this in the Word of God. The Parable of the Vine and the Branch (John 15:1ff) plainly states this truth. Fruit is a result of the tightness between the vine and the branch. The branch does not do fruit; it simply grows fruit. The branch in proper relationship with the vine cannot help but do so! In the parable, Jesus allows for no excuses from the branch. The vine is responsible for the life giving sap. Purging will be applied to the branch as needed to enhance the growth of the fruit. No effort is required from the branch. Its entire responsibility is to respond to the vine. Relationship with the vine is the branch's only concern.

Ingrained in the very nature of the relationship between the believer and Christ is the by-product of ministry. It is not possible to be in intimacy with Christ and not flow with ministry. The base of all ministries is Christ. In the fullness of the Holy Spirit we are sourced (Acts 1:8). This brings us to a state of relaxation. Dependency and leaning are the qualities of our life. Satisfaction and fulfillment are found in this intimacy. This is a call to embrace Him anew! Let us deepen our relationship with Him! May our constant craving be for Him. Allow nothing to distract from Him. Do not ignore the circumstances of life, but allow them to focus you on Him. Do not increase your activities, but allow Him to source and motivate you. Then do not be surprised when ministry happens!

Acts 1:26

SECONDARY - SUPERIOR

And they cast their lots (Acts 1:26). Most people have definite questions concerning this method of discovering the will of God. It is significant to notice that this method was never used again in the New Testament church. Pentecost had a distinct affect on the communication level between God and man. Did the early disciples rush ahead of God and use a questionable method for determining the will of God?

Let us understand at the beginning, lot casting was only one element in the entire procedure. This business meeting was initiated by the Scriptures and prayer. Peter was a part of the one hundred and twenty who **continued with one accord in prayer** (Acts 1:14). No doubt the Holy Spirit was directing him in the necessity of choosing another apostle. Also, the Holy Spirit gave them distinct wisdom concerning the qualifications for the possible candidates (Acts 1:21-22). They were deeply aware of the necessity that an apostle had to have been with them **all the time that the Lord Jesus went in and out among us.** This reduced the possibilities down to the group called "the seventy others" (Luke 10:1). There were only two among the one hundred and twenty who could qualify. A choice had to be made between these two individuals, Joseph and Matthias.

Those gathered in the upper room had every reason, both in Biblical precedent and teaching, to believe that God would make His will known through the casting of lots. There was nothing incorrect in their procedure. The author of Proverbs certainly set the standard for settling disputes and discovering the will of God.

> *The lot is cast into the lap.*
> *But its every decision is from the Lord (Proverbs 16:33).*

> *Casting lots causes contentions to cease,*
> *And keeps the mighty apart (Proverbs 18:18).*

The exact method in this case for casting lots is unclear. The actual Greek word for *cast* in this verse (Acts 1:26) means giving. So a literal translation would be, **And they gave them lots.** While this is unclear, the next phrase gives some clarification. It says, **and the lot fell on Matthias.** These two clauses together seem to indicate that each of the two names were written on a small stone and placed into a clay vessel. This vessel was shaken and the first stone to fall out would indicate the man who was chosen by God.

Luke introduces the two candidates to us in this way. **And they proposed two: Joseph called Barsabas, who was surnamed Justus, and Matthias** (Acts 1:23). We do not want to be guilty of assuming Luke is implying more than he is. But it is likely that he is inferring that Matthias was not rated as highly as Joseph in their minds. Not only does Luke name Joseph first, but he states two surnames. This shows that Joseph was held in great respect. He was called faithfulness and innocence or of a quiet and unassuming nature. His other name, Justus, implies outstanding honesty. Even though Joseph might have been the preferred choice of the group; God chose Matthias. There appears to be no hesitation on the part of the one hundred and twenty disciples to embrace Matthias as the one chosen by God. They believed the choice of the lot was the choice of God.

However, we are still faced with the fact this method was

Part Eight: A God Ordained Board Meeting: His Place

never done again by the early church. Why? There is no discussion of it at all. No one ever suggests casting of lots and is rebuked for it. It seems something profound happened which impacted them, and there is no question in anyone's mind that casting of lots was no longer a valid means of finding the will of God. A far superior way has now appeared! Pentecost has come!

In light of the method of casting lots, I want to discuss with you two contrasts. They are contrasts between the old and the new. Perhaps it will help us to understand our position in Jesus.

Relationship

Nothing we are going to discuss is for the purpose of undermining either the Scriptures or the acts of the early group of Christians. After the study of this great event, I am convinced they acted according to the will of God. However, in this final statement which gives the SOLUTION of the whole matter (Acts 1:26), I find a contrast between the acceptance of Judas as an apostle and Matthias. It seems to be significant that the Greek word Peter uses to refer to Judas' relationship with the apostles is different than the one Luke writes concerning Matthias.

Luke writes, *And they cast their lots, and the lot fell on Matthias. And he was numbered with the eleven apostles* (Acts 1:26). The Greek word translated *he was numbered* is a compound word. It begins with the Greek word meaning "together" or "with." The second Greek word means "according to." Then the last one means "to count or compute." This last word is the root word. It is where we get the idea of calculus. It has to do with a method of analysis and calculation using a special symbolic notation. It is a perfect description of the old system. Casting lots was a part of this Old Testament system. It was a method of calculating, measuring, and attaining. Notice the emphasis is on the idea of a method.

As you know, this is the focus of religion. What is the right method for receiving from God what is needed? The major question is "What should I do?" The focus is on accomplishment and completion. I can expect God to honor His commitment to bless me after I have done the law, kept the commandments, and accomplished the oral tradition. Regarding prayer, the issue is always "Did I pray enough?" The concern of fasting is "How many meals is enough?" When have I given enough money in the issue of sacrificial giving. In the realm of the Old Testament law there seems to be no end. This is the language used to express Matthias' inclusion in the apostleship.

Now this is contrasted to the language used for Judas' inclusion in the apostleship. In Peter's speech concerning Judas, he states, *"For he was numbered with us and obtained a part in this ministry,"* (Acts 1:17). The Greek word which is translated *numbered* is also a compound word. It begins with the Greek word meaning "with" or "to." It continues with the Greek word meaning "to count." This is the Greek word from which our word "arithmetic" originates. Peter is simply saying as far as Jesus and the other apostles were concerned, Judas was counted as one of them. There were no walls or barriers between them. They did not look upon Judas with suspicion. Judas was one hundred percent embraced, included, and accepted in the apostleship.

This Greek word is a relational term. The New Testament is an experience of relationship. It has the connotation of an embrace. This is seen clearly in the method used to select Judas as an apostle. Jesus was in oneness with the Father. Luke tells us, *Now it came to pass in those days that He went out to the mountain to pray, and continued all night in prayer to God* (Luke 6:12). It was from this time of prayer He knew exactly which disciples were to become apostles. He did not cast lots, but His choosing leaped out of the intimate relationship He had with the Father. They were being drawn into this same relationship. Mark records in his Gospel account a brief view of the calling of

Part Eight: A God Ordained Board Meeting: His Place

the twelve disciples. He wrote, **Then He appointed twelve, that they might be with Him and that He might send them out to preach,** (Mark 3:14). The tone of the position of the apostle as Jesus chose them was far beyond ministry. They were not called to the performance of certain ministry activities. They would not do any ministry until they had been with Him. The context of the calling of the apostles in the Gospels carries with it the thrust of relationship. Jesus, Who is in strong relationship with the Father, is praying all night to receive the mind of the Father. Through the intimacy of their relationship twelve individuals are selected to enter into this same kind of oneness with Jesus.

Now the picture is somewhat different with the choosing of Matthias. While there is prayer involved (Acts 1:24) the methodology is somewhat more calculating. It has the style of the Old Testament about it. Matthias is a full fledged apostle with the approval of God upon him, but the tone is more calculated than relational.

Perhaps you have known someone who spent their entire time with you calculating and measuring. They are always pleasing rather than accepting. It was hard to offer relationship to them for they are analyzing everything you do and say. You are constantly under a microscope in their presence. Everything you say is being questioned in their mind. Why did you say it? Did you have some hidden meaning when you said it? Were you talking about them? When you finally get away from them, you breathe a sigh of relief.

There are other people with whom you spend time (not too many of them). You can kick off your shoes even if your feet stink. You can relax and simply be who you are. There is no scrutiny or measuring. They accept you. You are in relationship! There is an embrace of intimacy which produces security. Nothing needs to be proven or accomplished. You are enabled to dream together.

This gives us the tone of difference between the Old Testament and the New Testament. What kind of relationship do you want with God? It is very difficult to live in a calculating relationship with God. You always fall short. There is no deed performed well enough. The basis of the relationship can never be performance; it must be love. The New Testament calls us into **accepted in the Beloved** (Ephesians 1:6). **He chose us in Him before the foundation of the world** (Ephesians 1:4). It is the wonder of **having** been **predestined ... to adoption as sons by Jesus Christ to Himself** (Ephesians 1:5). Did you hear the tone of these verses? It is all in Him! There is an acceptance through Christ. You are in His embrace! Intimacy with God is yours!

Response

And they cast their lots, and the lot fell on Matthias (Acts 1:26). The Greek word which is translated *cast* is in the indicative mood. This means it is a simple statement of fact. It is straight forward information. Also it is in the active voice. This means the subject is responsible for the action of the verb. The one hundred and twenty from the upper room were responsible for the action of casting the lots. In this sense they are the source of the activity. It is initiated from them.

This is contrasted with the actions of those disciples in the early church after Pentecost. There is an entirely new kind of action coming from the disciples. We have been calling it "response." There was established in the experience of Pentecost a relationship between the disciples and God. They had seen evidence of this in the life of Jesus. They had tasted something of it when Jesus **gave them power over unclean spirits, to cast them out, and to heal all kinds of sickness and all kinds of disease** (Matthew 10:1). They touch it when for the first time they enter into prayer (Acts 1:14). However, the reality of it was not comprehended until the Day of Pentecost. These disciples entered into an intimacy with God which paralleled

Part Eight: A God Ordained Board Meeting: His Place

the relationship between the Father and Son.

The examples of this are so numerous we cannot list them. The early church had gathered together in Antioch. It was the first place the early disciples were called "Christians" (Acts 11:26). Saul had been with this group for one year. Barnabas and Saul were their primary teachers. They were having tremendous results in ministry but *as they ministered to the Lord and fasted, the Holy Spirit said, "Now separate to Me Barnabas and Saul for the work to which I have called them,"* (Acts 13:2). This group continued to pray and fast. Then they *laid hands on them, they sent them away* (Acts 13:3). This is a far different procedure than the first recorded business meeting (Acts 1:15-26).

The early disciples moved from the outward calculating of the will of God to the inward relationship of His presence in guidance. They moved from God manipulating lots to communicate His will to His voice speaking to them. It is a fulfillment of the prophecy of Jeremiah, *"But this is the covenant that I will make with the house of Israel after those days, says the Lord: I will put My law in their minds, and write it on their hearts;"* (Jeremiah 31:33). No longer will they rely on tablets of stone which record the desires of God. Now, they will know God and experience His mind and heart.

While the early disciples had something of a ceremony and sent Barnabas and Saul out on the first missionary journey, the Scripture states, *So, being sent out by the Holy Spirit, they went down to Seleucia and from there they sailed to Cyprus* (Acts 13:4). This expresses a definite tone of personal involvement. There is nothing expressed which indicates anything of the disciples and their action. This is all being orchestrated by the Divine. There is a new communication level which has been established. Even this is different from the final statements of the replacement of Judas as an apostle. *And they cast their lots, and the lot fell on Matthias. And he was numbered with the eleven apostles* (Acts 1:26). Never again will man revert to casting of lots to determine the will of God. Now we know God.

I fear we have not been captured by this high level of intimate relationship. Each time we revert back to our own activities, however sincere we might be, we violate the very intimacy He desires to have with us. Is it possible to have such an intimate relationship with God? Can we know Him until His voice directs our path? This is not simply an issue of method and technique. Strategy for discovering the will of God is a direct reflection of our intimacy level with Him. Casting of lots is a sign we are not living in His heart!

During the period of four hundred years between the Old Testament and the New Testament, the Spirit of the Lord was silent in Israel. There were no prophetic utterances. This silence left them with only dice as a means through which God might communicate His will to them. But now the Spirit of Jesus is resting not only on a few prophets, but on the whole people of God. Intimacy with God has been established on an entirely new level.

The decisions of the early church were going to come from this intimacy with the Spirit of God. Peter was being summoned by the servants of Cornelius. **"Then the Spirit told me to go with them, doubting nothing,"** (Acts 11:12). We have already dealt with the Scripture above which tells us people were chosen for special roles by the communication of the Holy Spirit (Acts 13:2). It was in the letter which came from the Jerusalem conference concerning the Gentiles which indicates a consensus came to the group because of this new level of intimacy with the Holy Spirit. **For it seemed good to the Holy Spirit, and to us, to lay upon you no greater burden than these necessary things** (Acts 15:28).

What an opportunity we have in the fullness of the Holy Spirit! Let us seek the heart of God for intimate relationship. May our strategies and methods reflect the direct communication of the Holy Spirit in our lives!

S

ABOUT THE AUTHOR

Stephen Manley has found through the saturation of the Word the message of the cross. It is beyond an event; it is a style. Thus, the cross is not a piece of wood or an emblem, but it is the heart of the person of Christ. Cross style is the Christ style. He must be central. As an international evangelist, Stephen has taken this message to the world.

After 41 years in itinerant evangelism, Stephen Manley felt a clear call from God to come off the road for the purpose of starting the Cross Style School of Practical Ministry. In 2009, Stephen launched and became the lead pastor of Cross Style Church in Lebanon, Tennessee to create the ministry platform for future students.

The Cross Style School of Practical Ministry was launched with a desire to not only train up men and women in the Word, but to give them practical hands-on experience in ministering to a lost and dying world.

Stephen's life, testimony, and preaching has been used throughout the last six decades to touch, influence, and transform the lives of countless people around the world. For Stephen, his life is wrapped up in a total saturation of Jesus and the Word of God. Time in the Word is more than an activity or duty to schedule in his day. It is the delight of his heart and the focus throughout his day because it draws him deeper into intimacy with Jesus Christ. He wants his "moment-by-moments" saturated with the Person of Jesus and the Word. He longs for Jesus to ever increase and expand in and through His life. As he once wrote:

*"Jesus is present in every situation of my life. There is no conversation in which I do not feel His presence.
He participates in all my recreation. He is everywhere I go. Who would want to be without Him? He is the protection for my life. He is the fragrance I constantly smell. He is the flow of my spiritual blood giving me life.
He is my constant nutrition making me healthy.
I cannot survive without Him. I am a Jesus pusher!!!!*

*I want to push Him on you.
I want you to join me in this obsession.
You do not have to work at it; it is not a discipline.
It is as natural as breathing.
Please let Him pull you to His heart."*

Learn more about Stephen Manley and the ministry of Cross Style at: **CrossStyle.org**